Information Technology for Librarians and Information Professionals

LIBRARY INFORMATION TECHNOLOGY ASSOCIATION (LITA) GUIDES

The Library Information and Technology Association became part of Core: Leadership, Infrastructure, Futures, also a division of the American Library Association, in September 2020. Guides published in this series retain the series title LITA Guides.

Marta Mestrovic Deyrup, PhD
Acquisitions Editor, Core, a division of the American Library Association

The Library Information Technology Association (LITA) Guides provide information and guidance on topics related to cutting-edge technology for library and IT specialists.

Written by top professionals in the field of technology, the guides are sought after by librarians wishing to learn a new skill or to become current in today's best practices.

Each book in the series has been overseen editorially since conception by LITA and reviewed by LITA members with special expertise in the specialty area of the book.

Established in 1966 and integrated as part of Core in 2020, LITA provided its members and the library and information science community as a whole with a forum for discussion, an environment for learning, and a program for actions on the design, development, and implementation of automated and technological systems in the library and information science field.

Approximately twenty-five LITA Guides were published by Neal-Schuman and ALA between 2007 and 2015. Rowman & Littlefield and LITA published the series 2015-2021. Books in the series published by Rowman & Littlefield are:

Digitizing Flat Media: Principles and Practices
The Librarian's Introduction to Programming Languages
Library Service Design: A LITA Guide to Holistic Assessment, Insight, and Improvement
Data Visualization: A Guide to Visual Storytelling for Librarians
Mobile Technologies in Libraries: A LITA Guide
Innovative LibGuides Applications
Integrating LibGuides into Library Websites
Protecting Patron Privacy: A LITA Guide
The LITA Leadership Guide: The Librarian as Entrepreneur, Leader, and Technologist
Using Social Media to Build Library Communities: A LITA Guide
Managing Library Technology: A LITA Guide
The LITA Guide to No- or Low-Cost Technology Tools for Libraries
Big Data Shocks: An Introduction to Big Data for Librarians and Information Professionals
The Savvy Academic Librarian's Guide to Technological Innovation: Moving Beyond the Wow Factor
The LITA Guide to Augmented Reality in Libraries
Digital Curation Projects Made Easy: A Step-By-Step Guide for Libraries, Archives, and Museums
Change the World Using Social Media

Information Technology for Librarians and Information Professionals

Jonathan M. Smith

ROWMAN & LITTLEFIELD
Lanham • Boulder • New York • London

Published by Rowman & Littlefield
An imprint of The Rowman & Littlefield Publishing Group, Inc.
4501 Forbes Boulevard, Suite 200, Lanham, Maryland 20706
www.rowman.com

6 Tinworth Street, London, SE11 5AL, United Kingdom

British Library Cataloguing in Publication Information Available

Library of Congress Cataloging-in-Publication Data

Names: Smith, Jonathan M., 1978- author.
Title: Information technology for librarians and information professionals
 / Jonathan M. Smith.
Description: Lanham : Rowman & Littlefield, [2021] | Series: Library
 Information Technology Association (LITA) Guides | Includes
 bibliographical references and index. | Summary: "This comprehensive
 primer introduces information technology topics foundational to many
 services offered in today's libraries and information centers. Written
 by a librarian with extensive experience as a technology specialist in
 libraries the book clearly explains concepts information technology
 principles with an eye toward their practical applications in
 libraries"—Provided by publisher.
Identifiers: LCCN 2020052090 (print) | LCCN 2020052091 (ebook) | ISBN
 9781538120996 (cloth) | ISBN 9781538121009 (paperback) | ISBN
 9781538121016 (ebook)
Subjects: LCSH: Libraries—Information technology. | Library
 employees—Effect of technological innovations on. | Knowledge
 workers—Effect of technological innovations on.
Classification: LCC Z678.9 .S64 2021 (print) | LCC Z678.9 (ebook) | DDC
 025.00285—dc23
LC record available at https://lccn.loc.gov/2020052090
LC ebook record available at https://lccn.loc.gov/2020052091

To my wife, Katrina,
and my children,
Aliyah and Genevieve.

Contents

List of Figures and Tables

FIGURES

TABLES

Preface

Information technology (IT) is an integral part of many library activities, to the point where every librarian and information professional is expected to have at least some expertise with information systems. To make the best use of those systems and to shape future activities and workflows, it is necessary to have a basic understanding of IT.

This comprehensive primer introduces IT topics foundational to many services offered in today's libraries and information centers. Written by a librarian, it clearly explains concepts familiar to the IT professional with an eye toward practical applications in libraries. This book serves as an introduction to IT written with the library science student or accidental library technologist in mind. It will also function as a reference for professionals needing foundational information on a variety of IT topics.

Library and information science literature thoroughly covers traditional library technology topics such as integrated library systems and digital libraries as well as some emerging technology services. However, there is very little that deals directly with the foundational concepts that support those technologies or the day-to-day IT work that many librarians find themselves either directly responsible for or that they need to understand to work closely with their organization's IT department. It is the purpose of this book to cover the breadth of technology as it relates to libraries and to provide a solid introduction to most of the subjects that a librarian may face.

Chapters begin with a basic introduction to a broad IT topic then go into enough technical detail of relevant technologies to be useful to the student preparing for library technology and systems work or the professional needing to converse effectively with technology experts. Major topics covered include technology management, strategic planning, computer support, networking, information security, server administration, web development, and software and systems development. Chapters also include information about emerging technologies and services like makerspaces, 3-D printing, and immersive technologies, as well as traditional library technology such as integrated library systems, automated storage and retrieval systems, and digitization.

OVERVIEW OF THIS BOOK

Information Technology for Librarians and Information Professionals contains twelve chapters. Each chapter covers a foundational topic and includes a chapter summary, a list of key terms, a set of questions for review and discussion, and a couple of suggested activities that apply what was covered in the chapter and encourages deeper exploration. Chapters conclude with a bibliography for further reading, a list of relevant resources, and cited sources.

Chapter 1, "Information Technology in Libraries," begins by establishing the historical context for technology in libraries by reviewing developments over the past sixty years. It then discusses IT governance, the structure and roles within IT departments, and gives descriptions for employee positions. Finally, three issues are introduced: ethics of IT, user privacy, and equitable access.

Chapter 2, "Technology Management and Support," covers a range of topics applicable to providing user support and managing hardware and software within the library. User-centered support is discussed, as are the help desk, issue tracking, documentation, and software licenses. Mobile technology support and IT accessibility are discussed as well. The chapter finishes with an introduction to project management.

Chapter 3, "Computer Hardware and Software," goes into some technical detail about computer hardware and software. It introduces the reader to all of the major hardware components of a computer along with some suggestions on how to assess their specifications. This chapter also introduces some basic computer architecture concepts and reviews major operating systems.

Chapter 4, "Computer Management," introduces the reader to some of the main activities that a computer technician will undertake while managing computers. This includes computer administration, application installation, networking, and deploying images. Maintenance activities covered include data backups, cloud storage, malware protection, and other basic maintenance tasks. This chapter concludes with an introduction to several trends: desktop virtualization, Google Chromebooks, tablet computers, and "bring your own device."

Chapter 5, "Networking," gives an overview of network architecture, including different types of networks, network topologies, and geographic areas. It then introduces the major hardware components of a network, followed by a review of network administration topics such as user authentication, network security, and troubleshooting. This chapter closes with introductions to several related topics: Internet2, the internet of things (IoT), and net neutrality.

Chapter 6, "Server Administration," introduces several infrastructure topics from server hardware components to virtualization to cloud service models. Next it reviews server operations, including operating systems and server administration. Finally, this chapter introduces a number of different server roles that might be used by a library.

Chapter 7, "Information Security," begins with a broad overview of information security management, including privacy issues, regulations and policies, and library application security. Next it introduces many of the security threats facing information systems, such as social engineering and ransomware. Methods for protecting personal computers are discussed and the final section of the chapter introduces a number of network security tactics.

Chapter 8, "Web Design and Development," is separated into three sections, with the first section addressing website architecture and including topics such as the anatomy of a webpage, web server architecture, programming languages, and developer tools. The second section addresses web development, including the roles on a web development team, a description of the web design process, and a review of different design strategies. The final section introduces the semantic web, web application programming interfaces (APIs), web analytics, and web accessibility.

Chapter 9, "Software and Systems Development," covers several foundational development topics from the perspective of the library technologist. It begins with a discussion of the software development process, including business analysis and the project proposal, then goes into a description of the systems development life cycle. The next section provides an introduction to programming, including some code examples using pseudocode, then provides an overview of common programming languages. The section on database design gives an introduction to relational database design and an introduction to structured query language programming. The chapter concludes with a brief overview of two software development topics: APIs and open source software.

Chapter 10, "Specialized and Emerging Technology Services," begins with a discussion of creative and innovative spaces in libraries. Most of the rest of the chapter reviews different services and technologies that may be offered in libraries, including digital media labs, makerspaces, and 3-D printing, among others. The chapter concludes with an overview of future trends for libraries: artificial intelligence, blockchain, and IoT.

Chapter 11, "Library Management Technologies," addresses technologies that have developed specifically to provide solutions for libraries. An overview of the library management system is given from the perspective of the technologist, followed by a brief introduction to electronic resource management. Next, the chapter focuses on digital collections, including equipment and digitization practices. The final section reviews a number of collection and space management technologies, including self-checkout, book lockers, radio frequency identification, and automated storage and retrieval systems, among others.

Chapter 12, "Technology Planning," begins with a section about acquiring technology, including a discussion about budget planning and a description of the technology evaluation and selection process. The next section focuses on strategic technology planning, with a description of the entire planning process and the final planning document. The technology perspective of continuity planning and disaster recovery is covered next, with the continuity plan covered first; disaster response, mitigation, and recovery next; and risk management strategies last. This chapter concludes with a brief discussion about managing change.

Acknowledgments

While writing this book, I was inspired by the expertise and ingenuity of my fellow library technologists who solve complex problems and develop innovative solutions on a daily basis. Much about library IT work is not glamorous, yet it is essential to the services that libraries provide today. It is also impossible to be an expert in all technology subjects, so I am indebted to my colleagues who continually investigate, innovate, and share their knowledge.

To be a technologist is to be a lifelong learner and I believe that most library workers are at least a little bit of a technologist—whether they think of themselves that way or not.

I would like to thank Dr. Karen G. Schneider for her endless support and encouragement during this project as well as in my day job managing library technology and experimenting with emerging technology services. I also thank Charles Harmon for his eternal patience and guidance during my first book project. I know that I am not alone in listening to music at times while working, so I would like to acknowledge the musicians whose work aided my own creative process: Jóhann Jóhannsson, Hildur Guðnadóttir, Steven Wilson, and Insomnium. Finally, I want to thank my kids for their patience while their father spent time on weekends and vacations working on this book, and my wife, Katrina Smith (a librarian as well), for both her personal and professional support of this project.

Jonathan M. Smith
Santa Rosa, California

1

Information Technology in Libraries

The influence of information technology (IT) on the library world is undeniable. It is woven into nearly every service that libraries provide, whether the library user interacts directly with technology or the library worker uses technology in providing the service. It is a matter of course that all library positions involve some level of skill with IT, from operating personal computers and software, including library management systems, databases, and office productivity software, to designing new technology-based services, planning implementations, and administering complex IT infrastructures. As technology becomes ever more pervasive in the work libraries do, many positions are blending the skills and training of library and information professionals with that of IT professionals, resulting in emerging roles that capitalize on both.

Libraries have a long track record of using new developments in technology and have contributed to many developments as well. As forward-thinking as many in the profession are, it is important to examine new technology critically, as we would any other new service, and to not be carried away by the possibilities. At the same time, innovation occurs when we are not afraid to experiment and try something new. Failure breeds success. A spirit of innovation that is grounded in critical assessment will result in the best possible services for library users.

This chapter begins by establishing a historical context and reviews general technological developments over the past sixty years alongside developments that have taken place in libraries. The chapter then discusses the place of IT in organizations, some particulars of IT governance, and the role of the library in it all. Next, it goes into some detail about the structure of an IT unit, illustrates a library IT department, and describes a number of different positions with responsibility for technology. Lastly, the chapter touches on three issues: ethics of IT, user privacy, and equitable access.

HISTORY OF INFORMATION TECHNOLOGY IN LIBRARIES

Throughout time, libraries have capitalized on IT as well as contributed to the development of original technologies for their own benefit. The codex and the printing press are examples of early technologies that have had a major influence on libraries. The development of the card catalog in the late eighteenth century revolutionized access to library resources. Microphotography led to the development of microfilm in the early twentieth century and was adopted widely as a means of preservation as well as a method for greatly increasing collections while efficiently using space.

Computers and related digital technologies have transformed information storage and retrieval, and consequently libraries, much as they have society at large. Library services have been similarly affected. IT (also known as *information and communications technology*) refers to the combination of hardware, software, and services that people use to manage, communicate, and share information. As the IT industry continues to innovate, libraries will continue to use new developments in an effort to provide ever more equitable and better services and resources.

Information Technology in the 1960s

The 1960s were the age of the mainframe computer, and saw the first applications of computers in libraries. The machine-readable cataloging (MARC) standard was developed at the Library of Congress by Henriette Avram in the late 1960s.[1] It is an international standard still in use today for the digital description of bibliographic items such as books, and was key to the automation of libraries. Library staff were able to access the MARC records stored in a mainframe computer by using terminal workstations—thus were the first digital library management systems born.

The foundations of the internet were laid in the late 1960s by the Advanced Research Projects Agency (ARPA) of the US Department of Defense. The project sought to develop a method for digitally sharing messages and data between organizations. Known as ARPANet, the first network went live in 1969 and connected computers located at the University of California at Los Angeles, Stanford University, the University of California at Santa Barbara, and the University of Utah.[2]

This period also saw rapid developments in computer hardware. These advancements were described by Moore's law, which originally said that the number of transistors on an integrated circuit would double every year—essentially resulting in processing power that would increase exponentially. The law was revised in 1975 to say that the number of transistors would double every two years. Although a projection of a historical trend and not actually a physical law, Moore's law turned out to be fairly accurate for the next forty years. It demonstrated that computing power had simultaneously grown more powerful while also dropping in price.

Information Technology in the 1970s

For most of the 1970s the computing experience was dominated by terminals that connected to mainframes and workgroup computers. Then, in 1977, the first generation of mass-market personal computers were released, subsequently changing the entire landscape as computers came to be used in homes and schools in addition to libraries and businesses. Released that year were the Commodore PET, with the option of 4 KB or 8 KB of RAM; the Apple II, from the company founded by Steve Jobs and Steve Wozniak; and the TRS-80, which was produced by Tandy Corporation and sold in RadioShack stores. The 1970s also saw the development and release of the Xerox Alto, which is credited as the first computer whose operating system used a graphical user interface (GUI) and featured an input device called a *mouse*.

ARPANet continued to grow and develop, and libraries began experimenting with online information retrieval by means of connecting to a remote computer. Starting in 1971, MEDLINE, otherwise known as MEDLARS Online (Medical Literature Analysis and Retrieval System), gave libraries a way to access the National Library of Medicine's *Index Medicus*. Another early information retrieval product was Lockheed's DIALOG. The first online public access catalogs (OPACs) were developed, with the Ohio College Library Center (OCLC) and Dallas Public Library early pioneers. These first OPACs strongly resembled a digital form of card catalogs, with the ability to search records by title, subject, and author.

An important milestone in the history of computer operating systems was the development and release of UNIX, which would later become the foundation of a number of open-source operating systems.

Information Technology in the 1980s

In the 1980s, mainframes gave way to the client-server model as networks became more common. Along with ARPANet, a number of other networks were also developed, so a common protocol was needed in order to link them. Transmission control protocol/internet protocol (TCP/IP) became the standard to which many corporations and research organizations migrated, allowing networks to merge and the internet to take form. The first public online service providers appeared, with Compu-Serve, Prodigy, and America Online becoming available to consumers throughout the 1980s.

Home computing experienced a boom as mass-market personal computers (PCs) began to appear in homes and more companies joined the market to offer competing products. The IBM PC became available in 1981, followed by an assortment of "clones" from different makers known as *IBM compatibles*, running an operating system from Microsoft called MS-DOS (Microsoft—Disk Operating System). Other notable PC releases included the Texas Instruments TI-99 4/A (1981), the Commodore 64 (1982), and the Apple Macintosh (1985)—which was the first PC with widespread adoption to feature a GUI and a mouse for input.

Libraries experienced several significant technological developments. OPACs became more advanced, to include keyword and boolean searching, and were designed to interact with software developed to manage traditional library functions such as acquisitions, cataloging, and circulation. Combining these software modules into a single package resulted in the first integrated library systems (ILS).

The formulation of the international Z39.50 standard took place, a protocol for information retrieval over TCP/IP networks that enabled libraries to remotely search databases and exchange information.

CD-ROM technology was introduced in the mid-1980s, and was quickly adopted by information vendors and libraries as it was easier and cheaper than the prevalent method of online information retrieval. Rather than a library paying hourly rates to use an online service, a library patron could sit at a personal computer with an optical disk drive, and directly search and access information stored on the CD-ROM.[3]

With the availability of mass-market application software, libraries began to make computers available as a service to patrons for uses beyond information retrieval, to include providing access to productivity and educational software.

Information Technology in the 1990s

Much of the technology developed in the 1980s experienced rapid growth and widespread adoption in the 1990s. While personal computers became more prevalent in business and education settings, local area networks were also becoming more common. Researchers applied Metcalfe's law to telecommunications networks to demonstrate that the value of a network increased greatly with every connected user. The internet continued to grow, and in 1991 the World Wide Web (WWW) became publicly available. Early web browsers included NCSA Mosaic, Netscape Navigator, and Microsoft's Internet Explorer. With the rise in popularity of the WWW, web search engines and e-commerce sites used information-retrieval methods, and many other web-based technologies became increasingly important in libraries. The advancements made in online information retrieval would eventually inform a new generation of web-based library search interfaces.

Significant operating systems released for personal computers during the 1990s included the open-source operating system Linux (1991), Microsoft Windows 3.1 (1991), Apple's System 7 (1991), and Microsoft Windows 95 (1995); operating systems developed by competing companies, such as Commodore, Texas Instruments, and others, fell by the wayside. Apple introduced the all-in-one iMac G3 in 1998. Laptop computers were introduced, with adoption taking off following the establishment of the 802.11 Wi-Fi standard in 1997.

Advancements in library technology were mostly centered around the development of increasingly sophisticated ILSs, and greater use of online information retrieval. Dynix Automated Library System was originally released in the mid-1980s, and became one of the most widely adopted ILSs over the subsequent decade.[4]

Information Technology in the 2000s

As the web became more and more central to how users would seek information, libraries increasingly offered services online. Library websites developed to include web portals, online indices, finding aids, research guides, live reference services, digital libraries, and online exhibits. While library use of the web exploded, development on ILSs stagnated. So many subscription databases became available that federated searching was developed as a solution for sending a single search to multiple resources, then assembling the disparate results into one result set for the searcher.

In 2001, the Internet Archive became available to the general public via the Wayback Machine, a searchable archive of old web pages. Major digitization efforts were launched, including the Google Books Library Project, which initially involved several major research universities and the New York Public Library. In 2008, the HathiTrust was founded to be a repository and provide governance for library digitization efforts.

Wireless communication technologies were further developed, with new Wi-Fi standards that accommodated faster speeds and greater bandwidth. Smartphones were introduced, including the BlackBerry (2002) and the iPhone (2007); they were at first limited to email and personal organization, then later included web access and custom applications for communication and social media. Soon web developers had to design websites and applications with the relatively tiny screen of a mobile phone in mind.

Aside from the new smartphone market, other significant consumer releases included Mac OS X 10.0 (2001), Microsoft Windows XP (2001), and the Apple MacBook (2006).

Information Technology in the 2010s

In 2010, the Apple iPad was introduced and, along with other products produced by other companies, contributed to the rising adoption of the tablet computer. As of February 2019, 52 percent of American adults owned a tablet. The capabilities of smartphones continued to advance, and have become more widely adopted as well, with 81 percent of American adults owning one by February 2019, according to the Pew Research Center.[5] Mobile computing became widespread, and libraries and library resource vendors responded by developing custom applications for use on mobile devices; they have also developed websites that use responsive design that can adjust to a myriad of different screen resolutions rather than only a handful.

Data centers virtualized their servers or moved them to cloud service providers, completely outsourcing the infrastructure work involved. With the *cloud*, software as a service (SaaS) emerged, which is a model in which software applications are hosted in the cloud and accessed by a user via a web browser. Amazon Web Services offers many different models of cloud services, and Google offers a suite of web-accessible productivity applications.

Some library vendors also began offering cloud-based software to replace locally hosted library solutions, with OCLC Web-scale Management Services, Ex Libris Alma, and Serial Solutions 360 Resource Manager among them.

As the 2010s came to a close, the internet and the web had become firmly established as the dominant platforms for information seeking and exchange, and so have become central to many of the services that libraries provide.

INFORMATION TECHNOLOGY IN ORGANIZATIONS

The role of IT in an organization is determined by the policies and decision-making structure of the organization. Because of the influence that decisions regarding technology can have on members of the organization, a formal governance structure is essential to ensure that the best decisions are made for the organization, and the users that it serves.

Where the library fits into governance, and how IT responsibilities are divided between a central IT department and the library, depends on many factors, including the relationship between the library and external IT support, the skills available within the library, and the services it provides.

Information Technology Governance

Within any organization, there needs to be an established method for making decisions and setting policies that may have wide-reaching consequences. Governance of IT determines who will make the decisions, what the decision making process is, and how these decisions are communicated and enforced. Inclusive governance will incorporate input from stakeholders, not just those employed by the organization but also those in the communities that are served.

The library in particular should be concerned with opportunities for stakeholder input. IT does not operate in a vacuum and certainly the library will have multiple stakeholders. These stakeholders are not just the library patrons, but also the library employees. They need the ability to contribute their voices to the management and application of IT.

Organization-wide IT governance may take the form of a committee or set of committees led by managers and made up of both technology specialists and employees from units served by the technology unit. The committees may review and establish policies that influence the organization, procedures that involve the cooperation of multiple units, set major priorities, and create and monitor methods for feedback and accountability. It is important that governance is conducted within the framework of the organization's mission and goals, particularly when setting strategic directions.

The library's leader of technology should have a seat at the table in the parent organization's IT governance structure, both to represent library interests and to contribute expertise as an information professional. Where it makes sense, the library should also have representatives on any subcommittees or task forces. Even when the library representative does not have technology responsibilities central to their role, they can make important contributions by representing both the library's interests as well as the user's. An example of this is an instruction librarian serving on an academic technology committee, which might oversee technology use in classrooms and computer labs.

One of the things that helps determine the form of governance is the level of technology management and support that is centralized versus distributed. Many organizations have a mix of centralized and distributed responsibilities, so in practice it can be thought of as a spectrum rather than an either–or situation. An organization in which technology is completely centralized may have only one person in the library with part-time responsibilities, mainly acting as a liaison or representative to the centralized IT department. More often, there will be a mix of centralized and library-managed technology. Only the largest libraries will support the majority of their own IT—even then they may outsource some support, relying on cloud service providers for example.

There are pros and cons to both scenarios. Centralizing IT can result in much greater efficiency, eliminating the duplication of effort by employees and saving money through enterprise licenses and bulk purchasing. The organization will also benefit from standardization of technology and policies. On the other hand, distributed technology management will afford units with much greater flexibility, and the ability to customize solutions to their unique needs. Technology support may also be more responsive with greater attention paid to the local situation, but employees will not be able to specialize to the same depth as centralized support because individuals will often have broad technology support responsibilities.

Depending on the balance of organization-wide technology responsibilities, it may be that the library itself is primarily responsible for setting technology policy. Because technology is pervasive throughout library services and functions, the library's leader of technology should be a member of the library's senior leadership group. This could take many forms, including a department head sitting on a council of department heads or an associate dean serving on the senior leadership team for an academic library. As at the enterprise level, IT governance needs to exist for the library as well, making shared decisions and incorporating stakeholder input.

The opportunity to collaborate with other libraries introduces an additional need for governance. Often in the form of consortia, there may be shared resources or some IT support centralized at a consortium office. Collaborative decisions will need to be made regarding shared resources, including the creation of policies and procedures. Partnerships may spell this out in a memorandum of understanding (MOU), a document that defines agreed-upon relationships between organizations and describes responsibilities and perhaps financial or workforce contributions.

Division of Duties

The division of responsibility for technology management and support between the library and a central IT department varies from institution to institution. Generally, IT management is organized according to either a centralized or decentralized model, but the reality for many may lie somewhere in the middle.

Services that are strong candidates for centralization include enterprise applications, information security, and infrastructure support—which could include networking, telecommunications, and data center management.

The library should at the least be responsible for administering library-specific applications, such as the ILS and interlibrary loan software, and management of the myriad online platforms they use, such as the library's website, discovery interface, digital libraries, and institutional repository. Many library applications and web platforms are mission critical, and require specialized knowledge and attention that library staff have training and experience with.

Maintaining control over user and desktop support can also be valuable to the library. Libraries specialize in user services, often priding themselves in being sensitive to user needs, and user support is a point-of-need service that requires a quick response to provide quality service that may not be possible from a centralized service.

Table 1.1. Example Division of IT Responsibilities

Model One	Model Two
• Central IT services ○ Networking ○ Security • Library IT department ○ Server administration ○ Web development ○ End-user support ○ Lab management ○ Digitization ○ Programming ○ Institutional repository	• Central IT services ○ Networking ○ Security ○ Server administration ○ Programming ○ End-user support ○ Lab management • Library IT department ○ Application administration ○ Web development ○ Digitization ○ Institutional repository

The division of responsibility for other areas of technology depends on the demands and skills within the library, and the willingness and responsiveness of central IT, in addition to management support and financial capability. Regardless of where lines are drawn, library employees will have to work well with IT staff. Library managers will need to collaborate with IT leaders to provide direction while library staff will need to work with IT staff to provide the best quality services to the library and its users.

One area that can benefit from shared responsibility is server administration. Maintaining a data center can be an expensive proposition, especially if central IT already supports one. For the library to do so would be duplicating efforts when the staff time could be assigned to more library-specific applications. On the other hand, administering their own servers does give the library greater control and flexibility over the applications and databases hosted on the servers. A good compromise can be for central IT to maintain physical servers or provide a virtual server environment while allowing library technicians administrative access.

As a guiding principle, libraries should manage services that need close attention to focus on library needs, and allow the centralization of services that would otherwise result in duplicative efforts and unnecessary specialization by library staff. The library should focus their energies where their expertise may have the greatest effect.

Librarians with technology responsibilities occupy a unique role, being close to the perspective of library patrons and employees, while also having a solid understanding of the possibilities and limitations of IT. In library circles they will be considered a technologist, while in IT circles they will be the library specialist. Communication skills are important, as they will be a liaison between the library and IT, with the responsibility of translating from one group to the other. The library technologist needs to be able to communicate equally well with administration also, because the final decision on matters relating to organizational strategy, finances, and policy often rests there.

Because the central IT unit is usually part of the same organization as the library, there may not be an MOU describing the relationship—as useful as that might be. But where the library is a customer, it is very useful for service-level agreements (SLAs) to exist. There may be an SLA for each functional area supported by central IT, which will describe the service with some detail, covering the topics as seen in textbox 1.1.

> **TEXTBOX 1.1**
>
> **Service-Level Agreement Sections**
>
> Description of the service
> Expected performance level, quality, or reliability
> Responsibilities of the service provider
> Responsibilities of the customer (in this case, the library)
> Method of requesting service
> Expected response and resolution time frame
> Complaint resolution
> Method of amendment and termination
> Glossary of terms

THE INFORMATION TECHNOLOGY UNIT

Department Structure

The IT unit of an organization is often divided into subunits, allowing for greater specialization. The fact is, IT is such a broad discipline that no one can be an expert in every area. To provide adequate support for any specialty requires in-depth knowledge that comes from training and experience.

Depending on the size of the organization, common IT divisions include user services, infrastructure support, and enterprise applications. Additional divisions that might stand on their own include web development, information security, and software development. Each unit or team may be led by a manager who has advanced expertise in that specific area, with additional skills in project management, planning, and communication.

The help desk is often the first point of contact for any problem reports or requests for services. Staff are trained to handle basic troubleshooting and to gather information, then to escalate or direct the issue or request to the appropriate functional-area team. Depending on the size of the unit, some of the staff may specialize in specific operating systems or applications.

User Services

User services may include responsibility for the IT help desk, user support (levels one and two), troubleshooting for hardware and software, computer lab management, workstation setup and repairs, application installation and support, operating systems support, printer management, project management services, consultation on technology solutions, user training, and documentation.

Infrastructure Support

Infrastructure support may include responsibility for data center management, server administration, networking, remote access, virtual server environment, user authentication, creation of user accounts, backups and disaster recovery, and the physical computing infrastructure.

Enterprise Applications

Enterprise applications may include responsibility for business applications, human resources applications, database management, email and calendaring applications, and financial management systems.

Web Development

Web development may include responsibility for web design, website maintenance, web application programming, website scripting, graphical design, section 508 compliance (accessibility), and website content editor training.

Information Security

Information security may include responsibility for network security, change management, security standards for business processes, security implementation for cloud computing services, and security audits.

Software Development

Software development may include responsibility for application programming, development and support of custom applications, customization of open-source software products, and user experience (UX) design.

The Library IT Department

When libraries first began moving from the physical card catalog to a computerized system, it was known as *automating* the library; therefore, a library that had a department dedicated to this task was often known as the library automation department. Subsequently, the ILS became widespread, the responsible departments starting taking on additional systems-related tasks, and it became more common for departments to be known as *library systems departments* and the librarian who specialized in ILS administration was known as a *systems librarian*.

The technology footprint in libraries has grown far beyond that of just library systems to be interwoven into all manner of traditional and emerging roles, and additional units and positions have been created to reflect this. Units and positions that hew closer to traditional IT responsibilities—such as server administration or web development—are often named as such and staffed by employees with the same training and certifications as IT professionals. Units and positions that hew closer to the library or archival world—such as digital collections—may have technology training incorporated into their regular and ongoing training.

Technology responsibilities are delegated in libraries in many different ways. Some may be assigned to units or teams, with some to individuals who may have other library responsibilities as well. One logical way is to divide roles into application administration (often termed *library systems*), user support, web services, and digital initiatives.

The ILS is an enterprise application that may have dedicated staff, or support may be split between traditional library and IT roles, with the application administrator being someone located in a technical services unit, and the server or database administrator located in the technology services unit. Of note, however, is that the responsibilities for server and database administration are being made extinct by hosted cloud or SaaS solutions.

The library technologist usually is not able to specialize to the same depth as other IT professionals because their responsibilities are often much broader. A strong library technology team is made up of people with a comprehensive set of technology skills that fit the library's needs, as well as a good ability to communicate. Their success depends on their ability to research a problem and to work with experts, including a vendor or external IT department.

Within the hierarchy of the library's organization, the technology services unit should be independent of technical services, public services, and other traditional library units because the unit serves everyone in the organization. Although many support issues are particular to a certain library realm, many solutions also affect the entire library and so should be independent of the bias implicit in particular library functions.

Technology Unit Positions

The size of the technology unit often determines how narrowly staff may specialize or whether they have additional duties that are not specific to supporting technology services. Some responsibilities may also be covered by an external IT department or outsourced to a vendor. Therefore, position descriptions for staff providing technology services are often a unique blend depending on the particular needs of the library. Regardless of the particular role, however, most positions require skills or experience at some level with project management, customer service, troubleshooting, and communication. Positions strongly influenced by traditional or emerging library roles include the following:

- Digital initiatives librarian
- Emerging technology librarian
- Systems librarian
- Electronic resources librarian
- Digital archivist

Positions that are traditional IT roles include the following:

- Server administrator
- System administrator
- Network support technician
- Web developer
- UX designer
- Helpdesk specialist
- Programmer
- Lab manager
- Project manager
- Systems analyst

Head of Information Technology or Library Technology Services

The leader of the library technology unit may have the title of *head, director, manager, coordinator*, or *associate dean*—as appropriate for the institution. This person should have a seat at the table with other senior library leadership. They will supervise the work of staff in the technology unit, prioritize tasks, provide project consultations, and juggle schedules and deadlines. As a manager, it is useful to have skills and experience with human resources, project management, diplomacy, and to be collaborative. They will create requests for proposals and establish required system specifications for vendors. They may also have to plan and manage a budget, as well as assess technology use and plan strategic technology directions for the library.

Systems Librarian

A systems librarian often has a library background, with experience in technical services functions such as cataloging and acquisitions. This position is the spiritual successor to the automation librarian and, although the ILS may be central to their work, they may have other technology duties as well. This position has more of a focus on application administration, and less on server administration—particularly with the trend of moving ILSs to the cloud.

Systems librarian is also used as a generic title in smaller libraries where there is only one person with technology support responsibilities. In those situations this position may have a broad technology role, or else fill in the support gaps not provided by an external unit—and could involve almost anything else technology related. In libraries where this role is found in technical services instead of the technology unit, it may share responsibilities for managing electronic resources or cataloging.

Database management skills and experience with technical services processes, as well as a general understanding of server administration and networking, are useful.

Digital Initiatives Librarian

The digital initiatives librarian often has a library or an archives background and focuses on digital projects that involve digitization and database management, which are often web based. Strong interpersonal skills and project management experience are important. Responsibilities may involve managing a digital library or institutional repository, planning new digital services and online strategy, and digitizing document, image, audio, and video collections. This role may have an archival focus and may involve the supervision of staff.

Web Developer or Web Services Librarian

The difference between a web developer and web services librarian lies in the balance of responsibilities between web development and librarianship. Larger units may have dedicated developers with an IT background, whereas others may blend web development with other library responsibilities. A web services department has staff that specialize in either web development or web design. Web development uses web programming and scripting languages, as well as database management. Web designers have a background in graphic design and UX design. This role may be involved with the OPAC or discovery layer because of the web interface component, as well as managing other web platforms used by the library.

Electronic Resources Librarian

The electronic resources librarian is usually a technical services role and is not found in the technology services unit, but the work performed has been greatly affected by technology. It involves managing online subscriptions, and it helps to be familiar with database management, authentication, proxy servers, and APIs.

Server or System Administrator

The server administrator, sometimes known as the *SysAdmin*, is an IT professional. Responsibilities include the installation of servers, virtual server environment administration, user account creation, backups and disaster recovery, server security, and change management. In smaller organizations, responsibilities may overlap with network administration and information security.

Network Administrator or Technician

The network administrator or technician may be responsible for both local and wide area network administration, configuring network servers and routers, physical cabling, network security, troubleshooting network problems, providing internet support, administering proxy servers, and firewall configuration. Larger organizations may have dedicated network security specialists.

User Support or Helpdesk Technician

The user support technician has an IT background and is the most user-facing of all IT roles. It requires strong customer service skills combined with technical aptitude. A broad knowledge of IT aids in troubleshooting issues and escalating problems appropriately.

Specific responsibilities may include computer hardware installation and troubleshooting, software installation and maintenance, creating technical documentation, user training, and peripheral support for hardware such as printers. Larger institutions may have a separate shop for maintaining and troubleshooting computer hardware. Hardware support in the library goes beyond computers and printers to include scanners, instructional technology, automated storage, audiovisual equipment, and equipment loaned to library users.

Programmer or Developer

The programmer or developer may customize existing applications as well as develop new ones. He or she will write code in programming and scripting languages, and often specialize in specific languages and operating systems.

Project Manager

The project manager is a traditional IT role that is making its way into libraries. The IT professional who is a project manager often holds certification in a certain school of project management. He or she does not necessarily need specialized IT experience so much as a broad understanding of IT. It is important to have a solid understanding of business processes and the ability to translate those into technology requirements. The project manager is a team leader who often manages schedules, budgets, and deadlines.

Security Specialist

Many organizations have an information security officer who is ultimately responsible for the security of the network and computer systems. Security specialists enforce policies and procedures to ensure that data remains safe. They monitor the network for vulnerabilities and threats, and create plans to protect the organization's information.

INFORMATION TECHNOLOGY ISSUES

There are many issues, trends, and topics of interest relating to IT, a number of which will be covered in later chapters. We start with a few foundational issues.

Ethics of Information Technology

As IT can have a profound influence on individual lives as well as on society, the application of moral principles is a serious consideration. Privacy, intellectual property, intellectual freedom, and equitable access are just some of the issues that raise ethical questions. Certainly, any time a library considers a new technology implementation or service, staff should consider how it will affect the user's rights. They should ask whether there is any conflict with professional values or those of the organization. For many, it is easy to focus on how a service or business workflow may be improved, or to be distracted by what is new and shiny. But we need to think of the potential cost. In some cases it will be enough to change the particulars of an implementation, but there may also be times when a service is in conflict with our ethics.

To help guide us in making these decisions, several professional organizations have established a code of ethics. The American Library Association (ALA) provides a number of statements and documents that inform the decisions that we make. The "Core Values of Librarianship" lists several values directly applicable to technology services, including access, confidentiality and privacy, democracy, and intellectual freedom.[6] The *ALA Policy Manual* further describes the core values, with section B.2 covering intellectual freedom, and section B.4 covering equity and access.[7] The "Library Bill of Rights" is another document that informs the professional ethics of librarianship.[8]

IT professionals also have several documents that advise their professional practice. The Institute of Electrical and Electronics Engineers (IEEE) governing documents include both a Code of Ethics[9] and a Code of Conduct.[10] The Association of Information Technology Professionals provides a Standards of Conduct to which all members are expected to adhere.[11] These documents establish a foundation on which a technologist can make informed, ethical decisions.

User Privacy

Although privacy is an issue that goes beyond technology, it has come to the forefront of policy and practice concerns given the amount of personal data that is collected, managed, and consequently accessible using IT. Businesses collect information from customers while simultaneously social media users are volunteering information online. Websites and mobile phones collect information on user behavior, often without the awareness of the user. Information can take the form of financial records, personal data, images, audio, geographic position system and other location-related data, and many others. Questions persist about who may access what information under what circumstances and how people can protect their personal information.

What information may a commercial entity collect? What can they do with that information? How can the government access information collected by others? What rights and protections do private citizens have?

Libraries also participate in the collection and management of user data, in addition to providing access to resources and organizations who may as well. The types of software that libraries use that collect and manage user information include library management systems, ILSs, interlibrary loan software, room reservation software, and online portals, in addition to security systems like closed-circuit television recordings.

The ALA Code of Ethics specifically addresses privacy and confidentiality: "We protect each library user's right to privacy and confidentiality with respect to information sought or received and resources consulted, borrowed, acquired or transmitted."[12]

The prevailing attitude among the library profession is that libraries should only collect data that they absolutely need, protect what they do collect, disassociate the data from the user when they can, and educate users about their rights as well as how to protect themselves.

Equitable Access

Digital information resources have greatly expanded the amount of information available and ease of access for many people. Nonetheless, there exists a digital divide whereby economics, culture, geography, or physical ability, among other factors, result in unequal access to and skills for using IT. Libraries play an important role in bridging the digital divide and providing equitable access to information and technology that patrons might not otherwise have.

The *ALA Policy Manual* (B.2.1.15) states, "All information resources that are provided directly or indirectly by the library, regardless of technology, format, or methods of delivery, should be readily, equally, and equitably accessible to all Library users."[13]

Libraries have a responsibility to eliminate barriers to equitable access that may exist in the IT they provide. When implementing IT solutions, it is important to be cognizant of issues of access and to actively avoid setting up barriers. When acquiring IT, consider methods of access and compare alternate solutions, as one product may be more accessible than another.

SUMMARY

IT is present throughout the library in many of the services provided and much of the work performed. Libraries have incorporated many technological advances throughout history, from the codex to the e-book, and the card catalog to the ILS. Many library developments have coincided with technological ones including the MARC record in the 1960s; the personal computer and advances in networking in the 1970s; OPACs, the ILS, and the rise of the internet in the 1980s; the WWW in the 1990s; mobile technologies and major digitization projects in the 2000s; and cloud-based services in the 2010s—just to name a few.

IT governance is an important concept for organizations because it determines who makes decisions about technology, what the decision-making process is, and how these decisions are communicated and enforced. It is essential that stakeholders, including the library and its users, have a role in governance. Another factor to solve is what technology will be supported in-house by the library and what responsibilities will go to an external unit. This will depend on many factors, and there are a variety of solutions in the real world.

Depending on the size of the organization, common IT divisions include user services, infrastructure support, enterprise applications, web development, information security, and software development. The library IT department should focus its energies where its expertise may have the greatest effect and avoid duplicating efforts of others. Positions in the library supporting technology require IT skills and expertise, much like IT professionals—although some will be of a specialized library nature that also require a library or archives background.

There are many issues and trends to pay attention to in the field of IT. At the core of what we do, however, are our values and ethics. Librarianship and IT both have established professional values and ethics to help guide the decisions we make in the application of technology to our work. User privacy is an important issue that has gotten much press lately, and is certainly a factor in librarianship. Libraries also play an important role in providing equitable access to resources and technology.

KEY TERMS

Ethics of IT

Equitable access

Federated searching

Information technology (IT)

Integrated library system (ILS)

IT governance

Library automation

Machine-readable catalog (MARC)

Memorandum of understanding (MOU)

Online public access catalog (OPAC)

Service-level agreement

Stakeholder

Software as a service (SaaS)

User privacy

World Wide Web

Z39.50

QUESTIONS

1. What are some of the key historical developments in information technology that have influenced libraries?
2. What is the ideal division of technology responsibilities between a library and an external IT department? Why?
3. What are the pros and cons of centralizing technology management and support?
4. Describe the subdivisions of an IT department and their specializations.
5. What are some examples of library positions that have a strong technology component?
6. Describe an ethical concern specifically as it relates to technology use by libraries. What professional guidance is available on the topic?
7. Is there an emerging technology that you believe could have a significant effect on libraries?

ACTIVITIES

1. Choose a library and map the technology decision-making structures of the library and the parent organization to which it belongs. What formal governance structures exist? Who is involved? Are there informal practices?
2. Choose a library and describe the division of technology responsibilities between the library and an external IT department.

FURTHER READING

Berzai, Lou. "How Ethical Theories Apply to IT Professionals." *CompTIA* (blog), Jun 27, 2017. https://www.aitp.org/blog/aitp-blog/2017/06/27/how-ethical-theories-apply-to-it-professionals/.

Burke, John J. *Neal-Schuman Library Technology Companion: A Basic Guide for Library Staff*, 5th ed. Chicago: Neal-Schuman, 2016.

Chong, Josephine L. L., and Felix B. Tan. "IT Governance in Collaborative Networks: A Socio-Technical Perspective." *Pacific Asia Journal of the Association for Information Systems* 4, no. 2 (2012): 31–48.

Fernandez, Peter D., and Kelly Tilton. *Applying Library Values to Emerging Technology: Decision-Making in the Age of Open Access, Maker Spaces, and the Ever-Changing Library.* Chicago: Association of College and Research Libraries, 2018.

Hoover, Jasmine. "Gaps in IT and Library Services at Small Academic Libraries in Canada." *Information Technology and Libraries* 37, no. 4, (2018): 15–26. https://doi.org/10.6017/ital.v37i4.10596.

Jurkowski, Odin L. *Technology and the School Library: A Comprehensive Guide for Media Specialists and Other Educators*, 3rd ed. Lanham, MD: Rowman & Littlefield, 2017.

Kelley, Keith J. *The Myth and Magic of Library Systems.* Waltham, MA: Chandos, 2015.

Laudon, Kenneth C. and Jane P. Laudon. *Management Information Systems*, 14th ed. Boston: Pearson Education, 2016.

Office for Intellectual Freedom and Jason Griffey. *Privacy and Freedom of Information in 21st Century Libraries: A Library Technology Report.* Chicago: American Library Association, 2010.

Ratledge, David, and Claudene Sproles. "An Analysis of the Changing Role of Systems Librarians." *Library Hi Tech* 35, no. 2, (2017): 303–11. https://doi.org/10.1108/LHT-08-2016-0092.

Woo, Melissa. "Ethics and the IT Professional," *EDUCAUSE Review*, March 27, 2017. https://er.educause.edu/articles/2017/3/ethics-and-the-it-professional.

RESOURCES

Association for Information Technology Professionals: https://www.aitp.org/
ALA, Access to Digital Information, Services, and Networks: http://www.ala.org/advocacy/node/35
ALA—Privacy Toolkit: http://www.ala.org/advocacy/privacy/toolkit
ALA—State Privacy Laws Regarding Library Records: http://www.ala.org/advocacy/privacy/statelaws
Association for Information Science and Technology: https://www.asist.org/
California State University, San Bernardino, IT Governance: https://www.csusb.edu/its/it-governance
Choose Privacy Every Day: https://chooseprivacyeveryday.org/
Data Detox: https://datadetoxkit.org
EDUCAUSE: https://www.educause.edu/
Electronic Frontier Foundation: https://www.eff.org/
Institute of Electrical and Electronics Engineers: https://www.ieee.org/
The Library and Information Technology Association: http://www.ala.org/lita/
The Library Freedom Project: https://libraryfreedomproject.org/

NOTES

1. Schudel, Matt, "Henriette Avram, 'Mother of MARC,' Dies," *Library of Congress Information Bulletin* (May 2006), accessed on June 3, 2019, https://www.loc.gov/loc/lcib/0605/avram.html.
2. Stewart, William, "ARPANET—The First Internet," *The Living Internet*, accessed on June 3, 2019, https://www.livinginternet.com/i/ii_arpanet.htm.
3. Michalak, Joseph A., "Observations on the Use of CD-ROM in Academic Libraries," *The Serials Librarian* 17, no. 3–4 (1989): 63–67. DOI: 10.1300/J123v17n03_08.

4. Breeding, Marshall, "The Chronicles of Dynix," *Smart Libraries Newsletter* 25, no. 6 (June 2005): 2, accessed on June 3, 2019, https://librarytechnology.org/document/11896.
5. "Mobile Fact Sheet," Pew Research Center (February 5, 2018), accessed on June 3, 2019, https://www.pewinternet.org/fact-sheet/mobile/.
6. "Core Values of Librarianship," American Library Association (July 26, 2006), accessed on June 3, 2019, http://www.ala.org/advocacy/intfreedom/corevalues.
7. "ALA Policy Manual," American Library Association (August 17, 2010), accessed on June 3, 2019, http://www.ala.org/aboutala/governance/policymanual.
8. "Library Bill of Rights," American Library Association (June 30, 2006), accessed on June 3, 2019, http://www.ala.org/advocacy/intfreedom/librarybill.
9. IEEE Code of Ethics," Institute of Electrical and Electronics Engineers, accessed on June 3, 2019, https://www.ieee.org/about/corporate/governance/p7-8.html.
10. "IEEE Code of Conduct," Institute of Electrical and Electronics Engineers (June 2014), accessed on June 3, 2019, https://www.ieee.org/content/dam/ieee-org/ieee/web/org/about/ieee_code_of_conduct.pdf.
11. "AITP Standards of Conduct," AITP San Diego, accessed on June 3, 2019, https://aitpsd.org/about-us/standards-of-conduct.html.
12. "Professional Ethics," American Library Association (May 19, 2017), accessed on June 3, 2019, http://www.ala.org/tools/ethics.
13. "B.2 Intellectual Freedom (Old Number 53)," American Library Association (August 4, 2010), accessed on June 3, 2019, http://www.ala.org/aboutala/governance/policymanual/updatedpolicymanual/section2/53intellfreedom#B.2.1.15.

2

Technology Management and Support

Similar to other library services, technology management and support should be oriented toward providing assistance to users by focusing on their needs and requirements. We must resist the temptation to design services around the possibilities and limitations of technology; rather, we should acknowledge user behavior, facilitate business processes, and work with the environment in which the technology is used.

Supporting technology from the library means that your role may change from service provider to user to somewhere in between with regularity. There will be times that you are providing technology help to users of the library or library employees, while at other times you will be the customer of an external vendor who is providing assistance. Depending on your situation and scope of responsibilities, your parent organization—be it the city government or university, for example—may provide a level of technology support for which your role may be to act as liaison between the library user and the parent organization's technology department.

This chapter begins by examining user support, including support levels, the help desk, the issue tracking system, and service-level agreements. Documentation is integral to technology management, so the chapter introduces the service catalog, user documentation, internal documentation, and asset management. Next it discusses software management, including software licenses and digital rights management. Mobile technology has its own set of concerns, as does accessibility of technology. Finally, the chapter introduces the basic concepts of project management.

USER SUPPORT

In a user-centered environment, user support takes a central role for the staff providing technology services. In the library this attitude often comes naturally with our focus on patron needs but it is still worth mentioning for those of us who are passionate about technology and can sometimes get excited about shiny things. The range of aid provided depend on a variety of factors—the mission of the unit, the needs of the users and organization, the level of assistance (or lack thereof) provided by the library's parent organization, and the resources made available.

Some typical user support activities include:

- Staffing a technology help desk
- Troubleshooting hardware, software, and network problems
- Evaluating technology products for procurement
- Establishing organization-wide technology standards

- Providing training to users
- Creating documentation
- Participating in or leading technology planning

It is important for user support staff to have a strong customer service ethic, an essential part of which are good communication skills. Those who have worked in library public services will be familiar with the reference interview. Providing technology assistance is quite similar—when troubleshooting a problem with a user you must negotiate the complaint to identify the real issue and resolve the problem to the user's satisfaction. There is an added element that a complaint brought forward by an individual user may surface broader issues in the technology environment that may affect others, as well.

Ask targeted questions that will narrow the complaint down to the actual problem. Find out what precisely is happening and what specific activity immediately preceded the problem. The more detail you can obtain, the better. Find out the exact sequence of actions, any specific error messages that may have been displayed, and whether there have been any recent changes made prior to the issue occurring (a change in configuration settings, installation of new software or hardware, etc.). Document everything you learn about the issue to aid others who may work on the resolution. Documentation will also help track what may be a recurring problem. If a particular workstation has repeated issues or several workstations exhibit similar problems, it may be symptomatic of a broader issue.

For the unit providing technology support, good communication relies on established channels and clear procedures for reporting issues. It is important that library staff clearly understand how to report issues as well as methods for escalation. If the library technology unit shares responsibilities with another unit, or if there are different reporting procedures depending on area (e.g., website problems versus computer workstation issues) these procedures need to be very clearly communicated. Library public services staff will often be the first to encounter user complaints and will need to know how to direct the user to begin resolving the issue.

Providing user support doesn't always have to be a face-to-face transaction. As problems can be reported remotely through telephone or email, assistance can also be given remotely. Beyond diagnosing and resolving an issue by communicating with the user, there is also software that allows the person providing aid to remotely control the user's computer. By using remote desktop software, the technician's computer can connect to the user's computer. The software takes input from the mouse and keyboard of the technician and sends it to the user's computer as if the technician were physically sitting at that computer, controlling it. Although this is mostly used for resolving software issues—viruses and malware, optimization, configurations—it can also be used to help diagnose hardware problems. Two common remote desktop applications are Apple Remote Desktop and Remote Desktop Connection by Microsoft.

Another type of remote support involves screen sharing, in which the technician gives directions to the user and is able to watch the output relayed from the user's monitor. This could be considered an intermediary level between a simple telephone call or chat session and the technician taking control using remote desktop software. In situations in which there are policies or security reasons not to give a technician direct access to a computer, this can be a good alternative.

User support can also be outsourced. If the organization lacks the expertise or resources, outsourcing can be a way to augment what is already provided. For example, an organization may have a need to provide assistance outside of regular business hours but lack the resources to make it available. An outside vendor could be contracted to extend the service beyond normal hours via telephone or chat. Of course, the downside is that a contracted vendor will have difficulty establishing personal relationships with the user population as well as a lack of intimate knowledge of the technology environment particular to the organization.

Support Levels

User support is often organized into multiple levels—or tiers—to accommodate escalating levels of complexity and increasing specialization. The way that this is actually accomplished will vary depending on a unit's expertise and scope of responsibilities, but it is generally divided into three tiers.

Tier One (or Level One) Support

The first tier of support typically consists of front-line staff—whether stationed at a help desk or responding to calls from users. Often the first point of contact for users, tier one support staff will provide information about policies and procedures, answer directional questions, and attempt troubleshooting for basic problems. They may follow a guide or knowledgebase in an attempt to resolve simple or common issues. They are responsible for creating a ticket to track the resolution of the issue, as well as recording the user's contact information, detailed information about the problem, and any steps taken while troubleshooting. If the first tier is not able to resolve the issue, it will be escalated to the next tier.

Tier Two (or Level Two) Support

The second tier of support handles more complex and specialized issues than the first level. Technicians working at the second tier may be more experienced and have specialization in specific areas, such as desktop computers, networking, or telecommunications. They will take over responsibility for the escalated issue and conduct advanced troubleshooting, informed by their expertise and referring to technical documentation. Tier two technicians communicate directly with the user as necessary to continue working on a resolution. In the case of desktop computer help, technicians may visit the users' workstations or connect remotely to work directly on the machine.

Tier Three (or Level Three) Support

In a three-tiered model, this is the highest-level support, responsible for handling the most difficult or advanced problems. The technician at this level often has deep expertise with specific applications, hardware, or systems. The issue may represent a new or unknown issue that requires a custom solution. Research and development might be involved at this level as well, although larger organizations will often handle that separately from user support.

On its face, it may appear that employing a three-tier model for user support would require a sizable technology unit. However, even a small library IT department could informally follow this model—student workers or public services staff at a help desk might provide tier-one assistance, with the library technology staff providing tiers two and three. Depending on the expertise of the library technology staff, the parent organization or a vendor might be responsible for tier three.

Help Desk

The technology help desk exists to provide users with a single point of contact for IT support. It can provide resolution for basic issues (tier one) and escalate more difficult problems. They often have access to the technology unit's issue tracking system, primarily for the purpose of creating tickets, which will then be handled by the technology unit. Help desks can be both outward and inward facing, handling requests from both external users as well as the organization's staff. Libraries that are part of a larger organization with responsibility for providing technology support may have access to the parent organization's technology help desk. Some organizations may embed technology help desks within the library even though administratively they report to a department outside of the library. In other cases, the library may operate a technology help desk for library patrons, or even integrate it into other library service points such as an information or circulation desk.

Similar to a library reference desk, the technology help desk may field queries from telephone, chat, and email in addition to walk-up users. If the technician assigned to the help desk is not able to solve the issue, he or she may escalate the issue to a higher level capable of more complex or specialized issues. Depending on the size and scope of responsibilities, specialized staff may have responsibilities delineated into the following areas:

- Workstation support: Responsible for deploying and supporting desktop, laptop, and tablet computers.
- Networking: Sometimes known as the *infrastructure team*, they are responsible for managing and supporting both the wired and wireless network, including network switches, wireless access points, network security, access controls, and authentication.
- Server management: Responsible for the management of server hardware and software, including physical servers, virtual servers, and the administration of servers in the cloud. This group could also have responsibility for server backups and access.

Some other staff may be assigned responsibility for telecommunications, including telephones, voicemail, and voice over internet protocol (VOIP); application support, including custom application software support and programming; and information security. These divisions of responsibilities are not hard and fast; rather, it depends on the size of the unit, its scope of responsibilities, and the available resources.

Issue-Tracking System

A primary tool for workflow management and documentation is the issue-tracking system. Sometimes known as *incident tracking*, this is a system in which a ticket (alternately called a *trouble ticket* or *support ticket*) is created for the purpose of having a single point of documentation for tracking work progress and other relevant information for an issue. The ticket is usually created at the moment that an issue is reported. Although it is often created by the technician who receives the initial request from a user, ticket creation can also be an automated process, generated when users submit a webform or else directly create the ticket themselves in the issue-tracking system.

When creating a ticket, it is important to provide as much information about the issue as possible, including basic information like:

- The precise equipment (e.g., which computer)
- Name of the user
- Name of the reporting staff (if different from the user)
- Location and time that the problem occurred
- Any error messages
- Any actions taken to try and solve problem

Tickets often have the ability to include other relevant information, as well as the ability to attach electronic documents.

Depending on the unit workflow, tickets can be assigned to particular staff or teams, which then update the ticket regularly while work is underway. Tickets will have a current status (unassigned, open, waiting, closed, etc.), an urgency (low, normal, or urgent), and can sometimes track time spent on a task. This makes it easy for staff to see at a glance what sort of progress has been made toward resolution.

Tickets can also be useful as historical documentation. For example, when a problem with a desktop computer is submitted, a technician can search for the computer ID number and produce all of the tickets that have previously been created for the same computer. Sometimes a pattern may emerge. The information is also useful when establishing justification for funding or producing documentation for a grant report.

Issue tracking systems are a typical part of customer support used by vendor and IT help desks. Strongly consider using one in the library as well, even for small teams, as it is useful not only for documentation purposes but also as an efficient method for updating team members about the work that has been done to resolve issues.

Service-Level Agreement

Sometimes it may be necessary to come to an agreement about exactly what and how a particular service will be provided. The service-level agreement (SLA) is a document detailing the expectations and responsibilities between a service provider and a customer. Usually the library is the customer in this arrangement, with a vendor or another unit in the organization taking the role of provider. SLAs are useful for setting clear expectations for both parties.

The SLA document often includes the following components:

- Type of service provided
- Description of the service
- Expected performance level (disruptions, downtime and uptime)
- Monitoring process
- Procedures for reporting issues and for escalation
- Response and issue-resolution timeframe
- Repercussions when the provider does not meet its commitment
- Customer responsibilities

The SLA is different from an operational-level agreement (OLA), which defines the relationship between support groups. An OLA describes the scope, responsibilities, communication channels, and expectations between units cooperating to provide technology services.

DOCUMENTING TECHNOLOGY

Documentation plays a critical role in managing and supporting technology. Whether the activity is creating instructions for users, documenting procedures for staff, or collecting externally created manuals and warranties, it is vital to create and maintain accurate documentation.

Service Catalog

To communicate to users what services are available, it is common to employ a *service catalog*. This could take the form of a public website or intranet webpage with services listed and organized, contact information for getting general help in navigating what is available, as well as guidance for obtaining assistance that is not offered. A service catalog typically details the party responsible for the service, contact information, categorization that allows it to be grouped with other similar services, which users have access, associated costs (which may take the form of chargebacks for internal users), and the procedure for making requests.

Within the IT discipline, there are frameworks for designing services so that they fit the needs of the organization. One of the most broadly adopted is the Information Technology Infrastructure

Library (ITIL). Originally developed in the United Kingdom, it is now owned by AXELOS, which also manages individual certifications of five levels. The framework is described in five volumes:[1]

- *ITIL Service Strategy*
- *ITIL Service Design*
- *ITIL Service Transition*
- *ITIL Service Operation*
- *ITIL Continual Service Improvement*

ITIL is not the only framework that the industry uses. The Microsoft Operations Framework and the ISO/IEC 20000 (from the International Organization for Standardization) are others.

User Documentation

Technical documentation should be written clearly and concisely, while communicating all of the necessary information and with an organization that will be logical to the user. Include images when it will be helpful. Keep in mind the target audience for the documentation. Library staff might be familiar with certain resources or policies that library patrons may not. Expecting a certain level of technical expertise from the user can be risky. In general, if you know your audience, you might be able to make some assumptions about technical ability, but it is wise to write at the most basic level that is reasonable. Provide a way to obtain additional information for the more advanced users.

As an example, you might have a 3-D printer available for library patrons to use. First-time 3-D printer users need documentation that walks them through the process of preparing their print job and using the printer. This might take the form of a handout, webpage, or video (perhaps supplementing some instruction that the user has received). Repeat users may not need detailed instructions but having a simplified set of general steps posted at the 3-D printer may give them the refresher they need to use it with confidence. For advanced users who want to try printing with different types of filament (material) or need help troubleshooting a print job that has gone awry, consider providing a manual— whether print or digital—with deeper and more detailed information at an easy-to-access location.

Collect documentation in a central location appropriate to the audience. For library patrons, ease of access is paramount, so the public website is a great option. If writing for library staff, an intranet, wiki, file share, or some other secure and staff-only location is fine. Even better is a central repository of staff-only documentation that also hosts other library documentation like acquisitions and circulation procedures. Then you could create a section for technology documentation with procedures, FAQs, instructions on how to obtain help, a software catalog, and so on.

Although it might be easy to put everything online these days, don't discount physical formats for documentation. They can take the form of brochures describing services, instructions posted at the appropriate location (e.g., self-checkout machines), or even print manuals.

Internal Documentation

With internal documentation, the intended audience is the technology support staff. This documentation describes resources (servers, computers, networks, etc.) and also includes procedures, troubleshooting guides, and SLAs. The issue-tracking system is a form of documentation, as are inventories. Be sure to keep documentation up to date and make notes in the appropriate places for any changes that take place. Internal documentation should also collect externally created information from vendors like user manuals, warranties, and contracts.

Warranties and contracts need to be accessible when a technician must contact a vendor for assistance. They may contain an identifier, like a contract number, that the vendor may request prior to providing help. They will also describe the level of service that the vendor will provide—which is particularly important if an item needs to be returned for maintenance or replacement. Some warranties will require that an authorized service provider repair equipment. If the technician attempting repair does not have the proper certification, he or she might void the warranty. For extended warranties, pay attention to the terms as the coverage may differ from the original or basic warranty.

Asset Management

Asset management is an important aspect of documenting and managing technology. You may have a financial or legal responsibility to maintain an accurate inventory of property purchased with institutional funds. Your institution may conduct regular audits, during which an auditor may have to verify the presence and location of each individual item that you are required to track. From the perspective of supporting technology, documenting assets is useful for tracking the location of items, planning refreshes and upgrades, and change management. Having a clear picture of the assets under your control will aid in strategic planning and encourage the redistribution of existing resources.

A spreadsheet or database listing relevant information can function as a simple asset management system. For physical assets, the documentation should include the following information at a minimum:

- Make
- Model
- Serial number
- ID number
- Physical location
- Acquisition date

Including additional technical information will help with support, assessment, and planning. (For more on assessment and planning, see chapter 12.) Using a desktop computer as an example, additional information to record might include the operating system, processor speed, storage capacity, memory, and network jack as well as the person, department, or function to which it is assigned. Your institution might also track assets as part of procurement management, but the information will likely focus on financial information—which, although useful, will leave out much of the technical information relevant to technology management.

It is important to continue tracking assets after they are taken offline and put in storage—even if they are destined for e-waste—so that they don't get lost before they complete the disposal process. When disposing of assets, there may be a procedure to follow from the property and finance management perspectives of the institution your library belongs to as well as data security steps that involve the wiping of data and destruction of computer hard drives.

Although a spreadsheet or homegrown database might be sufficient for your asset management, updating it is a manual process that will quickly become cumbersome the more information that there is to record and the larger the inventory. A number of software solutions are available with features that make it easier to track and manage assets. Some will scan your network for connected devices and build your inventory automatically. Some are integrated with other user support features like help desk or knowledgebase software.

MANAGING SOFTWARE

A software catalog is a central listing of the software maintained and provided for users. It includes a description of the software, the operating systems it is compatible with, who may use it, and instructions for how to obtain the software. Depending on how the computers are managed and whether users have administrative privileges for installing software, this may be a direct download, or it may be a method to request approval and installation. Be sure to carefully consider whether to allow users to install software on their own. There will be implications for technical support as well as the license terms a user may accept.

Not all software is designed for the individual user—enterprise software is meant as a solution for the organization. It often contains large datasets used by multiple people or teams. Examples include accounting, human resources management, identity management, and, as a library-specific example, the integrated library system. Enterprise software sometimes contains a suite of customizable applications or modules and may be centrally managed through an administration interface. The datasets may reside in a database on a server managed locally (whether physical or virtual) or on a cloud server.

Another way that software can be used is through the software as a service (SaaS) model. This is a cloud-type service in which the software actually resides on a central server that is usually accessed through a web browser. Office productivity software from companies like Google and Microsoft, as well as others, are a common example of SaaS. Depending on the information being communicated through the internet and stored on the vendor's servers, data security may be a concern.

Software Licenses

Software use and distribution is governed by copyright law. A software license grants specified permissions to the licensee for use, and depending on the license, possibly modification or distribution. Two broad categories that software often fall into are described as *proprietary software* and *open source software*. With a proprietary license, the copyright holder usually grants rights to use the software as intended, without the ability to modify or further distribute the software. Additional licenses can be purchased for individual installations or, in the case of volume purchases, for additional seats for a large number of users. Software maintenance and upgrades may be included in this license, although it is often limited to a set period and requires renewing the license to continue receiving upgrades.

Open source software (OSS) often grants the user rights to modify the software and may include access to the source code. Some common OSS licenses include the following:

GNU General Public License

A type of copyleft license, the GNU general public license (GPL) gives the user complete freedom to use and modify the software. The user may distribute the modified software under the condition that any derivative works be distributed under the same license (described as a *share-alike license condition*). It is a commonly used license for free and open source software.

Berkeley Software Distribution and Massachusetts Institute of Technology Licenses

The Berkeley software distribution (BSD) and Massachusetts Institute of Technology (MIT) licenses are similar to the GPL—the user has complete freedom to use, modify, and distribute—but without the distribution restrictions of the GPL. This means that BSD- and MIT-licensed software can be incorporated or developed into proprietary software.

Keep track of software licenses and product keys as the license number might be necessary to receive technical support from the vendor. It can also help to reduce costs by balancing the number of purchased software licenses to the number of licenses used. In other words, don't pay for what you don't need. Track your installations (or number of users, as appropriate) to make sure that you are in compliance with license volume and expiration, thus reducing legal risk. Set a reminder for annual license renewals and include them in your budget. It would not be good for users to lose access to software because you neglected to renew a license. If you find yourself up against a renewal deadline, talk to the vendor as they may be willing to give a temporary extension to your current license while the renewal is processed.

Digital Rights Management

Digital rights management (DRM) are the technologies used to control access to the functionality of copyrighted software. Not all software incorporates DRM; in fact, it is considered somewhat controversial in some circles. Richard Stallman, founder of the Free Software Foundation, refers to DRM as "Digital Restrictions Management."[2] However, it is common for proprietary software to use DRM. In some cases, following installation the software will not function until it is activated. In other cases, the software might function until a grace period has passed, after which the software will cease to function or else the functionality will be greatly reduced. This is the case with Microsoft Office, which will allow files to be viewed but not edited after the grace period has ended. DRM can be used to enforce a trial license, which might be limited by time or functionality. The software license might be feature-based, meaning that DRM will block certain features until they are unlocked by purchasing the appropriate key.

A product key is sometimes required to unlock or activate software after purchase. When software was primarily distributed on physical media, there was sometimes a series of numbers and letters printed on documentation that accompanied the installation media. Although each key may have been meant to be unique, it was not completely effective in preventing copyright infringement as the keys could easily be distributed. Some software now requires an internet connection during activation to verify that the key has not been used previously. Although some software conducts the key validation "behind the scenes" during activation, even in this age of digital distribution it is not uncommon to have to manually enter a product key during the installation or upgrade process. For software that requires an annual license renewal, a new key might be distributed with each renewal.

MOBILE TECHNOLOGY

Mobile technology has its own set of requirements and challenges for support. If the mobile device is something that the institution lends, it will reduce some of the complexity because the devices are known and probably selected because they work well in the institution's technology environment. Laptop computers, for example, could be of a standard make and model with identical operating systems and software configurations.

Libraries need to be ready for the devices that patrons bring with them—not to mention the use of personal devices by employees for work (also known as *bring your own device* [BYOD]). Mobile devices are primarily laptop computers, tablet computers (e.g., iPad), and smartphones. These devices will be used to connect to the wireless network, access online resources and institutional email, and print. Users may require assistance configuring and troubleshooting their devices to accomplish these tasks and more.

The technology infrastructure needs to be capable of handling increasing network connections as more and more devices walk into the library. They will also require electrical outlets for charging batteries or other options like charging lockers or inductive charging stations (wireless charging that uses an electromagnetic field to transfer energy). If employees are allowed to BYOD, there are security concerns for the risk of a data breach if a device with sensitive data or passwords is lost.

ACCESSIBILITY

As the library and its technology are focused on the user, we have ethical and legal obligations to ensure library resources and technology are accessible to users who have disabilities. The concept of universal design is something to keep in mind while designing library and technology services. It originated with the field of architecture but is being more widely adopted, including by the IT discipline. Universal design aims to create products that are usable by a diverse population with the broadest range of abilities possible. In addition to designing products to be accessible, many assistive technology tools can be used to help provide alternative means of access.

Accessibility concerns hardware as well as software and addresses many disabilities and impairments. Among the disabilities to consider are cognitive, visual, hearing-related, and dexterity disabilities. Section 508 of the Rehabilitation Act (29 U.S. Code § 794d)[3] requires federal departments and agencies to ensure (unless an undue burden) that individuals with disabilities have access to and use of information and data that is comparable with access available to individuals who do not have disabilities. This applies when developing, procuring, maintaining, or using electronic and information technology. Organizations that receive federal funds or are under contract with a federal agency are also required to comply.

Libraries most often encounter these requirements when purchasing technology and designing websites. Procurement processes usually have steps built in to address compliance. If implementation of Section 508 standards causes undue hardship, the library is required to provide an alternative means that allows disabled persons to make use of the technology. To aid the purchasing process, the Information Technology Industry Council, a trade organization with membership composed of IT companies, has developed a form that has been widely adopted in the IT industry. The voluntary product accessibility template (VPAT) is a table that the vendor is responsible for completing and making available to customers. In it the vendor explains how its product performs against the standards in the subsections of Section 508.

The Section 508 Standards for Electronic and Information Technology[4] are as follows:

- 1194.21 Software applications and operating systems
- 1194.22 Web-based intranet and internet information and applications
- 1194.23 Telecommunications products
- 1194.24 Video and multimedia products
- 1194.25 Self-contained, closed products
- 1194.26 Desktop and portable computers
- 1194.31 Functional performance criteria
- 1194.41 Information, documentation, and support

If, for some reason, the technology product is not fully accessible, you may be required to develop alternate means of access. In higher education some universities are requiring purchasers to develop an "equally effective alternative access plan" to address accessibility issues that a product is not able to accommodate. In some cases, this might include the use of assistive technology.

There are many examples of assistive technology, which are devices and software designed to aid people with disabilities.

- A screen reader is computer software that translates text to speech or braille (via refreshable braille display). It is sometimes used in combination with a screen magnifier.
- A screen magnifier is a software tool that enlarges the text or image on the computer screen.
- Speech recognition software, also known as speech-to-text software, will take spoken commands and input.
- Video magnifiers incorporate a video camera and a monitor. They can be used to view printed materials magnified on the monitor.

- A refreshable braille display can be connected to a computer and displays one line of text at a time using braille. This is usually accomplished by pins that raise and lower to display to appropriate braille characters.

Web accessibility is another important area to consider when developing resources and purchasing products. Many library resources are accessed via the web, so if we are to focus on the user, we have an obligation to design websites for accessibility and pressure vendors to do so as well. The Web Content Accessibility Guidelines are the official guidelines published by the W3C Web Accessibility Initiative. For more on web accessibility see chapter 8, "Web Design and Development."

PROJECT MANAGEMENT

Projects occupy a realm that is distinct from both ongoing operations and strategic planning. A project is a temporary activity with a desired outcome and a defined beginning and end. Projects occur regularly as a part of managing technology, so developing good project management skills is important for a successful and efficient technology unit. Project management is a developed discipline with education programs, certifications, and literature. Although the IT technician usually completes specialized training, all library staff managing technology should have at least a basic understanding of project management practices. Fortunately, there are many resources available—some written specifically from the library perspective.

In a nutshell, project management is the development of a project plan and the execution of the plan while remaining within defined constraints. During planning and execution, it is essential to consider the needs of the stakeholders, roles of all participants, project goals, cost, and timeline.

There are a number of different approaches and schools of thought on how to conduct project management. What method you select depends on the type and scope of the project, whether your institution has a preferred method, and the training that the participants have received. Even for small projects it is good to use project management practices. Over time you will develop personal preferences and may use an informal style of your own in some cases.

Basic Project Management

A traditional approach to project management, known as the *waterfall method*, uses five sequential steps: initiation, planning, execution, controlling, and closing (the names of the steps can vary depending on industry, but the concepts are similar). Although this method works well for smaller projects, it may not be a good fit for others with more complex requirements and risk.

Initiation

Initiation is clearly the beginning of a project. It may involve a request from a customer or the desire to undertake a project to implement a new or improved service. At this stage the nature and scope of the project are established, often in the form of a written project proposal. The proposal describes the purpose of the project, the overall goals, the general scope, and the expected duration of the project. Stakeholders should be identified. An analysis of stakeholder needs and review of current operations should be conducted, as well as a financial analysis of the cost and benefits. If the decision is made to proceed with the project, a document called a *project charter* can be written, which includes the proposal as well as the findings from the investigations conducted. Then the project moves to the next phase.

Planning

During the planning phase, the project details are established. Depending on the scale of the project, a team might be assembled to conduct the planning. The team identifies the main activities and the sequence of events that needs to take place. They estimate the resources needed for the activities, as well as the time needed and cost. From this information, a project schedule and budget is established. Next, a work breakdown structure, with increasing detail, assigns the tasks, deadlines, and deliverables. This document is referred to throughout the project to help keep the project on track and within scope. It is important that some risk analysis take place during planning to consider what challenges may be faced and how they will be dealt with. Once formal approval to begin work is obtained, the project may kick off and proceed to the execution phase.

Execution

Execution is the time to commence the project work. Everyone who is assigned to work on the project conducts their assigned tasks. The work breakdown structure details the expected deliverables during this phase and guides the work. It is important during this time to keep good documentation.

Controlling

The controlling phase occurs as the execution of individual tasks are conducted and deliverables achieved. Project performance is observed to identify areas where things may not be going according to plan. Timeline, cost, and scope are three areas in particular that the project manager keeps an eye on and makes adjustments as necessary to try to remain within the project constraints. If necessary, the project plan is updated as well.

Closing

Finally, the project finishes with the closing phase. All of the activities are finalized, final outcomes are delivered, and resources are released from the project. At this time, you may want to conduct a postimplementation review to analyze how well the project performed and produce a lessons-learned document.

Project Management Methods

Different methods of project management may be more appropriate to the project depending on the type, size, scope, complexity, stakeholders involved, and many other factors. These are just a few of the many project management methods and schools of thought that exist:

- The *agile method* originated in software development as a flexible alternative to the rigid form of the waterfall method.
- The Project Management Institute maintains a set of standards called the *Project Management Body of Knowledge* and a number of certifications, including the Project Management Professional.
- PRINCE2 (PRojects IN Controlled Environments) is a method and set of certifications originally developed by the United Kingdom Office of Government Commerce, and is currently maintained by AXELOS Ltd.
- *Scrum* is an iterative methodology that originated in software development and focuses on short timelines and quickly adapting to regular feedback.

Although much of the project management documentation can be created and updated using templates in common office productivity software, a number of specialized project management software solutions are available as well. These solutions can make it easier to do analysis on complex projects and may incorporate task management and communication tools for teams.

SUMMARY

The user should be the primary focus of technology services offered in the library. Not all technology users in the library are from the same communities: some are members of the general public and others are library staff. Each group has its own sets of skills and expectations. User support is often organized into three tiers of escalating complexity and specialization. The help desk is the first point of contact for users seeking assistance. An issue-tracking system and service-level agreements are tools for providing support.

Documentation plays a critical role in managing technology, and may take the form of a service catalog, user documentation, internal documentation, and asset management. Software has particular management aspects such as the software license and digital rights management. Mobile technology includes laptop computers, tablet computers, and smartphones—and introduces another set of requirements for support and technology infrastructure.

Libraries have ethical and legal obligations to ensure that resources and technology are accessible for all users. Section 508 of the Rehabilitation Act establishes federal requirements for accessible technology, and the Web Content Accessibility Guidelines address web accessibility standards.

Project management is frequently used while managing technology and is a useful skill for all library employees. A project is a temporary activity with a desired outcome and a defined beginning and end. A traditional approach to project management, known as the *waterfall method*, uses five sequential steps: initiation, planning, execution, controlling, and closing.

KEY TERMS

Accessibility
Asset management
Bring your own device (BYOD)
Digital rights management
Documentation
Enterprise software
Help desk
Issue tracking system
Open source software
Product key
Project charter

Project management
Proprietary software
Section 508
Service catalog
Service level agreement
Software license
Universal design
User support
User support tiers
Voluntary product accessibility template (VPAT)
Work breakdown structure

QUESTIONS

1. Discuss how reference interview practices can be applied when providing technology support.
2. Describe the levels of user support in a three-tier system.
3. What training is necessary for frontline library public services staff to provide tier one technology support?
4. What are some different types of technology-related documentation? Who is the intended audience and where can the documents be found?
5. What are the implications of BYOD for library employees?

6. What is the library's role with regard to accessibility? What library services and resources does this affect?
7. What are the basic steps of project management? In your experience, how have you seen them followed?

ACTIVITIES

1. Investigate an IT unit. How are the user support tiers established? What are the escalation procedures?
2. Create an SLA for a specific technology service, describing the relationship between a central IT unit and a library.
3. Choose a library and describe the measures they are taking to ensure provided technologies are accessible.

FURTHER READING

Allan, Barbara. *The No-Nonsense Guide to Project Management*. London: Facet, 2017.

Beisse, Fred. *A Guide to Computer User Support for Help Desk and Support Specialists*, 6th ed. Boston: Cengage Learning, 2015.

Canuel, Robin, and Chad Crichton. *Mobile Technology and Academic Libraries: Innovative Services for Research and Learning*. Chicago: Association of College and Research Libraries, 2017.

Marchewka, Jack T. *Information Technology Project Management: Providing Measurable Organizational Value*, 5th ed. John Wiley and Sons, 2015.

Mates, Barbara T., and William R. Reed. *Assistive Technologies in the Library*. Chicago: American Library Association, 2011.

Note, Margot. *Project Management for Information Professionals*. Waltham, MA: Chandos, 2016.

RESOURCES

Accessible Technology Coalition: https://atcoalition.org/
AXELOS ITIL: https://www.axelos.com/best-practice-solutions/itil/what-is-itil
AXELOS PRINCE2: https://www.axelos.com/best-practice-solutions/prince2
GNU General Public License: https://www.gnu.org/licenses/gpl-3.0.en.html
National Library Services for the Blind and Physically Handicapped: https://www.loc.gov/nls/
Open Source Initiative licenses: https://opensource.org/licenses
PEAT Buy IT! Your Guide for Purchasing Accessible Technology: http://www.peatworks.org/Buy-IT
Project Management Institute: https://www.pmi.org/
United States Access Board: https://www.access-board.gov/

Project Management Software

Microsoft Project: https://www.microsoft.com/en-us/microsoft-365/project/project-management-software
Open Workbench: http://open-workbench.en.softonic.com/
OpenProj (open source): http://www.serena.com/products/openproj/index.html
Tom's Planner (web based Gantt charts): http://www.tomsplanner.com/

NOTES

1. "What Is ITIL® Best Practice?" AXELOS, accessed August 30, 2020, https://www.axelos.com/best-practice-solutions/itil/what-is-itil.
2. Richard Stallman, "Opposing Digital Rights Mismanagement," GNU, accessed August 30, 2020, https://www.gnu.org/philosophy/opposing-drm.en.html.
3. "29 U.S. Code § 794d—Electronic and Information Technology," Legal Information Institute, accessed August 30, 2020, https://www.law.cornell.edu/uscode/text/29/794d.
4. "Section 508 Standards for Electronic and Information Technology," United States Access Board, December 21, 2000, https://www.access-board.gov/guidelines-and-standards/communications-and-it/about-the-section-508-standards/section-508-standards.

3

Computer Hardware and Software

Computers are used in a wide and growing variety of ways, including programmable thermostats, microwave ovens, building security systems, and 3-D printers. Although many of those things are often found in libraries, this chapter focuses on the common personal computer. If you decide to delve deeper into more specialized cases, like embedded systems, you will find that many of the concepts translate.

Computer engineering is basically about the design and development of computer systems. This chapter introduces the component parts of a computer system by examining two major realms: hardware and software. It introduces the major physical components of the computer with an emphasis on the specifications to consider when measuring the capabilities of a computer system. The chapter also describe the basics of how software works and interacts with computer hardware.

Having a basic understanding of computer specifications and how a computer operates helps with the selection of the appropriate computer for the job and establishes a foundation for trouble-shooting problems.

COMPUTER HARDWARE

Hardware refers to all of the physical components that make up and interact with the computer. This includes the electronics—motherboard, central processing unit (CPU), memory, and storage devices—as well as some of the more mundane parts like cooling fans and the power supply. Hardware isn't limited to what you will find inside the computer; it also includes the case, cables, keyboard, and monitor as well. Although a laptop has a much smaller space in which to include all of the necessary components, it generally has similar parts and operates in a similar manner to a desktop computer.

Power Supply

If you were to open up a desktop computer case and look inside, one component that you would see is an unassuming box whose only real clue as to its function is the connection where the power cable plugs in. The power supply unit receives electricity from an external source, converts it from alternating current to direct currents, then distributes it to the hardware inside the computer that requires electricity.

Power supplies are rated in watts. This is the amount of electricity that the power supply is capable of providing for the computer's components—although not necessarily the amount it will continuously draw from the outlet. The greater the need of the components, the greater the draw on the power supply. A lightweight desktop computer primarily used for office productivity might have a power supply in the range of 180 to 300 watts, whereas a high-powered gaming system with a discrete graphics card may need upward of 850 watts. Computer vendors tend to include the appropriate power supply with prebuilt general-use computers. However, if the computer will be used for more demanding activities—such as gaming, multimedia editing, virtual reality, or machine learning—you will want to pay attention to the needs of the components. A number of vendors have power supply calculators on their websites to help with making an appropriate selection.

Motherboard

The motherboard is the computer's main circuit board. It is the largest board inside of the case, with many components either directly on the board, plugged into ports, or connected with cables. Some of the components that may live directly on the motherboard include the CPU (the processor), battery, memory slots, networking interface, and expansion slots. The battery in this case does not power the entire computer; rather, its main purpose is to provide power to the internal clock, the "real-time clock," so that it can keep time while the computer is turned off.

The chipset controls communications among the components and peripherals. Regardless of the motherboard manufacturer, chipsets are designed by either Intel or AMD to work specifically with their CPUs. Different chipsets can accommodate different classes of CPUs—such as high-performance CPUs—and determine which and how many components and peripherals they will work with.

Central Processing Unit

The CPU is a microprocessor that handles the flow of information to and from memory and uses mathematical and logical operations to conduct processing work as instructed by a computer program. It runs hot, so it normally has a heatsink placed directly on it and a fan to help prevent it from overheating.

There are several different aspects of a CPU to consider when evaluating the potential performance, the primary being the clock speed followed by the number of cores. Clock speed is currently measured in gigahertz (GHz); the higher the number, the faster the processor. CPUs typically fall on a scale between 2.0 GHz and 4.0 GHz, although there are already consumer models that go beyond 4.0 GHz. Another factor to consider is the number of cores on the CPU. Multicore processors actually have multiple processors on a single integrated chip. However, measuring overall processor performance it is not as straightforward as multiplying the clock speed by the number of cores. Increasing the number of cores improves performance for software that is specially written to take advantage of the opportunity to carry out multiple operations in parallel. In general, programs that tend to be more processor intensive, such as multimedia editing, are increasingly written to take advantage of multicore processors. Typical low-intensity activities like using the web or word processing don't make much use of multiple cores.

There are essentially two companies competing on the processor market: Intel and Advanced Micro Devices (AMD). They both have a large variety of products for varying levels of need with an assortment of specifications. One company's product isn't necessarily better than the other, and for general use both are just fine. The most important things to consider when selecting a CPU are the generation and the clock speed, paying greater attention to the specifications for more demanding activities.

Read-Only Memory

Read-only memory (ROM) often contains information or special software known as *firmware* that rarely changes, and is closely tied to the operation of the computer's hardware. The CPU accesses the instructions on ROM chips and does not change what is stored, except in rare cases.

Random Access Memory

When people speak of the computer's memory, they are usually referring to random access memory (RAM). The CPU has very little on-board memory to store the data it is working on, so RAM is the workspace that it reads and writes to while processing operations. You can also think of RAM as the computer's short-term memory. It is not meant to store data that is not being actively worked on and in fact requires electricity to retain data. After you power off a computer, the data stored in RAM disappears. To keep from losing data that you have been working on, you typically save it to a storage device—like the computer's hard drive or a universal serial bus (USB) flash drive. The next time you work on it the CPU will grab the relevant data from storage and move it to RAM to begin work.

When a computer runs out of space in RAM, it will turn to the hard drive to create virtual memory with which to have a larger workspace. This results in more work moving data around; consequently processes slow down as reading and writing data to the hard drive is much slower than to RAM. Fortunately, increasing the amount of RAM in a computer is one of the easiest and cheapest ways to improve a computer's performance.

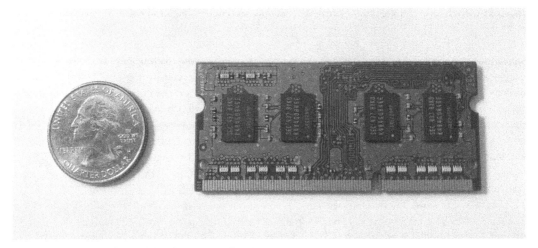

Figure 3.1 A 4 GB SO-DIMM with a quarter for size

A memory module, also called *dual inline memory module* (DIMM) is a rectangular circuit board on which integrated circuits chips are mounted. The DIMM is plugged into a slot directly on the motherboard, which often has multiple slots to accommodate more than one memory module. It is important to select a DIMM that matches the specifications of your computer as there are a variety of types and using the wrong type could potentially damage the computer. SO-DIMM, for example, is made for small form-factors such as laptops and is roughly half the size of a regular DIMM for a desktop computer.

The amount of memory on the module is measured in megabytes (MB) or gigabytes (GB). To describe how much RAM a given computer has, one simply adds together the amount of memory on each module. For example, if a computer has four DIMMs of 512 MB each, the computer is said to have 2 GB of RAM (1,024 MB is equal to 1 GB). Alternately, two DIMMs of 1 GB each also equals 2 GB of RAM in the computer.

Another factor is the speed of the RAM, measured in megahertz (MHz). For typical office productivity, faster RAM won't have the same effect as simply increasing the amount (to a point). If you are running busy servers or memory-intensive programs like 3-D modeling, you may notice a difference.

The generation of the technology used is noted by appending a number to the acronym *DDR*, which stands for *double data rate*. DDR3 is found in computers made after 2007; currently the most common generation DDR4 is found in computers made after 2017 and DDR5 is expected to have its first consumer release in 2021.

Mass Storage

Whereas RAM is the short-term memory of the computer, the mass storage is the long-term memory. *Mass storage* is a generic term that refers to pretty much anything you can save files and programs to—the hard drive, USB flash storage, CD-R, even floppy disks. First, this chapter focuses on the primary storage device, which is usually located inside of the computer, as opposed to removable media or cloud storage.

The primary storage device is often referred to as the *hard drive*. This is where the operating system (OS), programs, and many files are found. It doesn't require a source of electricity to maintain its memory, so shutting down the computer will not result in losing everything that you have saved. The capacity of storage devices is usually measured in GB or terabytes (TB). There are two types of mass storage devices commonly used for primary storage, the older hard disk drive (HDD) and the newer solid state drive (SSD). SSDs are a faster, smaller, and newer technology than HDDs but they are also more expensive for the amount of storage space. Prices are falling, however, and it won't be long until SSDs have completely replaced HDDs as the primary storage device of choice.

Inside of an HDD is a stack of disks (also called *platters*) on which an arm will read and write data by magnetizing a coating on the surface of the disks. Picture a record player to imagine how the computer accesses the data on the HDD. The platters spin rapidly while the arm moves back and forth to access different areas on the disks. The rotational speed is one measure of performance for an HDD with 7,200 rotations per minute (RPM) currently the most common. Older HDDs may be 5,400 RPM, whereas high-end computers might have a 10,000 RPM HDD and servers often have a 15,000 RPM HDD. Another measure of performance is the transfer rate. This describes how quickly data is read from and written to the disk, measured in Gigabits per second (Gbit/s).

SSDs do not have any moving parts and thus are not prone to mechanical failure like an HDD. They can even take some physical shock—imagine how rough we are with our laptops and mobile phones. Instead, an SSD uses integrated circuit chips—much like a USB flash drive—to store data. It is not volatile (unlike RAM), although the data degrades over a period of time that is much shorter than an HDD. It is not good practice to rely on an SSD for long-term archival backups. The advantages of SSDs over HDDs are that they are more compact and feature much faster transfer rates, resulting in a shorter startup time for the computer and load times for programs.

At this time, the price point per GB of storage is still much higher for SSDs than HDDs, but it is dropping and SSDs will soon replace HDDs as the most common primary storage device. The type of mass storage you select depends on how you intend to use the computer. If quick load times are most important, select an SSD. If you need large amounts of local storage, consider pairing an SSD with an HDD, which is still the way to go for large amounts of storage because of the price difference. For typical office productivity, go with an SSD for better performance and if storage becomes an issue, most desktop computers can accommodate additional internal drives. Because of the file sizes involved, situations in which you might need a lot of storage include multimedia editing and digitizing images. Rather than simply purchasing the largest HDD you can get your hands on, you might consider alternative solutions such as an external HDD, using the local network to store files on a server, or even cloud storage solutions.

Also pay attention to the form factor of the SSD. Serial AT attachment (SATA) was originally developed for HDDs, but it is also the most common type of SSD. The SATA SSD is usually 2.5 inches, which is fine for most laptops but smaller than the 3.5-inch hard drive bay still found in many desktop computers. However, this is easily solved with an adapter that can be secured in the location of the hard drive bay. SATA is slower than newer form factors like the M.2, AIC, and U.2—but is still much faster than an HDD and fine for most situations.

Removable Media

The removable media category of hardware refers to all of those storage media that are temporarily plugged in or inserted into the computer, then removed. This encompasses optical disks, media cards, USB flash drives, and external HDD or SSD drives. The USB flash drive (also called a *USB stick* or *jump drive*) is perhaps the most common removable media because of its compact size and portability. However, with the popularity of cloud storage and the ability to access it from potentially any device, use of USB flash drives will probably decline. External hard-drives, however, are a convenient way to add a large amount of local storage. They usually connect to the computer via USB cable, and if you need to access the files on a different computer, it is a simple matter of unplugging the drive, going to the next computer and plugging it in.

Media cards use flash memory in a similar manner to USB flash drives, and come in many shapes and sizes. In the early 2000s there were a number of competing formats—Compact Flash, Memory Stick, and SmartMedia being a few. Some computers had multiple slots to accommodate the wide variety of shapes. In recent years, the industry has settled on the secure digital (SD) card as an accepted standard. If a current laptop or desktop computer has a media card slot, it is usually for an SD card. There are three sizes of SD cards: the standard SD card, the smaller miniSD, and the smallest, the microSD. MicroSD cards are used in mobile phones, portable gaming devices, and physical computing platforms like the Raspberry Pi. An adapter in the shape of a standard SD card allows you to use a microSD with a computer that has a standard SD card slot.

Figure 3.2 A microSD card and an SD card adapter with a quarter for size

As software increasingly moves to the internet for distribution, and first USB flash drives then cloud storage have become widespread, optical media drives have been disappearing from computers. In large part, they are no longer included in laptops, thus saving space and weight, as well as removing a potential point of mechanical failure. External optical drives that are accessed via USB cable are now the standard way to use Blu-rays, DVDs, and CDs with a computer that doesn't have an internal drive. Both internal and external drives are usually capable of writing to optical disks—although each type of disk uses different although similar technology, so be certain that you are using the correct disk for the drive. Disks that can be written to only once are labeled *CD-R*, *DVD-R*, and *BD-R* (Blu-ray Disk—Recordable). Disks that can be written to, erased, and written to again, over and over are *CD-RW*, *DVD-RW*, and *BD-RE*.

Physical Ports

Ports are the many interfaces through which the computer communicates with external devices—often peripherals. It used to be that a computer had different ports for different tasks, and different types of connectors to accommodate the various communication standards of the peripherals. Over time many of those ports have disappeared in favor of a common technology known as the *USB*.

Peripheral Ports

USB is a commonly used industry standard for connecting a computer to a peripheral device. In addition to facilitating communication between the computer and the device, it also provides enough power so that some devices don't need an additional power source. Over time the USB standard has been revised to provide faster transfer speeds and greater power. USB 2.0 was introduced in 2000 and has a transfer rate of 480 Mbit/s. USB 3.0 was introduced in 2008 with a transfer rate of 5 Gbit/s, and is visually marked by a blue port. USB 3.1 was introduced in 2013 and has a transfer rate of 10 Gbit/s, and, like USB 3.0, has a blue port. Newer versions are backward compatible with older versions, although you may not benefit from the higher transfer rate.

The USB port and cable also comes in a variety of shapes. USB type-A is a flat rectangular shape commonly found on a computer or other host device. Usually this is also the power source. USB type-B is often found on the peripheral and is a different shape from type-A. USB also comes in mini, micro, and proprietary shapes (think older iPhones and iPads). USB type-C was introduced in 2014 and changes things in that it provides a much greater amount of power, the cable endpoint is reversible (meaning you don't have to worry about plugging it in the right way on the first try), and it is capable of being used by both the host and the device.

Thunderbolt is another standard for connecting peripherals to a computer and is most commonly found on Apple products. Thunderbolt has much higher transfer rates than USB and is capable of powering displays, connecting to Ethernet (via an adapter), and daisy-chaining devices. Thunderbolt 3 uses the same shape as the USB-C.

Many peripherals are available in wireless varieties that use the Bluetooth standard for connecting to a computer or other device. For computers that don't have Bluetooth built in, a USB Bluetooth dongle can get the job done.

Video Ports

Many different types of video ports are in use today. Fortunately, there are also adapters in almost every combination of the common types. The ubiquitous video graphics array (VGA) has been around since 1987 and continues to be found both on legacy equipment as well as modern monitors and projectors. VGA carries analog video, has a connector with 15 pins, and has a maximum resolution of 2048 × 1536. Digital video interface (DVI) was introduced as the successor to VGA in 1999. The DVI specification is compatible with VGA—although not with the connector, which, depending on the variety, has up to 29 pins. DVI also has a maximum resolution of 2048 × 1536 and typically carries only a video signal and not audio.

Figure 3.3 Video cables, left to right: VGA, DVI, HDMI

The three most common current video interface technologies are DisplayPort, high-definition multimedia interface (HDMI), and the previously mentioned Thunderbolt. They all use digital signals and include the audio data along with the video data. Whereas DisplayPort is the more common standard of the three for connecting a computer to a monitor and HDMI is common for connecting to televisions, both types are often found on both desktop computers and laptops. Thunderbolt is the standard typically used on Apple computers.

Networking Ports

Although wireless networking is becoming widespread, it is still very common, and in some cases more practical, for computers to have a wired connection to a network. It used to be that computers had a special card called the *network interface card* plugged into an expansion slot that included a port for the networking cable. Now it is far more usual for the network interface and port to be integrated into the motherboard.

The speed of data transfer for a wired connection depends on many factors external to the computer, but, all things being equal, a wired connection using a category 5e (Cat5e) cable can support up to 1 GB/s. A newer standard that uses Cat6 cabling theoretically offers transfer rates up to 10 GB/s, although of course that depends on other components in the network, like the router, being similarly capable.

In general, wired networking is faster, has greater stability, and is more secure than wireless networking. It can be hard to beat the convenience of wireless, however, and it is improving in all of those areas as well. It would be wrong to automatically assume that wired connections are for desktop computers and wireless is for laptops. Many desktop computers are shipping with built-in Wi-Fi, giving the user flexibility of choice. On the other hand, as laptops get thinner and lighter, some are ditching the wired networking port altogether.

Expansion Slots

Several expansion slots are found directly on the motherboard. These are provided so that the functionality of the computer can be extended by expansion cards—printed circuit boards usually designed for a specific purpose. Many of the features now integrated into the motherboard began life as expansion cards, including networking, storage drives, and audio. The number of available slots vary based on the form factor and design of the motherboard, but they typically use a standard known as *peripheral component interconnect express* (PCIe).

These days the most common use of an expansion slot is for discrete graphic video cards. Although the motherboard usually has an integrated graphics controller, which is fine for powering a monitor and conducting normal office productivity work, more demanding graphic processing requires a dedicated graphics card. It is even possible to link some card models together for super-powered graphics rendering. Depending on the make of the video card, this is known as *Scalable Link Interface* if made by Nvidia or *Crossfire* if made by AMD.

Input/Output Devices

Computer peripherals are synonymous with input/output (I/O) devices, and can be categorized as either input devices, output devices, or both. These are the devices used to communicate and interact with a computer. Input devices take information and send it to the computer. Examples of input devices include a keyboard, a mouse, an image scanner, a video game controller, and a microphone. Output devices provide information from the computer. Examples of output devices include a monitor, a speaker, a printer, a projector, and a refreshable braille display. An I/O device performs both functions and can include devices like a touch screen, a virtual reality headset, and storage devices like a USB flash drive or the hard drive.

When selecting I/O devices, there are factors to consider beyond performance. Ergonomics and accessibility become particularly important if the devices are meant to be used by a group of people whose abilities are unknown. As mentioned in chapter 2, "Technology Management and Support," Section 508 applies to hardware as well as software. If the device does not meet accessibility standards, then an alternate method of accomplishing input, output, or both should be provided.

COMPUTER SOFTWARE

Whereas *hardware* refers to the physical components of the computer, *software* is the digital data that controls, and responds to, the hardware. Software exists on a number of levels, with the lowest-level programmed in machine language directly executable by the CPU. High-level programming languages are closest to natural human language and so are easier for human programmers to understand. It is what the majority of software applications are written in.

Computer Architecture

The design and organization of a computer system is called *computer architecture*. Being a digital machine, the foundation of computer architecture as well as software is binary code, a base-2 number system represented by zeros and ones. Table 3.1 shows how counting in binary relates to counting in decimal, a base-10 number system and the one we are most familiar with.

Table 3.1. Counting in Binary

Decimal	Binary
0	0
1	1
2	10
3	11
4	100
5	101
6	110
7	111
8	1000
9	1001
10	1010

Each digit is known as a *bit* (b), and a string of eight bits is known as a *byte* (B). The byte has become the standard unit for memory as each byte can represent one of 256 characters, including all alphanumeric characters. This is why we normally see memory capacity described in bytes—be it on the scale of kilobytes (1,024 bytes) or megabytes (1,024 kilobytes), and so on. The reason a kilobyte does not equal precisely 1,000 bytes goes back to the use of a base-2 number system. Two to the tenth power equals 1,024. See Table 3.2 to see how we measure data in bytes.

Table 3.2. Measuring Data

KB	1 kilobyte = 1,024 bytes
MB	1 megabyte = 1,024 kilobytes
GB	1 gigabyte = 1,024 megabytes
TB	1 terabyte = 1,024 gigabytes
PB	1 petabyte = 1,024 terabytes

Software that is programmed directly to the hardware inside the computer is called *firmware*. It is as close to the hardware as software can get. It directly controls the hardware and is not meant to change frequently, if ever. This is different from a device driver, which is used as a translator between the OS and hardware. A driver allows the OS to provide input to and receive output from hardware.

Boot Process

When a computer is turned on it goes through a complicated series of self-tests and software startups until a state is reached where the OS is loaded and ready for input from the user. The term *boot* comes from the idiom "to pull oneself up by one's bootstraps" and is based on the idea that a computer starts up without external input, beginning with a very simple program that starts a chain of successively more complex programs.

When the power comes on, the computer first looks at a location for firmware that will then run a power-on self-test to check all of the hardware and configuration settings. For many years, the firmware in use was basic input/output system (BIOS). In recent years however, BIOS has been phased out in favor of the unified extensible firmware interface (UEFI), and hardware maker Intel ended support for BIOS entirely in 2020.[1] Apple Macintosh, on the other hand, adopted UEFI's predecessor, extensible firmware interface (EFI), in the mid-2000s when it switched to an Intel architecture.

After the firmware (BIOS, EFI, or UEFI) have completed checking and configuring the hardware, it loads the boot manager into memory, which determines the location of the OS kernel and uses a boot loader to run it. If the computer is set up with more than one OS, the boot process may pause at the boot manager so that the user can select which OS to load. At this time control of the computer is handed over to the OS kernel, which loads the OS and a number of applications and services, including the graphical user interface (GUI—sometimes pronounced "gooey").

Operating Systems

The OS is the main piece of software that runs on a computer. It manages hardware and software resources, provides the main user interface, and serves as the platform on which software applications run. The choice of OS affects what applications are available to the user as well as the environment in which a user operates. Although different operating systems operate differently under the hood, the user's needs and expectations often dictate the selection of an OS. In some cases, the applications needed to conduct business may limit the options; other times an enterprise environment that is largely based on a particular OS may dictate choice. Variety may be the spice of life, but variety of applications and operating systems greatly increases the complexity of support.

Microsoft Windows

By far the most common family of operating systems is Microsoft Windows, with an overall world-wide market share of around 80 percent (depending on your source for statistics).[2] Because of the widespread use of Windows, it is also a popular target for viruses and malware, so the importance of keeping a Windows installation up to date cannot be overstated. Microsoft engineers are continually working not only to improve the OS but also to fix bugs and patch security flaws. However, Microsoft will not work to fix problems with each OS forever, so there are a few dates to pay attention to.

During the mainstream support period, Microsoft actively works to improve the OS by adding functionality, improving efficiency, eliminating bugs, and patching security vulnerabilities. After the end of mainstream support, they will no longer develop improvements, which also means that the latest versions of software applications may no longer work, but Microsoft will continue to release security updates for the OS. After the end of extended support, all development activities for the OS will cease. At this point, it is considered unsupported so using it risks not only incompatibility with current software applications but security vulnerabilities.

Table 3.3. Microsoft Windows Lifespans

Operating System	General Availability	End of Mainstream Support	End of Extended Support
Windows Vista, SP2	January 30, 2007	April 10, 2012	April 11, 2017
Windows 7, SP2	October 22, 2009	January 13, 2015	January 14, 2020
Windows 8.1	October 18, 2013	January 9, 2018	January 10, 2023
Windows 10	July 29, 2015	version dependent	

For a number of years, the product life cycle was planned so that the "end of mainstream support" would take place roughly five years after the OS was released to the public, and the "end of extended support" was roughly ten years later. With the release of Windows 10, Microsoft has changed its product life cycle. Version updates take place twice per year with support for Home and Pro editions lasting eighteen months, and support for Enterprise and Education editions lasting thirty months.[3] The version naming scheme uses *YYMM* where *YY* represents the last two digits of the year and *MM* the month of release. For example, Windows 10 version 1809 was made available in September 2018.

Apple Macintosh

Apple macOS (previously known as OS X) is the second most popular family of operating systems, with a 20 percent market share in North America.[4] It is generally considered to be safer than Windows as it is targeted by viruses and malware less frequently, but it is not immune as some people erroneously believe. The macOS comes preinstalled on all Apple Macintosh computers. In 2001 Apple released a fully redesigned OS related to Unix that they dubbed Mac OS X 10.0. Since then, they have released regular updates, while changing their naming scheme a few times. With the release of macOS High Sierra in 2017, a new file system called Apple File System was introduced, which was optimized specifically for flash storage and SSDs as well as having an increased emphasis on file encryption for enhanced security. Unlike Microsoft, Apple famously does not publicize when they end support for a macOS version. Fortunately, it is free to upgrade to the latest version, assuming the hardware isn't too old or underpowered.

Table 3.4. Macintosh Operating Systems

Name	Version	Release Date	Notes
El Capitan	OS X 10.11	September 30, 2015	HFS+ file system
Sierra	macOS X 10.12	September 20, 2016	HFS+ file system
High Sierra	macOS X 10.13	September 25, 2017	APFS file system
Mojave	macOS X 10.14	September 24, 2018	APFS file system
Catalina	macOS X 10.15	October 7, 2019	64-bit applications only
Big Sur	macOS 11.0	November 12, 2020	Support for ARM64 processors

Like other Apple products, macOS is tightly integrated with the Apple ecosystem making it easy for the user to move between Apple devices. Apple's *Continuity* technology allows the user to start editing a document on an iPad, for example, then continue working on the document on a linked iMac. Similarly, phone calls and text messages can be made on a linked computer; a web page can be viewed on an iPhone then moved to a MacBook; and using the Universal Clipboard content can be copied in one device, then pasted in another.

Unix-like Operating Systems

There is a large family of related operating systems that have roots in Unix—with some being open-source and others closed-source. Unix and related operating systems are far more commonly used on server hardware and embedded systems than for desktop and laptop computers, although there are some notable examples of the latter.

Linux operating systems are free and open-source software that use the Linux kernel as their foundation. Being open-source means that the source code is freely shared for anyone to examine and contribute improvements. Although the operating system may be free to download and install, there are some companies whose business model is to provide support. Some popular Linux distributions include Linux Mint, Ubuntu, Debian, elementary OS, Tails, fedora, and openSUSE. The different distributions have different strengths, and may have been tailored to particular situations or uses, such as K–12 education, information security and privacy, or running on old hardware. Although communities exist around specific Linux distributions (often shortened to "distros"), documentation is of uneven quality and depth, which can make support tricky if you are not paying for a commercially supported version such as Red Hat or SUSE.

Chrome OS is a Linux-based operating system developed by Google as a lightweight platform that uses the Chrome web browser as the main user interface. Chromebooks are laptops that run Chrome OS, and, as they are inexpensive and easy to administer, they have become massively popular in the K–12 education market. Chromebooks tend to have very little mass storage space because the assumption is that most of what the user will do is on the web and stored in the cloud.

Other Unix-like operating systems include BSD and its derivatives; Solaris, which was originally developed by Sun Microsystems and is now owned by Oracle; and macOS, which is the current operating system for Apple Macintosh computers.

Application Software

Application software, also referred to as *application programs*, is the category of software that a user interacts with to perform certain tasks. Typical examples of applications include office productivity suites, media players, and video games. They can be general purpose, like a spreadsheet program, or tailored to a specific purpose, such as interlibrary loan software. The application can be thought of as sitting on top of the operating system, making use of the system software such as device drivers and system utilities. When a user decides to launch an application, the computer will load it from the storage location into memory, where it can execute the software.

Cloud-based software uses a thin-client arrangement where the actual processing work is done by a remote computer or server and the user interfaces through a lightweight client application—usually the web browser. A common example of this is web email. Because the heavy lifting is done remotely, the hardware requirements for the user's computer are much lower. This business model is known as *software as a service* (SaaS). Microsoft (Office 365) and Google are two well-known providers of SaaS, but vendors in the library industry are also increasingly offering solutions that take advantage of this technology.

Chapter 9, "Software and Systems Development," provides an introduction to programming languages and the software development lifecycle.

SUMMARY

Computer hardware refers to the physical parts of the computer, including all of the electronics. Components are either directly on or else connected to the motherboard—which is the main circuit board. The CPU conducts logical operations and controls the flow of information to and from memory, which acts as the workspace for the CPU. Information is saved in a mass storage device, such as an HDD or SSD drive, or on removable media. External devices interact with the computer via physical ports.

Computer software controls and responds to computer hardware. The lowest level software is binary code, composed of zeros and ones. There are many levels of software on a computer, with firmware being the closest to the actual hardware. The boot process starts with a single instruction, which begins a series of successively more complex and higher level programs until the operating system is loaded and ready for user input.

KEY TERMS

Binary code
Boot process
Byte
Cat6 cable
Central processing unit (CPU)
Computer architecture
Firmware
Hard disk drive (HDD)
Input/output (I/O) device
Integrated circuit chip
Linux
macOS

Mass storage
Microsoft Windows
Motherboard
Operating system
Power supply
Random access memory (RAM)
Read-only memory (ROM)
Removable media
Solid-state drive (SSD)
Universal serial bus (USB)
Video ports

QUESTIONS

1. List the component hardware of a computer.
2. What are the options for storing digital information? Consider mass storage and removable media. What are the pros and cons of each?
3. List the different types of video ports.

4. List I/O devices and whether each provides input, output, or both.
5. What are the hardware specifications of your computer?
6. Describe the boot process.
7. What OS and version does your computer use?

ACTIVITIES

1. Use a PC builder website or tool to create custom computers at different price points (e.g., $700 and $1,400). Compare your custom computer with a prebuilt computer at the same price point from a major vendor like Dell or HP. How do the specs of your computer compare to the prebuilt computer? (Newegg Custom PC Builder: https://www.newegg.com/tools/custom-pc-builder/)
2. Open a computer case and identify and photograph each of the hardware components listed in this chapter.
3. Replace or add a hardware component to a computer, for example, the hard drive, RAM, or a graphics card. Write step-by-step instructions that describe the process.

FURTHER READING

Andrews, Jean, Joy Dark, and Jill West. *CompTIA A+ Guide to IT Technical Support*, 9th ed. Boston: Cengage Learning, 2017.

Mueller, Scott. *Upgrading and Repairing PCs*, 22nd ed. Indianapolis: Que, 2015.

White, Ron, and Timothy Edward Downs. *How Computers Work: The Evolution of Technology*, 10th ed. Indianapolis: Que, 2015.

Ward, Brian. *How Linux Works: What Every Superuser Should Know*, 2nd ed. San Francisco: No Starch Press, 2015.

RESOURCES

Cooler Master Technology (power supply calculator): http://www.coolermaster.com/power-sup ply-calculator/

Crucial (memory and SSD tool): http://www.crucial.com/usa/en/advisor

Fry's (hardware vendor): https://www.frys.com/

Newegg (power supply calculator): https://images10.newegg.com/BizIntell/tool/psucalc/index.html

Tom's Hardware (reviews): https://www.tomshardware.com/

NOTES

1. Peter Bright, "The PC BIOS Will Be Killed Off by 2020 as Intel Plans Move to Pure UEFI," *Ars Technica*, November 22, 2017, https://arstechnica.com/gadgets/2017/11/intel-to-kill-off-the-last-vestiges-of -the-ancient-pc-bios-by-2020/.
2. "Global Operating Systems Market Share for Desktop PCs, from January 2013 to July 2018," *Statista*, accessed on November 28, 2018, https://www.statista.com/statistics/218089/global-market-share -of-windows-7/; "Desktop Operating System Market Share Worldwide," Statcounter, accessed on November 28, 2018, http://gs.statcounter.com/os-market-share/desktop/worldwide.
3. "Windows Lifecycle Fact Sheet," Microsoft, last modified on November 13, 2018, https://support.mic rosoft.com/en-us/help/13853/windows-lifecycle-fact-sheet.
4. "Desktop Operating System Market Share North America," Statcounter, accessed on November 28, 2018, http://gs.statcounter.com/os-market-share/desktop/north-america.

4

Computer Management

For the technician responsible for managing computers in any setting, whether a small office or a multibranch library system, the basic tasks and concerns remain the same. With increased scale comes additional concerns about workload but there are enterprise tools that help manage the scope. A single chapter about computer management cannot possibly cover all of the tasks involved, particularly as they relate to variations in operating systems and even between different versions of the same operating system. Even so, we can introduce the main computer management responsibilities of the IT department.

This chapter provides an overview of the typical activities and tools associated with computer management. When configuring computers, the tasks involve the administration of individual computers, application installations, some basic computer networking, and the deployment of disk images. Computer maintenance tasks include data backups, cloud storage, and protection from viruses and malware. The chapter also reviews some of the other main maintenance tasks and discusses how and when to replace aging computers. Finally, the chapter introduces several trends related to computer management, including desktop virtualization, tablet computers, bring your own device (BYOD), and the Google Chromebook.

CONFIGURING COMPUTERS

Managing a computer involves configuring the operating system, applications, and network connections so that it meets business needs while conforming to the local technology environment.

Computer Administration

The computer user with administrative privileges has the ability to configure settings; install hardware and software; and add, remove, or update other user accounts. In general, it is good practice for a user's everyday account to be a standard account rather than an administrator. This will limit the type of trouble the user can get into and is good practice even for personally owned computers that are used by only one person. Having a separate administrator account will make it harder to accidentally change settings or install unwanted software but is not much of an inconvenience because the user does not have to switch accounts, but is prompted to enter an administrator username and password when trying to make changes that require administrator access.

On a Microsoft Windows computer there are a few places that centralize many of the tasks and reports that an administrator finds useful. With Windows 10, many of the utilities previously found

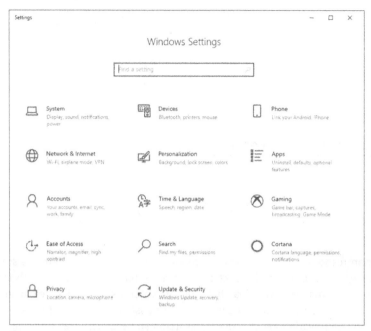

Figure 4.1 Screenshot of Settings in Microsoft Windows 10 Home
Used with permission from Microsoft.

in the Control Panel are now in the user-friendly Settings app. The Control Panel still exists for the time being, however, and serves as one way to access the Administrative Tools folder and Computer Management application.

On macOS many of the most common tasks and settings are located in the System Preferences, as seen in figure 4.2. There you have access to settings for security and privacy, displays, printers, networks, sharing, users, parental controls, and accessibility, among others. For the more advanced user, the Utilities folder, located in the Applications folder, contains useful applications such as activity monitor, console, disk utility, keychain access, system information, and terminal, among others.

Although Windows and macOS both have features that can help control the type of access a user has and activities they can do, there are also third-party solutions that make it easier to manage a large number of computers. Programs like Faronics Deep Freeze and Fortres Grand Clean Slate are particularly useful in situations in which you want to have tighter control over what a user may do or to prevent the user from making any permanent changes to the computer. These programs can be set to return the computer to a predetermined state when it is rebooted. These programs can make it easier to maintain large computer labs and classrooms where computers have multiple users.

Installing Applications

When considering a software application for installation, it is important to first evaluate several aspects: whether the computer meets system requirements, how it interacts with the network environment, and what type of license is needed. System requirements list the minimum specifications that a computer must have to be capable of running the software. It will list things such as the operating system version, amount of memory (random access memory [RAM]), mass storage space, and perhaps the graphics requirements. For the network environment, consider whether the application requires internet access, has special firewall rules, or needs access to local network resources. Inves-

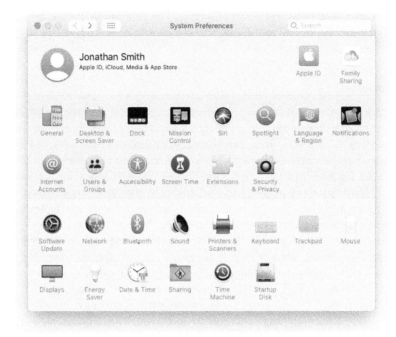

Figure 4.2 Screenshot of System Preferences in macOS 10.15.6
macOS is a registered trademark of Apple Inc.

tigate whether your organization already has a license for the application and whether a site license or an individual license will be needed.

The actual installation process for many applications is often straightforward. On the Windows operating system it is usually a simple matter of double-clicking the installer program icon and walking through a few guided configurations. When missing an obvious installer, locate a setup.exe or install. exe file to begin the process. Before running an installer, it is good practice to close other applications that are running as they may interfere with the installation process. The installer will automatically distribute portions of the application to the appropriate locations and update the Windows Registry as well as other configuration files maintained by the operating system.

When it is time to remove an application, it is important to use the uninstall process rather than deleting the application launcher or folder. Parts of the application may reside in different locations within the system and system configuration files will need to be updated. Many applications can be removed by right-clicking on the icon and selecting "uninstall." Other applications may need to be removed via the Apps menu in the System portion of the Settings menu. The old-fashioned Programs and Features in the Control Panel is an alternate solution for removing applications.

An application installer on macOS is usually a disk image and has a .dmg file extension. Double-clicking the icon mounts the disk on your system as if it were a disk drive. Double-clicking the program icon installs it on your system and may involve dragging the program icon into the Applications folder. After installation, the disk image needs to be ejected. To uninstall an application, you simply move the icon to the Trash, then empty the Trash.

Installing applications onto a Linux operating system is a far more manual process and can differ depending on the Linux distribution. Linux operating systems depend on repositories to distribute most software. First you have to connect with the repository in question, then locate the application package to download, unpack it, and install it. The application may have dependencies (related applications) that also need to be installed to function. The application installation process can be done from the command line as well as the graphical user interface, which gives the user even greater control. The advanced user can even download and compile the application from the source code.

Networking Computers

Beyond connecting to the internet, connecting computers to a local area network (LAN) has many uses. Computers can share resources such as directories and files as well as peripherals like printers, scanners, and external hard drives. They can also access other devices connected to the network such as copiers, printers, storage, and servers. Networked computers can be set up to use authentication protocols like Lightweight Directory Access Protocol (LDAP) and Microsoft User Experience Virtualization (UE-V), which allow a user to have a consistent experience regardless of the computer they log onto. Remote administration software allows an administrator to conduct maintenance and troubleshooting of networked computers without having to physically visit each one.

Networked computers become easier to manage when you use system management software rather than physically touching every individual computer to configure, maintain, and troubleshoot. Microsoft System Center Configuration Manager (SCCM) is a well-known solution that can manage large numbers of computers using a variety of operating systems, including macOS.

Chapter 5, "Networking," dives much deeper into network architecture, protocols, and management.

Deploying Disk Images

Not too long ago technicians would have to manually set up every individual computer, installing the operating system and applications, and configuring all of the settings—a time-intensive operation. To make setting up computers more efficient, it is now common to make an *image* of a model computer setup that has all of the applications installed and the system configured in a standardized way, and clone it to the new computer. A disk image is essentially a copy of an entire storage device (e.g., a hard drive). Cloning greatly increases efficiency because it cuts out tasks that would have to be repeated for each computer and also eliminates a source of human error.

With networked computers, cloning images can be taken to another level of efficiency. By using a product like the Microsoft Deployment Toolkit, you can deploy images over a network to the connected computers. This is ideal for situations in which you have many computers to set up that would otherwise be similar or identical in their configuration, like a public computer lab.

Some computer vendors also offer a service in which they install an image that the customer has preconfigured before they ship out the computers.

MAINTAINING COMPUTERS

Computer management also involves the maintenance undertaken to sustain performance and prevent problems. Maintenance is made up partly of tasks that can be automated, like regular backups and malware scans, and partly of manual tasks that are handled periodically to improve system performance and check for problems.

Backups and Cloud Storage

Having a solution for backing up computers is important for situations in which lost or destroyed data would be problematic and is also a normal part of a disaster recovery plan. The reason for the data loss can range from an accidental file deletion affecting a single computer to a catastrophic event affecting many computers such as a fire or a flood. Backup software automates the process for networked computers and can be scheduled to take place at times when network traffic is low, such as overnight. If the backups are being stored on a local server, that server should also have a redundant backup somewhere off site in case a disaster affects the local server room as well. It is recommended practice to test restoring backups to ensure that everything will work the way that you expect when you actually need it.

Not every computer needs to be backed up, though. Computers in public labs that don't store user data probably don't need to be backed up. It is also becoming common for users to rely on cloud storage for saving data, thus making local backups of data unnecessary. Cloud storage has additional benefits like making the user's files accessible from other internet-connected devices. If the device is set up to sync files to the local machine, files can be available when there isn't a network connection and then the files stored in the cloud are updated the next time the device connects. Using cloud storage as an enterprise solution can eliminate some work for the local support team because there will not be local storage servers to maintain. There are trade-offs beyond the financial cost to consider when relying on a third-party, such as the reliance on the vendor for data security and privacy.

Local backups and cloud storage are both good options for recovering data, but if the issue is related to the computer system, sometimes restoring it to an earlier state is enough to solve the problem. For example, an application update might have gone awry and caused the application to become unusable. In this situation it could be desirable to have the computer go back in time to a point before the update took place. Microsoft Windows has a feature called System Restore that automatically creates a snapshot of the system every time you install a new program, a new device driver, or a Windows update. You can also choose to create restore points manually in the configuration settings. However, this feature is not turned on by default in Windows 10, and has to be enabled. One way to do this is to turn on system protection in the system properties. Keep in mind that the system restore is not a full-blown backup of data and files on the computer; it only backs up the system files and settings.

Time Machine is the backup software that is part of macOS. It can back up to an external hard drive connected to a computer or over the network to a server. In addition to backing up data and files, Time Machine also backs up system settings and applications. Because it runs on a regular schedule and keeps previous backups (up to a point) it is possible to roll back to a previous version of an individual file—as well as the entire system.

Viruses and Malware

The first step in protecting computers from viruses and malicious software (malware) is to always keep up to date with patches to the operating system. This is one of the simplest actions that you can take—and it can be automated. Microsoft, Apple, and other operating system developers continually work to patch vulnerabilities in their software that a virus or other malware might try to exploit.

Operating systems also have some built-in security features to help combat malware. In Microsoft Windows 10, Windows Defender Security Center is the control center for several security components including Windows Firewall and the built-in antivirus software Windows Defender. Windows Firewall is the communications gatekeeper for an individual computer, restricting network traffic in and out based on security settings. Windows Defender operates much like third-party antivirus software, with the ability to scan new internet downloads as well as conduct full-system scans for viruses and other malware.

MacOS is well known for being secure, a reputation earned in part because it isn't targeted by viruses nearly as often as Windows. Nonetheless, macOS does have a number of features designed to secure the operating system, although it does not include an antivirus program. Gatekeeper is a feature that helps prevent malicious software that may have been downloaded from being installed on the computer. It checks to see whether the software has come from a trusted source or if it is on

Figure 4.3 Screenshot of Windows Defender Security Center in Microsoft Windows 10 Home
Used with permission from Microsoft.

a blacklist of dangerous software prior to installation. MacOS also has a built-in personal firewall that can be accessed in the Security & Privacy section of the System Preferences.

Third-party antivirus software is also available for both Windows and macOS. There are many programs available, including established names such as Sophos, Kaspersky, McAfee, Avast, and Trend Micro. It is critical to make sure that antivirus software is set to automatically update with the latest virus definitions. Otherwise the computer will not be protected from the latest exploits and malware out in the wild.

Chapter 7, "Information Security," goes into much more depth with computer security, privacy, and malware.

Computer Maintenance

There are not many maintenance tasks to be done on hardware beyond cleaning fans and keyboards of dust and other particles, so most of the work focuses on software maintenance that you can undertake to help prevent performance degradation. Consistently updating the operating system and applications is the first and most obvious maintenance task. In an enterprise environment, keeping all of the computers on the same software version will reduce the complexity of support.

A place to start with periodic maintenance is to review the applications that are installed for any that are unnecessary, and to uninstall them. This is also a good time to examine the start-up programs, as these increase the boot time for the computer and use memory while it is running.

Over time, temporary files will pile up and random file fragments will be orphaned on the hard drive. A disk cleanup utility deletes temporary and orphaned files, including those created by web browsers, in order to clear some storage space and improve system performance. One is provided as part of Windows and there are third-party utilities available as well.

As applications come and go during regular computer use, the registry fills up with broken and old entries that are no longer needed and can slow the computer down. Windows doesn't provide a registry cleaner, so a third-party solution like CCleaner or Glary Utilities is necessary. These third-party solutions often have many additional features such as a disk cleanup function.

With hard disk drives (HDD), defragmentation is a necessary task for periodic maintenance. As a hard disk fills up, it places file fragments wherever it can locate space on the disk platters. As files and programs become increasingly fragmented, this means that the mechanical components of the hard drive have to work harder to recall all of the fragments, resulting in mechanical wear and longer load times. The Defragmentation and Optimize Drives utility uses the free space on the hard drive to move around all of the file fragments like a puzzle in order to make files as physically contiguous as possible. For solid state drives (SSD), however, which do not have any moving parts, defragmentation as a part of regular maintenance isn't necessary. While files do become fragmented, an SSD operates very differently from a HDD. Windows recognizes this difference and, although it conducts scheduled defragmentation in the background, it is not nearly with the same regularity and scope as with the defragmenting of HDDs.

Replacing Computers

As a computer ages the cost of providing support and maintenance increases. A refresh strategy should be part of a greater technology plan guiding the overall acquisition and support of technology. The generally accepted industry practice is to replace a computer every four to five years. Replacing a large number of computers at one time can be cost prohibitive, so a refresh strategy staggers computer purchases in such a manner that an even number of computers are being replaced every year. An ideal situation for a four-year refresh cycle is to replace 25 percent of the total computers at a time—both to spread out the financial impact and the demand on staff time.

Just because a computer has aged out of a program doesn't mean that its usefulness has come to an end. Older computers can be rotated to areas or uses that are less demanding. Upgrading and replacing hardware components is an option for extending the life of a computer. Desktop computers are easier to upgrade than laptops because they are much roomier inside, although, depending on the laptop model, it certainly is possible to upgrade some parts. Adding RAM often has the biggest effect on performance, and it is a fairly straightforward matter to install. The hard drive is also a good candidate for replacement as a new drive with improved specs can decrease load times and increase storage space.

When it is time to get rid of a computer, don't just throw it in the trash. There are programs that accept donations of technology and may be able use or upgrade older technology. Failing that, computer components are made of materials that can be harmful to the environment and should not go straight to the landfill. The United States Environmental Protection Agency certifies recyclers, and maintains information on their website about recycling electronics. Your state and local governments may provide information as well.

TECHNOLOGY USE POLICIES

Creating documented and published technology use policies helps establish an understanding of what behavior is expected of users, and what technology support will be provided. They should be used to make clear the expectations and responsibilities for each party, as well as any consequences or legal liabilities. Having these policies documented and posted in a public location like the website will serve to protect both the library and the patrons.

Separate policies may apply to different technologies as well as different user groups. Begin a policy document with a simple statement of purpose: what is the intended use of the technology and who is it meant to serve? Depending on the type of technology, it may address issues of safety, intellectual property, intellectual freedom, copyright, privacy, and security. It may express the expectation that the technology will only be used for lawful purposes. The policy may also address more practical issues such as time limits or training prerequisites. The consequences for breaking or abusing policies should also be made explicit such as fees and fines, a suspension of privileges, and the reporting of unauthorized or illegal activity to the authorities.

When there are safety concerns regarding equipment, establish the rules and guidelines for equipment use and make them known to the users. Be clear about how to use the equipment in an appropriate manner and whether any training or certification is required. You may want to consider a user agreement that makes evident potential liabilities.

Although not policies, some basic procedures might be grouped with the policy statement. These might include procedures for gaining access to the technology, making reservations, the method for obtaining help or support, and where to find further information about how to use the technology.

Support Policies

It can also be useful to publish the support policies of the technology support unit. This describes what type of services are available and, if there are different user groups, who may receive what type of service (such as at an academic library where faculty and students might receive different services). It includes the computers, equipment, operating systems, and application software that is supported and the method for obtaining support. It should note where the policy applies—such as in a specific computer lab or classroom—and that nonstandard hardware and software may not be supported.

The support policies may be included with the service catalog of the technology unit, or with documentation about technology standards. The standardization of technology helps to establish expectations for support, and promotes the adoption of standard technologies, thus encouraging a more consistent environment both for the user and the support technician. A technology standards document lists the supported hardware and software, and may also provide recommended specifications. Establishing standards means there will be fewer technologies and versions of technologies for technicians to maintain expertise with, resulting in more consistent support and reducing support costs.

TRENDS IN COMPUTER MANAGEMENT

The trends covered in the following section are not cutting edge; rather, they are well established trends at varying levels of adoption that you may already have some familiarity with.

Desktop Virtualization

Some libraries are using desktop virtualization for public computer labs where there are large numbers of computers to maintain. Virtualization separates the hardware aspect of the computer from the software while still providing a seamless experience for the user. Virtual desktop infrastructure is a type of client-server computing arrangement in which the operating system is hosted on a server in a centralized data center rather than locally on the computer a user is directly interacting with. The user has a regular experience with the computer using the operating system and various applications as if they were running on the local machine, yet the client computer relays all input and output over the network to the host server where the actual processing takes place, including the running of applications and storage of data.

There are a number of benefits to this setup. For example, a traditional computer lab has many individual computers, each needing to be configured and maintained, resulting in a very high cost of staff time. A more efficient lab setup takes advantage of a single computer image that is configured once, then deployed to many machines—however, each of these machines still needs to be maintained individually after the image is deployed. System maintenance for a computer lab using desktop virtualization requires only that the primary image be maintained, resulting in staff time savings.

Additionally, because much of the processing work is handled by the server, the hardware requirements for the client workstations can be much lower than usual. This can extend the life of older equipment that would be underpowered according to current standards, or inexpensive new low-powered equipment can be acquired.

There are some tradeoffs, however. Virtualization requires a larger investment in enterprise server hardware and a network capable of the increased traffic, as well as the requisite staff knowledge and skills.

Google Chromebook

Chromebooks have recently become a popular computing option in the K–12 education setting because of their low cost and ease of enterprise administration. For similar reasons, some libraries include Chromebooks in their fleet of lending laptops. They have light hardware requirements because the Chrome OS moves most of the computing to the cloud by using web applications in an internet browser, including the Google suite of applications. There is very little local storage as Google Drive is the cloud storage option tied to Chrome OS. A limitation, however, of using the Linux-based operating system is the inability to install Microsoft Windows– or Apple Macintosh–compatible applications.

Ultimately the decision to deploy Chromebooks rests on the intended use. If user requirements will be met by working in a web environment, using web applications for productivity and the cloud for storage, then the low cost and ease of management may mean Chromebooks are a good choice. If the user needs applications that have to be installed on a computer in Windows or macOS and a comparable web-based alternative isn't sufficient or simply doesn't exist, then the cost and staff time savings may not be worth it.

In addition to Google's Chromebook products that feature the Google-developed Chrome OS on their own hardware, a number of manufacturers design and produce laptops that use Chrome OS such as the well-known companies Acer, ASUS, Dell, Samsung, HP, and Lenovo. For organizations there is Google Chrome Enterprise, a cloud-based management solution.

Tablet Computers

Tablets come in many different shapes and sizes, with some sharing attributes with mobile phones while some others cross over into laptop computer territory with full blown computer operating systems. The majority of tablet computers currently fall somewhere in the middle, featuring touch screens and operating systems designed for mobile use. Apple's iOS only runs on Apple-produced hardware like the iPad, while Google's Android is a Linux-based open source operating system used by a number of tablet manufacturers. Customized versions of Android are also used on the Kindle Fire and the Nook.

Mobile device management (MDM) solutions provide a way to configure, update, and manage devices such as tablets and other devices in an enterprise environment. Apple Configurator is an application offered by Apple specifically for configuring iOS devices. There are also third-party solutions that offer more features for a price, such as JAMF (formerly Casper), VMware AirWatch, and Cisco Meraki Systems Manager. Some of these solutions support multiple operating systems and other devices beyond tablets such as desktop computers and mobile phones. They can be used to manage devices assigned to specific users as well as fleets of devices used in a lending program.

When lending devices will be used by multiple users, IT staff need to ensure that each user has a similar experience and that any personal data is wiped from the device after use, much as in a public computer lab. One way to accomplish this is by setting up a default profile, with predetermined apps and content, that the device can be restored to after each use. Storage carts can be used both to secure and charge devices between each checkout. But as devices come in many different form factors, one size does not always fit all.

Bring Your Own Device

It is a fact of life that many users will bring their own mobile devices into the library. Although the mobile operating system market share is roughly split between iOS and Android in North America,[1] the fact is a huge variety of operating system versions and hardware may visit the library, including laptops, mobile phones, and tablet computers. The extent to which the library provides services and support for patrons and staff who bring devices varies. At a minimum, local wireless infrastructure should have enough coverage and bandwidth to accommodate connections from all over the building. In reality, however, users walk in with such a huge variety of devices, operating systems, software, and device capabilities that the user has to assume at least some responsibility for configuration and troubleshooting.

If the library does provide services for users who bring their own devices, they need to be prepared to support at least a few of the most common varieties. If printing from devices is offered, be prepared with instructions on how to print from multiple operating systems for laptop computers, phones, and tablets. Staff may desire to use personal devices to access email, so be prepared with configuration options for different clients. MDM can also be used to manage personal devices brought in by staff. Microsoft Intune, a cloud-based MDM that manages iOS and Windows devices, is one such solution.

SUMMARY

Computer management is the collection of activities in which the computer system is configured for the user and maintained to sustain performance. The computer administrator has the ability to configure the system, install applications, and set up network connections. A disk image of a model system can be cloned to other computers, saving time for the technician and reducing the possibility for user errors. Regular backups of both the system and data are important for recovery after problems occur. Cloud storage is an option for data backup and recovery. Regular system updates and malware scans as well as periodic manual maintenance on the system helps to prevent problems.

Several trends can affect the options for how technology is managed. Desktop virtualization offers an alternate way to manage computers and can extend the life of hardware. Tablet computers and the Google Chromebook are two devices that have different needs from regular computers. That users will bring their own devices into a library's technology environment is inevitable; how they will be managed is the question.

KEY TERMS

Antivirus software	Google Chromebook
Bring your own device (BYOD)	Mobile device management
Cloud storage	Refresh cycle
Computer administration	System preferences
Control panel	System requirements
Defragmentation	System Restore
Desktop virtualization	Tablet computer
Disk image	Technology use policy

QUESTIONS

1. What are some of the actions that can be taken to protect a computer's data?
2. If a user requests that a specific application be installed on their computer, what information do you need to evaluate the request?
3. List and describe regular computer maintenance tasks.
4. List the issues that technology use policies should cover.
5. What are some of the implications of library patrons bringing their own devices into the library?
6. Are there any computer management trends that you would add to those discussed in this chapter?

ACTIVITIES

1. Perform maintenance on a computer and describe the steps that were taken.
2. Select a computer management trend from the chapter and describe how it has affected a specific library.
3. Investigate the technology environment in a library—what are the different operating system versions that they support? How are they managed? What efforts are made to backup user data? What is the process for getting rid of computers that are no longer needed?

FURTHER READING

Connolly, Matthew, and Tony Cosgrave. *Using iPhones, iPads, and iPods: A Practical Guide for Librarians.* Practical Guides for Librarians, no. 10. Lanham, MD: Rowman & Littlefield, 2015.

Gleason, Ann Whitney. *Mobile Technologies for Every Library.* Lanham, MD: Rowman & Littlefield, 2015.

Halsey, Mike. *Windows 10 Troubleshooting. Expert's Voice in Windows.* South Yorkshire, UK: Apress, 2016.

Pogue, David. *Windows 10: The Missing Manual*, 2nd ed. Sebastopol, CA: O'Reilly Media, 2018.

Pogue, David. *macOS Mojave: The Missing Manual.* Sebastopol, CA: O'Reilly Media, 2018.

Rawlins, Ben. *Mobile Technologies in Libraries: A LITA Guide.* Lanham, MD: Rowman & Littlefield, 2016.

Stokes, Jeff, Richard Diver, and Manuel Singer. *Windows 10 for Enterprise Administrators: Modern Administrators' Guide Based on Redstone 3 Version.* Birmingham, UK: Packt, 2017.

Willse, Elizabeth. *Using Tablets and Apps in Libraries.* Library Technology Essentials, no. 11. Lanham, MD: Rowman & Littlefield, 2015.

RESOURCES

Apple, iOS Deployment Reference: https://help.apple.com/deployment/ios/

Apple, macOS Deployment Reference: https://help.apple.com/deployment/macos/

Apple, Mobile device management settings for IT: https://help.apple.com/deployment/mdm/

CCleaner: https://www.ccleaner.com/ccleaner

CNET, Download.com: https://www.download.com

Faronics Deep Freeze: https://www.faronics.com/products/deep-freeze

Fortres Grand Clean Slate: https://www.fortresgrand.com/products/cls/cls.htm

Glary Utilities: https://www.glarysoft.com/

Google, Chrome Enterprise: https://cloud.google.com/chrome-enterprise/

Microsoft Deployment Toolkit documentation: https://docs.microsoft.com/en-us/sccm/mdt/

Microsoft, System Center: https://www.microsoft.com/en-us/cloud-platform/system-center

Microsoft, System Center Configuration Manager Documentation: https://docs.microsoft.com/en-us/sccm/

United States Environmental Protection Agency, Electronics Donation and Recycling: https://www.epa.gov/recycle/electronics-donation-and-recycling

Mobile Device Management

Apple, Apple Configurator: https://support.apple.com/apple-configurator
Cisco Meraki Systems Manager: https://meraki.cisco.com/products/systems-manager/
JAMF: https://www.jamf.com/
Microsoft Intune: https://www.microsoft.com/en-us/microsoft-365/enterprise-mobility-security/microsoft-intune
VMware AirWatch: https://www.air-watch.com/

Antivirus Software

Avast: https://www.avast.com/
AVG: https://www.avg.com/
Kaspersky: https://usa.kaspersky.com/
McAfee: https://www.mcafee.com/
Sophos: https://www.sophos.com/
Trend Micro: https://www.trendmicro.com/

NOTES

1. "Mobile Operating System Market Share North America," Statcounter, accessed on January 1, 2019, http://gs.statcounter.com/os-market-share/mobile/north-america.

5

Networking

Many people are used to being connected to the internet and to others at all times through their mobile phones, and through computers at work, at school, and at home. Yet it is important to also keep the digital divide in mind. Even with the scale of mobile phone adoption in the United States and Canada, there are those for whom libraries are their primary means of access to the internet. The internet, and through it a vast amount of information, as well as the ability to communicate with friends, colleagues, and people around the world, are made possible by computer networking.

The internet is just one part of the greater topic of networking. The smallest libraries often have at least a simple network in place—even if it just consists of an employee workstation, a printer, and a search station for patrons. As that network grows by adding workstations and other devices, and is further connected to other networks, the complexity grows as well. It is likely that a library network will include multiple employee workstations, public computer workstations, shared resources such as printers, servers, scanners and other devices, and be connected to other networks at a campus or organizational level, as well the internet and world wide web. As networks grow they become complex very quickly.

Having a solid understanding of computer networking will be greatly helpful for library employees, whether they are tasked with some level of support for the network or working with those who are.

This chapter introduces some of the most relevant concepts and practical topics for the technician from the perspective of the library. It begins with network architecture, which is the design of networks from the local level to the regional level. Next, it describes the most common hardware components used in a local network, such as what you would see in a library. The chapter finally covers some practical issues for the network administrator, and then some current topics and trends including, Internet2, the internet of things, and net neutrality.

NETWORK ARCHITECTURE

The architecture of a network is the design that describes how computers on a network are connected. It includes the hardware, software, and protocols used, and maps out their connections. Each device on the network has an address that uniquely identifies that device to others on the network. In this way, devices don't have to be directly networked to each other, but can address data to a specific device; the data is then passed along by other devices along the route until it reaches the destination.

Network Types

Networks are often categorized into two different types: wired and wireless. Virtual networks could be considered a third type, as they can incorporate both wired and wireless connections. In a library setting, it is likely that the local network will incorporate a mixture of network types.

Wired Network

Connections in a wired network are made physically, often using Ethernet cable. Most desktop computers, servers, and many other networking devices have a network interface controller (NIC) where one end of the Ethernet cable plugs in. For laptop computers that don't have an Ethernet port, it is possible to use an adapter that plugs into an available universal serial bus (USB) or Thunderbolt port. Although the cabling most commonly found in home and office settings is a type of twisted-pair cabling that resembles a telephone cable, coaxial cable and fiber optics are used in networking as well.

Given the option between an Ethernet and a wireless connection to a network, it is usually recommended to use the physical cable. Ethernet has significant advantages over wireless, including faster speeds and stronger security. Wireless does offer the advantage of mobility—an important factor in libraries when considering space design because wireless lends itself well to flexibility in space use, and users today come with an expectation for mobility. But when desktop workstations are used and mobility is not a factor, a wired connection is the preferred solution.

Wireless Network

Wireless networking generally uses radio waves, whether it uses the Institute of Electrical and Electronics Engineers (IEEE) 802.11 standards (commonly referred to as *Wi-Fi*) or a cellular network. Bluetooth and infrared are two other wireless technologies used for transmitting data between devices in relatively close proximity. In an office setting like a library, Wi-Fi is generally used to provide wireless access to the network. Most mobile devices, be they laptops, tablets, or phones, have wireless networking capabilities. Many desktop computers also have wireless built in, and for those that do not it is easy to add wireless capabilities with an expansion card or a USB Wi-Fi dongle.

Wireless devices connect to the network through a wireless access point (WAP), which can handle connections from multiple devices simultaneously. The WAP is usually connected to a router with an Ethernet cable, with the router directing traffic and making the connection to the larger network. In the case of home networking, the WAP and router are often combined into a single device, which then connects to a cable or digital subscriber line modem for internet access.

The radio frequency bands used by Wi-Fi are most commonly 2.4 GHz and 5 GHz, which are further divided into channels. As Wi-Fi is radio, it is susceptible to interference, including from other Wi-Fi signals. General practice is to set up a WAP to broadcast on the channel with the least use. But since adjacent channels overlap, it is most common to use the three nonoverlapping channels—1, 6, and 11—which can operate concurrently without interfering with each other.

The IEEE created and maintains the 802.11 standard used for Wi-Fi. As new standards are released, backward compatibility is built into new WAPs to ensure the continued operability of older Wi-Fi-capable devices. Beginning with the 802.11ax standard, a new generation-based naming scheme will be used to make it simpler for consumers to understand. Older standards 802.11n and 802.11ac will also get generation-based names because they are still in use. Table 5.1 lists Wi-Fi standards with their generation and release dates as well as the theoretical max data rate that they are capable of. Max data rates aren't as straightforward as one might hope; because there are some different ways to calculate the rate, there are many mitigating factors such as the number of connections, and they are, after all, theoretical. But it does give you an idea of the leaps and bounds in data rates that each generation of Wi-Fi takes.

Table 5.1. Wi-Fi Standards

IEEE Standard	Generation	Release	Frequency	Max Data Rate
802.11b	n/a	Sept. 1999	2.4 GHz	11 Mbps
802.11g	n/a	June 2003	2.4 GHz	54 Mbps
802.11n	Wi-Fi 4	Oct. 2009	2.4/5 GHz	450 Mbps
802.11ac	Wi-Fi 5	Dec. 2013	5 GHz	1.3 Gbps
802.11ax	Wi-Fi 6	Sept. 2020	2.4/5 GHz	9.6 Gbps

Virtual Network

Whereas both wired and wireless networks depend on the physical layout and direct connections of the network devices, a virtual network exists as a logical layer on top of the physical network. In this manner, the virtual network can have different pathways and even a different topology from the physical network. A virtual local area network (VLAN) can be defined by the network administrator using software to separate resources that share the same physical network, rather than physically adjusting cabling and connections. This way there might be a VLAN for library staff that is separate from a VLAN for library patrons, preventing patrons from accessing employee-only resources such as shared files or printers located in staff areas—despite sharing the same physical network infrastructure.

A virtual private network (VPN) can exist over network infrastructure that includes larger networks such as the internet, and can connect networks to each other logically. They often feature strong security measures, such as encryption, to protect data while it travels between endpoints within the VPN. A practical application for libraries is allowing employees to join the organization's VPN remotely, from some geographic location off-site, thus gaining access to all of the VPN's resources as if the computer had a direct physical connection to the local network. Traffic from the VPN-connected computer will also appear as having originated from the VPN's host network location when leaving the network.

Network Topology

Connect two devices together so that they can communicate—whether physically with a cable or wirelessly—and you have created a network. This is the simplest network topology, known as a *point-to-point topology*. A network topology describes the form and arrangement of devices on the network. The geographic or physical location of devices don't matter so much as the connections and pathways between the network devices. The greater the number of connections between devices, the more robust the network. If there is a connection on the network that many devices depend on, then a failure at that point could affect all of those devices, whereas if there are multiple connections then data can travel down an alternate pathway that took over for the failed connection. Of course, increasing the connections also increases the complexity and consequently the cost of support.

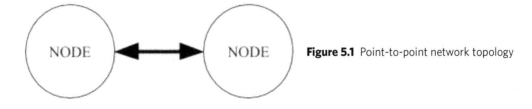

Figure 5.1 Point-to-point network topology

Linear

The point-to-point network from our first example of two connected devices could be expanded by connecting each device, or node, on the network to a second, creating a line of nodes. Connecting devices in this way is known as *daisy chaining* and our point-to-point network now has a linear topology. Data can move in either direction along the network, but it does have to pass each node on the network until it arrives at the destination. A network node is any device on the network where data might originate, pass through, or end up. This includes printers, scanners, switches, routers, and other devices, as well as computers.

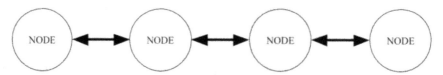

Figure 5.2 Linear network topology

Ring

Aside from linear, there are several other common network topologies. If you connect the endpoints of a linear topology to form a circle, then you have a ring topology. Like the linear topology, data can pass in either direction, but it will never have to travel the entire length of the network because it can always travel the shortest distance of two possible pathways to the destination. By having an alternate path to each node, we can also compensate for a single break in the network.

Figure 5.3 Ring network topology

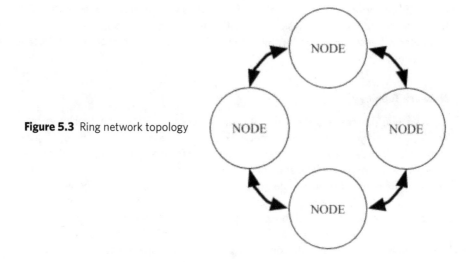

Bus

A bus network topology is similar to the linear topology, except that each node is connected to a common cable, or backbone, rather than another node. A failure at a single node won't affect the other nodes, but a break in the bus will disrupt the network. The bus topology was one of the earliest used for computer networking.

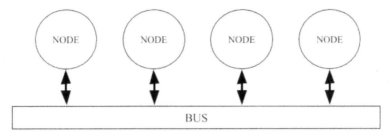

Figure 5.4 Bus network topology

Star

One of the most common topologies currently is the star topology. In it, all nodes are directly connected to a central hub, which relays data from the originating node to the destination node. This is one of the simplest networks to set up as there is no disruption to the network when adding additional nodes. It is also robust in the sense that a failure at a single node or a cable will not break the network. Instead the hub represents a risk as a single point of failure. A common example of the star network is a wireless environment, where multiple wireless devices connect to a single WAP.

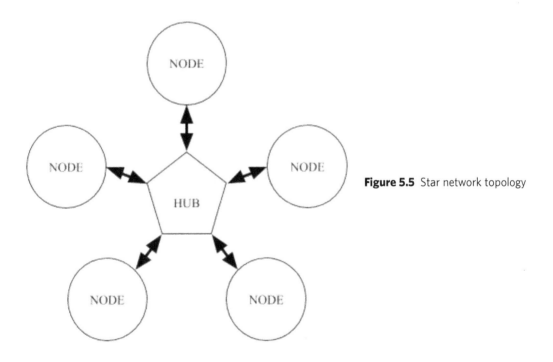

Figure 5.5 Star network topology

Mesh

When some nodes are connected to more than two other nodes it is known as a *mesh topology*. In this model there are multiple pathways that data can take between end points. If every node is connected to every other node, it is a fully connected mesh network. This is the most robust network possible as there is no single point of failure, but also the most expensive to set up because of the amount of connections needing to be made for each node.

Networking

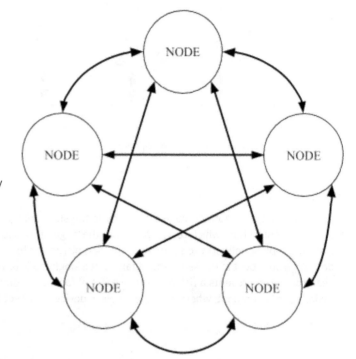

Figure 5.6 Mesh network topology

Hybrid

Hybrid topology combines two or more different topologies into a network. This represents the fact that a network need not be limited to a single topology. It is easy to imagine as small networks of different topologies can be connected to each other to form larger networks. An example of a hybrid topology is multiple star networks connected by a bus topology.

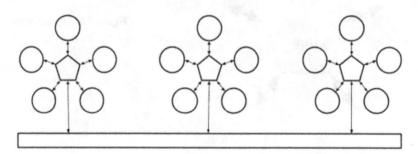

Figure 5.7 Hybrid network topology

Geographic Area

Networks can also be described by the physical or geographic area that they encompass. There are many ways to describe area networks, and the number of types vary depending on who you talk to. The following are the four you are most likely to encounter with regard to a library.

Personal Area Network

Your personal workstation and the devices connected to it constitute a personal area network (PAN). Wired connections are commonly made with a USB or Thunderbolt cable and wireless connections with Bluetooth or infrared. Devices that can be connected in this way include computers, laptops, tablets, smart phones, printers, and mass storage. One of the devices can also act as a gateway to another network, such as when a laptop is tethered to a cell phone, with the cell phone providing access to the internet.

Apple devices that run macOS or iOS include a feature called *AirDrop* that allows the user to transfer files between two devices wirelessly, without needing to be connected to a greater network. In the April 2018 update to Windows 10, Microsoft released a similar feature called *Nearby Sharing*.

Local Area Network

A local area network (LAN) typically connects computers and other devices in a home, building, or small group of nearby buildings. This is most likely the type of area network that you will encounter in a library setting. The communication medium for a LAN may consist of Ethernet cables or Wi-Fi, or a mix of the two. Devices on the LAN may include multiple computer workstations, printers, switches, routers, and firewalls, among other devices. The LAN can be connected to other networks nearby as well as via the internet. It may also have servers dedicated to providing specific services to the devices on the network, such as print servers, storage servers, email servers, web servers, and specialized application and database servers.

Campus Area Network

A campus area network (CAN) links together LANs within a limited geographic area, and may provide access to external networks and the internet. Not all libraries may be part of a CAN. It is commonly used in situations in which a single organization has multiple LANs to connect and has the advantage of being able to share resources throughout the CAN. Examples are often found on university campuses, multiple-building government centers, and corporate campuses. Different LANs within the CAN may serve different or specialized functions accessible by users in connected LANs, such as a data center that provides the majority of server resources or campus-wide directory services such as the Lightweight Directory Access Protocol (LDAP). If the CAN provides the gateway to networks external to the organization, such as the internet, then this area is a focus for network security and is described as the *network edge*.

Wide Area Network

A network that covers a very large area, connecting many different network owners, can be classified as a wide area network (WAN). Communications on a WAN can travel long distances, even around the world; the internet can be considered a WAN. Communication through a WAN is typically over leased lines featuring technologies such as fiber optics, asymmetric digital subscriber lines, cable, and cellular.

NETWORKING HARDWARE

In addition to the client workstations and servers, a number of hardware components perform specific functions for a network. Sometimes multiple functions are performed by a single device, as in the case of a home internet gateway, which functions as a basic switch, WAP, and router, all in one.

Network Interface Controller

The NIC is the hardware on a device such as a computer workstation or server that transmits and receives data, whether over wired Ethernet or via Wi-Fi. Each NIC has a unique media access control (MAC) address that is stored permanently in read-only memory. The MAC address is important because it identifies your computer to the network and is sometimes referred to as the physical address of your computer—in contrast to an IP address, which is logical and may be assigned.

Cabling

The prevalent form of cabling in LANs uses Ethernet over twisted pair. The cables resemble telephone wiring; twisted-pair technology was first commonly used for analog telephone communications. These days there are two standards in common use, with Category 6 (Cat 6) cabling replacing the more ubiquitous Cat 5e because of its ability to transmit data at a much faster rate. However, to take advantage of Cat 6 data rates, devices on the network also need to be capable of transmitting at an equivalent or better rate. Fortunately, Cat 5e and Cat 6 are both backward compatible with older hardware, even using the same RJ-45 connectors as previous standards, so network components can be upgraded piecemeal rather than wholesale.

Table 5.2. Ethernet Cabling Specifications

Standard	Bandwidth	Max Data Rate	Cable Length
Cat 5e	100 MHz	1 Gbps	100 m
Cat 6	250 MHz	10 Gbps	50 m
Cat 6a	500 MHz	10 Gbps	100 m

Coaxial cable predates twisted pair for use in Ethernet networks and is still commonly used in home networking with a modem to receive internet provided by a cable internet service provider. Optical fiber cable is found more often in large networks. It is more expensive than twisted pair, but can transmit over much longer distances while also carrying greater bandwidth.

Switch

Switches connect the computers within a network, directing traffic from one destination to another. They come in many different sizes—from a small desktop switch with four ports to rack-mounted switches with forty-eight ports. Each device that is plugged into the switch has a unique MAC address and the switch learns to associate each occupied port with the appropriate MAC address. As data reaches the switch, it looks at the destination MAC address and directs the data to the appropriate port. Switches used in the home or small office are often unmanaged switches that are plug-and-play, and simply work. Enterprise-level switches can have a variety of features and many configuration options, including the ability to remotely manage and monitor the network using the Simple Network Management Protocol.

Router

A router connects networks and subnetworks (also known as *subnets*). A simple example consists of two separate networks each using a star topology with a group of computers connected to a switch at the center of the star. Each of the switches is then connected to a single router, thus connecting the two networks. It is the router's job to direct network traffic between networks and subnets, including forwarding traffic on to the next router. Although our example is simple, imagine three or four networks connected to a router and that router connected to several other routers that each have their own connected networks. It becomes complex quickly. As there may be multiple pathways data might take to reach its destination, the router determines the best pathway and forwards the data along to the next node in the optimal route.

Firewall

Crucial components of network security are firewalls. They separate a network from external data sources and control access to the network. One is often used on the edge of a network where it connects to the internet, and is configured to allow certain types of traffic through specific ports while denying others. They can also be configured to permit traffic from trusted sources to pass while denying others. A firewall can be both hardware and software based, where a physical router behaves as a firewall or in the case of a personal workstation with a software-based firewall as a component of the operating system. Firewalls don't have to exist solely on the edge of the network, and in fact having multiple layers means greater control over the type of traffic moving around within a network.

Wireless Access Point

A WAP, alternately referred to as an *access point*, is the network device that facilitates a wireless connection to the network for wireless capable devices. In your home you may be familiar with a device that combines the functionality of a WAP with a router, and possibly also a modem, but the WAP used in enterprise settings is usually dedicated to the task of providing wireless connections. The WAP is then physically connected with Ethernet cabling to a router, consequently providing access to the LAN.

Because Wi-Fi uses radio frequencies as a communication medium, the WAP will have one or more antennas—although the antenna may not be visible and may be hidden inside the casing. There is some signal degradation to the radio waves as they pass through physical obstructions such as walls, although the material makes a difference in how much the signal degrades. Radio waves by their nature are also susceptible to interference from other electronic devices including other WAPs.

When you set up the WAP you have to give a name to the service set identifier (SSID). This is where you determine the name of the Wi-Fi network that is broadcast to wireless devices looking to connect. When more than one WAP has the same SSID, it is assumed that they are part of the same network, so that if the signal connecting a device to a WAP grows weak and there is a stronger signal with the same SSID available, they perform a handoff, thus transferring the device's connection to the WAP with the stronger signal.

NETWORK ADMINISTRATION

Network administration covers the day-to-day concerns of managing a network. In some cases the network is administered from within the library; in other cases the library network will be part of a larger organization's network, with management of the network coming from the parent organization. Large IT departments have a team of technicians providing network support with responsibilities ranging from physically pulling cables to remote management of network devices. Some may specialize in specific areas such as network security or user management. Libraries who manage their own network may have one or two technicians who have other responsibilities as well. Some of these tasks, such as pulling cables and installing network jacks, can be contracted to outside vendors.

The Network Administrator

The person responsible for designing, maintaining, and managing the network infrastructure is known as the *network administrator*. Depending on the size of the organization, management of the network is often handled separately from computer user support. When problems are reported by an end user, it may first be handled at the technology help desk, where a support technician documents the complaint and then determines that the problem is networking related and so escalates the issue to the network support team. In smaller organizations, it may be that staff fill multiple functional roles and need a broad range of knowledge rather than specializing solely in networking. For example, it is fairly common for staff involved in the network management to also be responsible for server administration. In libraries that rely on a parent organization for network management, library staff providing technology support will need to be familiar enough with networking to solve the most basic problems and to recognize when an issue needs to be escalated to the network management team.

The responsibilities that often fall under network administration include designing expansions and updates to the network, ensuring the security of the network, managing network software, administration of the user management system (e.g., LDAP), replacing network hardware, monitoring network performance, and troubleshooting network problems. Networking specialists can earn professional certifications that demonstrate their expertise. Among the certifications available are the CompTIA Network+ certification, the Cisco Certified Network Associate (CCNA), and the Microsoft Certified Solutions Associate (MCSA), which allows you to specialize in different Microsoft technologies such as Windows Server.

Networked Printing

In a small home office, it might suffice to share a printer that is attached to a computer with other users on the network, but in an environment with many users and multiple printers a print server is often set up to manage and direct print jobs. The print server may be a workstation connected to the network and several printers. It may use print server software that, beyond managing a queue of print requests and directing them to the appropriate printer, may also include features that conduct accounting for resource management, payment processing, and printing from mobile devices.

User Authentication

LDAP is a common protocol used in networks for authenticating users and granting access to shared resources. From the user's perspective, he or she is able to login to computers on the network by supplying an account name and password, whereupon those credentials are passed through the network to the authentication server for validation. If the credentials are valid, the user gains access to the network including access to shared files, printers, and other resources according to their permissions. It is the network administrator who creates the user accounts and assigns permissions to users on the authentication server.

Active Directory is a Microsoft service on Windows server operating systems that uses LDAP. It resides on the network server that controls the domain using software such as Windows Server 2019. A domain is a network that is centrally managed by servers that are known as the *domain controller*. Although it is possible to use macOS computers with Active Directory, many of the Windows features cannot be used.

An alternative to Windows Server is Samba, an open-source domain controller designed to operate on Linux, Unix, and Unix-like machines, such as macOS. It can also be integrated with Active Directory.

Network Security

When securing the network, care must be taken to guard against external and internal threats alike. Threats may come from other networks as well as from within, and attacks may try to gain unauthorized access to files or control of network resources. By gaining access to the network attackers might attempt to steal confidential information including credit card numbers, passwords, social security numbers, and other personal data. They can then use that data to conduct further hacking, make unauthorized purchases, or else sell the confidential information.

While problems with viruses, worms, and Trojan horses tend to be seen as security issues for individual computers, strong network security will help protect against these attacks as well as aid in preventing their spread from an infected computer. There are some basic measures that you can take to help keep the network secure: keep all software patched and up to date, always use strong passwords, limit the number of people who have access to administrative accounts, limit user access to network resources only to situations where there is a need for them to have access, and be conservative with user access levels—only granting read and write access when appropriate.

A firewall is a key component to protecting a network from external intrusions as it is capable of monitoring incoming and outgoing traffic, and preventing certain types of traffic. Firewalls can also be used to isolate portions of a network by using them as a gateway to enforce different rules for traffic accessing that part of the network. One of the ways to control access beyond the firewall is to limit the type of traffic that can pass through the firewall by limiting the ports that are open. Software ports are associated with specific services and protocols, and are assigned a number. For example, HTTP uses port 80, whereas FTP uses port 21. If you wanted to allow web traffic but not FTP you would open port 80 in the firewall and leave port 21 closed.

Another vulnerability to network security is inherent in wireless networks as data is remarkably simple to intercept using Wi-Fi sniffing tools. These tools have legitimate uses for monitoring wireless networks and testing security but in the wrong hands can also be used for eavesdropping on unprotected networks. Libraries have a responsibility to the privacy of their users, and as it is simple to snoop on open Wi-Fi networks, utilizing encrypted Wi-Fi is a fundamental task for network security. Wi-Fi Protected Access (WPA2) is the current industry standard for encrypting Wi-Fi and, although not perfect (nothing is), it goes a long way toward establishing a secure environment for users.

Often public Wi-Fi networks in hotels, airports, and coffee shops use a captive portal to authenticate users and grant them access to the internet. The problem with captive portals is that the device is already connected to the network before having to click through to accept terms and possibly enter a simple password. A captive portal is not a replacement for an encrypted network, and can lull users into a false sense of security.

Troubleshooting

The general troubleshooting process for networks is similar to troubleshooting other technology-related problems with the added dimension that a single problem can affect many, many users. As the source of what appears to be a networking problem may be with a specific computer, a resource connected to the network such as a printer, a server, or the network infrastructure itself, a good first step to identifying the problem is to figure out who is affected.

Is the problem isolated to a specific workstation? Is it a specific user, regardless of the workstation they use? Is it localized to a portion of the LAN? Is it the entire building? Is the entire region affected, or perhaps the world? Is it a specific service provided locally, or perhaps via the internet? Obviously, you may not have the ability to do anything about some situations. If the internet goes down for an entire region, it may be time to get a cup of coffee and straighten up your office—after you alert your users, of course. If the problem is with a specific, cloud-based service, don't be too quick to blame the service; there may actually be issues with your network configurations such as the firewall. Either way, this is a time to reach out to the service provider's technical support. As you determine the extent of users who are affected by the problem, you will hone in on the source of the problem.

There are many tools in the network administrator's toolbox for troubleshooting network problems. A number of them can be run from the command line, and are useful for making quick checks of different aspects of the network. Command Prompt is a utility that has been on Windows operating systems since the early days, and gives power users the ability to interact with the system using text commands. It is often referred to as *CMD* or *CMD.EXE* because of the file name. On Unix-like operating systems, including macOS and Linux, a utility called Terminal serves as the command-line interface. Although experienced administrators may be very comfortable using CMD, Microsoft started including an additional utility called PowerShell since Windows 7 that is far more powerful and closer in capability to the Unix Terminal. When using the commands that appear in Textbox 5.1 (as well as others) you can add parameters to the command to display specific information or take specific actions.

TEXTBOX 5.1

A Sample of Network-Related Commands

ipconfig (Windows) or ifconfig (Unix): Display computer's IP settings
ping: Check the connection to a machine using IP address or hostname
route (Windows) or netstat (Unix): Display local routing table
tracert (Windows) or traceroute (Unix): Display path to a machine using IP address or hostname

---

TOPICS AND TRENDS IN NETWORKING

Internet2

In 1996 some leading higher education institutions came together to form Internet2, to create a high-performance, cutting-edge network with which to solve common problems, conduct research, and produce innovative technology solutions. Internet2 now includes more than 400 universities, government agencies, and regional education networks, and through them more than 100,000 community institutions—as well as many corporations and research and educational organizations around the world. Do not confuse Internet2, which is essentially a networking consortium, with Web 2.0, which is a concept that describes certain website technology and user behavior.

A service of Internet2, the InCommon Federation provides a trust framework for education and research institutions to provide securely managed access to online resources. One way this is accomplished is through a certificate service for servers. Also known as *secure socket layer* (SSL) certificates or web server certificates, it informs the end user visiting the website that the site is indeed who it claims to be—not a fake—and establishes a secure connection between the server and the end user.

The InCommon Federation also supports secure, single sign-on (SSO) solutions that use Security Assertion Markup Language (SAML) and federating software such as Shibboleth. The direct benefit to libraries of SSO is the ability for users to access resources from different applications and sources while only having to validate their credentials once per session.

Eduroam is a service that provides a way for users from a member organization to gain network access when visiting another member organization. If a student of a university that is a member of Eduroam were to visit a library at another member university, they would be able to log on to the Wi-Fi network using the same credentials they use at their home institution. The idea here is not that all member organizations have access to a pool of user data, but that the visited organization will trust the user's home institution to authenticate the user, thus keeping the user's credentials secure.

Internet of Things

The internet of things (IoT) is not a specific technology or protocol; it is the concept of a vast network of everyday objects communicating and interacting with each other. These objects range from full-blown computers and servers to what would normally be noninternet–enabled or even nonelectronic devices. In the home we are seeing consumer devices that include smart light bulbs, thermostats, dishwashers, coffee makers, door locks, refrigerators, and the list continues to grow. Many of these devices can be programmed to behave a specific way, to respond to their own sensors or data from other connected devices, and can be controlled from a central hub in the home or even remotely on an internet-connected mobile phone or computer.

Since IoT involves networked devices, these devices are as vulnerable to threats like hacking and viruses as any other networked device. So far, IoT devices do not have a great track record for the strength of their security and, although a coffee maker may not be an attractive target in itself, it may be the weak link that provides an attacker access to more secure devices on the same network. There are also privacy concerns, not necessarily from a security standpoint, but in the sense that vendors may be collecting large amounts of data from the devices. Other issues with IoT include fragmentation of protocols and standards, interoperability between devices from different vendors, and the scale of networking that will be needed to accommodate the number of connections and bandwidth of all of those smart devices.

IoT devices may use any number of different communication protocols, including Bluetooth low energy, radio frequency identification (RFID), near-field communication, ZigBee, and Wi-Fi among many others. In an effort to coordinate the many communication methods used, as well as to try to simplify the adoption of IoT for consumers, IEEE established standard 1905.1 in April 2013. The new standard is branded as *nVoy* and provides support for Wi-Fi, Ethernet, multimedia over coax, and powerline networking (which takes advantage of existing electrical lines).

Adoption of IoT by libraries seems low at the moment, but interest is strong and a number of libraries are experimenting with applying it to library services. Some of these pilot projects have been written about. See "Further Reading" at the end of the chapter for a list of articles. IoT offers many interesting possibilities for libraries. Environmental monitoring and climate control can lead to more efficient use of energy as well as valuable support for archival and rare materials. Some libraries already use RFID-tagged items; IoT presents the opportunity for enhanced inventory control as well as innovative ways to link the physical collection to an online library system. Combined with smart way-finding it could be possible to recommend items based on the physical location of the user. IoT-linked sensors can go far beyond simple gate counts to assessing physical space use throughout the building.

Net Neutrality

Net neutrality is not so much a technical networking topic as it is a policy issue, controversial in some circles and actively being debated by technology experts, commercial internet service providers (ISPs), and legislatures. *Net neutrality* is the concept that a neutral network should treat all traffic equally, and not discriminate based on content, source, type, protocol, or any other classification. In practice this means that ISPs should not give preferential treatment or restrict certain types of traffic, nor should they charge consumers based on the content they want to access.

Advocates of net neutrality are concerned that ISPs may take the role of gatekeeper by restricting access to certain content or content types with bandwidth throttling—that is intentionally slowing the transmission speeds—or entirely blocking access unless the user pays additional charges. Additionally, it would be possible for ISPs to prioritize certain content—perhaps from certain providers—thus giving an advantage to that content or service provider.

Net neutrality opponents argue that the significant rise in the amount of bandwidth used requires additional investment to expand and improve the network, and that charging based on the amount of bandwidth or type of content is a fair way to fund necessary work. They argue that regulation in the form of net neutrality will discourage financial investment and consequently competition and innovation.

The American Library Association (ALA) takes a position in support of net neutrality, summarizing their stance as follows:[1]

- The ALA endorses strong, enforceable net neutrality rules such as those adopted by the Federal Communications Commission (FCC) in 2015, which banned blocking, throttling, or degrading of any lawful internet content.
- The ALA opposes "paid prioritization" for internet traffic as an inherently unfair practice.
- The ALA supports efforts to protect net neutrality in federal court.
- The ALA supports legislation that preserves the competitive online markets for content and services.
- The ALA supports state-level efforts to preserve net neutrality protections for consumers and institutions like libraries.

The FCC has issued several decisions regarding the classification of internet services and any regulation, although it has reversed a number of positions during the presidency of Donald Trump. Most recently, as of this writing, several states have sought to enact their own rules about net neutrality, including California's Senate Bill 822, known as the California Internet Consumer Protection and Net Neutrality Act of 2018. The national debate about net neutrality is ongoing.

SUMMARY

Networking is an important topic for libraries because it is used to provide access to so many of the resources that they provide. A network can be formed by as few as two devices that are connected and communicating with each other. Network architecture describes the design of the network connections, including information about hardware, software, and protocols. Several different aspects of networks can be described, such as the type of network, the topology of the connections, and the scale of the geographic area.

There is hardware built to serve a particular purpose for the network, including the NIC, cabling, switches, routers, firewalls, and WAPs. The network administrator manages the network, and is concerned both with the design and the day-to-day operations. They manage the configuration of network devices, user authentication, and network security among other things, and may be involved in troubleshooting problems.

Of the networking topics to be aware of, Internet2 offers a number of services of particular interest to academic organizations. The IoT trend is still in the early stages of experimentation as far as libraries are concerned, but is worth keeping an eye on as it offers some very useful applications. Net neutrality is a hot and rapidly developing topic and the field of librarianship has a relevant voice to add to the conversation.

KEY TERMS

Network architecture
802.11
Category (Cat) 6
Ethernet
Firewall
Internet of Things (IoT)
Local area network (LAN)
Net neutrality
Network administration
Network interface controller (NIC)

Network topology
Router
Single sign-on (SSO)
Switch
User authentication
Virtual network
Virtual private network (VPN)
Wireless access point (WAP)
Wireless networking

QUESTIONS

1. Compare wired networking with wireless networking. In what situations is wireless networking preferred to a wired network connection? What are the drawbacks?
2. List and describe the different network topologies.
3. List the types of geographic networking areas and provide examples.
4. List and describe networking hardware.
5. What are some of the measures that can be taken to keep a network secure?
6. Describe a use case scenario for using an IoT technology in a library.
7. What are the latest developments in net neutrality?

ACTIVITIES

1. Do an assessment of wireless speed at a library or other public building. Use a mobile device and a bandwidth testing website or app. Test different locations inside and outside of the building and record the results. Be sure to try often overlooked locations such as stairwells, basements, and hallways as well as office and study areas. Which areas had the fastest bandwidth? Were there examples of slow bandwidth where you would expect otherwise? Are there other factors that might affect your results, such as the amount of people present (more devices)?
2. Use a network modeling tool to model a home or small office network. Show any computers, printers, televisions, and IoT devices on the network as well as their connections to network hardware such as switches, routers, and WAPs.

FURTHER READING

Booth, Char. "Hope, Hype, and VoIP: Riding the Library Technology Cycle." *Library Technology Reports* 46, no. 5 (2010).

Breeding, Marshall. "Smarter Libraries through Technology: Beyond IP Authentication: The Need to Modernize Access to Library Resources." *Smart Libraries Newsletter* 37, no. 12 (2017): 1.

Cameron, Dell. "California Net Neutrality Bill Signed into Law." *Gizmodo*, September 30, 2018. https://gizmodo.com/california-net-neutrality-bill-signed-into-law-1829402679.

Gibson, Darril. *Microsoft Windows Networking Essentials.* Serious Skills. San Francisco: Wiley, 2011.

Halsey, Mike, and Joli Ballew. *Windows Networking Troubleshooting.* Windows Troubleshooting Series. Apress, 2017.

Massis, B. "VPNs in the Library." *Information and Learning Science* 118, no. 11 (2017): 672–74. https://doi.org/10.1108/ILS-10-2017-0099.

Meyers, Michael, and Scott Jernigan. *CompTIA Network+ Certification All-in-One Exam Guide.* New York: McGraw-Hill Education, 2018.

Satterwhite, Ellen. "Net Neutrality Updates: What the Future Holds in Mozilla Case." *American Libraries*, February 4, 2019. https://americanlibrariesmagazine.org/blogs/the-scoop/2019-mozilla-net-neutrality-updates/.

Spacey, Rachel, Adrienne Muir, Louise Cooke, Claire Creaser, and Valérie Spezi. "Filtering Wireless (Wi-Fi) Internet Access in Public Places." *Journal of Librarianship and Information Science* 49, no. 1 (March 2017): 15–25.

Xu, Gordon F., and Jin Xiu Guo. "Improving Library User Experience: Wi-Fi Network Assessment." *Journal of Library Administration* 58, no. 8 (2018): 806–34.

Internet of Things

Bradley, Jonathan, Patrick Tomlin, and Brian Mathews. "Chapter 4: Building Intelligent Infrastructures: Steps toward Designing IoT-Enabled Library Facilities." *Library Technology Reports* 54, no. 1 (2018): 23–27.

Enis, Matt. "Voice Activated." *Library Journal* 143, no. 6 (2018): 28–29.

Hahn, Jim. "The Bibliotelemetry of Information and Environment: An Evaluation of IoT-Powered Recommender Systems." *Proceedings of the ASIS&T 2018 Annual Meeting*, 55, no. 1 (2018): 151–160.

Hahn, Jim. "The Internet of Things: Mobile Technology and Location Services in Libraries." *Library Technology Reports* 53, no. 1 (January 2017): 1–28.

Hoy, Matthew B. "Smart Buildings: An Introduction to the Library of the Future." *Medical Reference Services Quarterly* 35, no. 3 (2016): 326–31.

Kyriakos, Stefanidis, and Giannis Tsakonas. "Integration of Library Services with Internet of Things Technologies." *Code4Lib Journal*, no. 30 (2015).

Massis, Bruce. "The Internet of Things and Its Impact on the Library." *New Library World* 117, no. 3/4 (2016): 289–92.

Monica Maceli. "EnviroPi: Taking a DIY Internet-of-Things Approach to an Environmental Monitoring System." *Code4Lib Journal*, no. 42 (2018).

Wójcik, Magdalena. "Internet of Things—Potential for Libraries." *Library Hi Tech* 34, no. 2 (2016): 404–20.

RESOURCES

ALA, Network Neutrality: http://www.ala.org/advocacy/net-neutrality

Cisco, certifications: https://www.cisco.com/c/en/us/training-events/training-certifications/certifications.html

Coalition for Networked Information: https://www.cni.org/

CompTIA Network+: https://certification.comptia.org/certifications/network

EDUCAUSE, 2018 Trends and Technologies: Domain Report: https://www.educause.edu/ecar/research-publications/trends-and-technologies-domain-reports/2018/overview

Eduroam: https://www.eduroam.org/

IEEE standards: https://www.ieee.org/standards/index.html

InCommon: https://www.incommon.org/

Internet2: https://www.internet2.edu/

Microsoft, Windows Server 2019: https://www.microsoft.com/en-us/cloud-platform/windows-server

Microsoft Certified Solutions Associate: https://www.microsoft.com/en-us/learning/mcsa-certification.aspx

Samba: https://www.samba.org/
Wi-Fi Alliance: www.wi-fi.org

Bandwidth Testing Tools

Broadband Now: https://broadbandnow.com/speedtest
Ookla Speedtest: https://www.speedtest.net/

Network Modeling Tools

Creately: https://creately.com/
LucidChart: https://www.lucidchart.com/
Microsoft Visio: https://www.microsoft.com/en-us/microsoft-365/visio/flowchart-software

NOTE

1. "Network Neutrality," American Library Association, accessed on March 11, 2019, http://www.ala.org/advocacy/net-neutrality.

6

Server Administration

In an IT organization the system administrator is responsible for managing the servers. These servers are often computers with specialized hardware and software designed to provide services over local networks as well as the internet. Some of these services might be as a print server, as a web server, or as a mail server.

The trend in server hosting for libraries has gone from individual computers as physical servers in the library to centralized data centers to virtualized servers to cloud service providers. This is an interesting time to support servers for libraries as many services transition to the cloud—and yet examples of all the previously mentioned scenarios remain. In fact, it is plausible that a library system administrator will be supporting servers and services from each scenario all at the same time.

Even in the library that uses cloud providers for nearly all of their services, it is important for the library technician to have an understanding of server administration because it affects other areas he or she may support such as the network, workstation support, web development, or application development.

This chapter begins by reviewing the infrastructure related to computer servers, from hardware components up to the cloud. Next, the chapter introduces some server operations topics, and then finishes by reviewing a number of services that are frequently provided using servers.

INFRASTRUCTURE

Although a server is indeed a computer, dedicated servers have specialized hardware features that allow them to perform reliably and provide services at a much higher standard than a typical desktop computer-turned-server would be able to. Organizations that support servers usually house them in a centralized data center, which is a much more efficient way to support an optimal operating environment, and provide for security and emergency systems in case of a power outage or natural disaster.

Servers are now commonly virtualized, instead of offering dedicated physical servers to individual services. This affords much greater flexibility with regard to the resources that may be allocated to a particular server. Cloud providers also take advantage of virtualization in the services that they offer customers. It is useful to remember, however, that moving your servers to the cloud is in actuality moving to a vendor's physical data center out there, somewhere.

Hardware

Most modern computers, even a lightweight laptop, could function as a server at some level. Dedicated servers have many of the same hardware components that you will be familiar with from desktop computers such as the central processing unit (CPU), random access memory (RAM), storage, and a motherboard. It is, however, expected to maintain maximum uptime and consistently high performance, so there are a number of specialized configurations in dedicated servers.

Hardware Components

It is critical for server hardware to be reliable and durable. Even a small interruption to a mission-critical service could be catastrophic for the organization or users involved. Fortunately, library services usually aren't a matter of life or death, but interruptions or failures of expected services can still be extremely unpleasant. Hardware intended for servers tends to be robust with redundancies built in to mitigate hardware failures and minimize downtime.

They often have multiple CPUs in order to increase the amount of processing that can be done simultaneously as multiple clients make requests of the server. They also have redundant power supplies in case one fails.

Servers use specialized memory called *error correction code* (ECC) RAM. ECC is a type of memory that helps detect and correct single-bit memory errors, which lead to data corruption. Servers often have large amounts of RAM compared with desktop workstations—with 16 GB to upward of 1 TB RAM.

Some components, like the hard drive, may be hot swappable—which means that components can be removed and replaced without shutting down the server, enabling the service to continue running uninterrupted. This is made possible in part by redundant storage set up to provide fault tolerance.

One way in which servers differ significantly from other computers is that they are meant to be administered remotely over a network instead of by a technician physically in front of the server. Tools such as secure shell (SSH), Virtual Network Computing (VNC), remote desktop, and Remote Server Administration Tools (RSAT) make this possible. Therefore, it isn't necessary for servers to have peripherals like a keyboard, mouse, or even a monitor. One peripheral in particular, however, can be critical in the case of a power failure—an uninterruptible power supply (UPS).

When selecting a server to purchase, make sure to be aware of what type of maintenance service is provided, and what the expected response time will be. Typically, you will pay more for a faster response, but depending on the service, a two-hour response is very different from same-day or even next-day response. Vendors will also want the ability to remotely connect to your servers to provide support.

RAID

Because a disk failure in the hard drive of a server could be catastrophic, servers often implement a method of distributing and replicating data across multiple disks known as *RAID* (alternately defined as *redundant array of inexpensive disks* and *redundant array of independent disks*). RAID combines a group of physical disks on a server into a single logical unit, consequently improving performance as well as protecting data. In this way, it is also possible to replace failed drives with minimal downtime.

Multiple levels describe the details of the RAID as implemented. It is also possible to combine RAID levels for enhanced performance.

Some of the most common RAID levels:

* RAID 0: Known as *striping*, this level distributes data across multiple disks, resulting in greatly increased read–write speeds. The more disks involved, the faster the reading and writing because it happens concurrently on all disks. The great disadvantage is that a failure on any single disk can result in the loss of all data because the files are spread out with parts on each disk.

- RAID 1: Known as *mirroring*, in this level the same data is simultaneously written to multiple disks, resulting in disks that mirror each other. In case of a disk failure, the RAID controller will use the good disk until the bad one can be replaced and the data copied over to it.
- RAID 5: Known as *striping with parity*, in RAID 5 data is distributed across multiple disks and parity data is also written to a disk. In this way the data lost when one disk fails can be reconstructed from the parity data. This is a common setup because it is both fast and fault tolerant; however, rebuilding a large disk can be quite slow.
- RAID 6: Known as *striping with double parity*, RAID 6 is similar to RAID 5 but has an additional set of parity data for each stripe. Writing data is slower than RAID 5 but the system can tolerate the loss of two disks.
- RAID 10 (also known as RAID 1+0): This is a combination of RAID 0 and RAID 1, using both mirroring and striping.

Server Form Factors

There are three different form factors for servers in common use: tower servers, rack-mount servers, and blade servers. Tower servers are similar to large desktop computers in appearance, with room for multiple hard drives inside and perhaps redundant power supplies.

Rack-mount servers are designed to fit into tall racks, or frames that can accommodate many servers stacked vertically—thus fitting many more servers into a small footprint than towers. The servers are a standard 19 inches wide and flat in appearance. The height of the servers can vary, but are usually described in terms of rack units (U) that equal 1.75 inches in height, according to the placement of the threaded holes in the rack frame. So a 2U server occupies approximately a space 19 inches wide by 3.5 inches tall in the rack, with a little space for airflow and to make it easier to remove individual servers without catching on each other. The height of the racks vary, with 42U being a common height. Racks are typically 36 inches deep, although the servers themselves are not always that deep. Some racks are designed to accommodate a shorter depth, and some have rails that allow the server to slide out like a drawer for servicing. However, having so many servers in close proximity can generate a lot of heat, and so airflow and cooling become paramount.

Blade servers are designed to save even more space than standard rack-mount servers. Some of the typical hardware components such as the power supply and networking interfaces are removed from the server and placed in an enclosure that can accommodate multiple servers—otherwise known as *blades*. In this way, rather than each server having its own power supply, cooling, and networking, a number of servers share those resources and save space in the rack. Blade enclosures are designed to fit into the standard 19-inch server rack.

Data Center

A data center is a dedicated place where servers and other shared resources are kept. Even if a library doesn't maintain a data center of its own, chances are that your servers will reside in one—whether it is a room controlled by your organization or by a cloud service provider. It is usually in a physically secure space with significant support for cooling, humidity control, and fire suppression, as well as an abundance of electrical power and networking. Uninterruptible power supplies (UPS) help keep services running during a short power outage, and onsite power generators provide electricity for a longer term. The data center should be prepared for natural disasters that may threaten its location as well.

Although many libraries do not maintain their own data centers, the days of servers hiding in library staff offices under desks and in closets should be long behind us. Servers that are not properly cared for are at a major risk for failure or security breach. If a library hosts mission-critical servers in this type of situation, they should immediately look into either moving them to their parent organization's data center or to a cloud provider.

Virtualization

One of the most common ways that servers are used currently is through virtualization—whether that virtual server lives in a data center on hardware under your direct control or in a cloud-service managed data center. One of the great benefits of virtualizing servers is dynamic scalability—the ability to add resources when needed and reduce resources when not needed. To do this with a physical server, it would be necessary to literally add hardware to the server in order to expand it; if it is underutilized there isn't a way to reclaim resources for other servers short of physically removing them. This is an expensive and inefficient practice when compared with the flexibility of virtual servers.

A virtual server is emulated using special software on a physical computer. The physical computer is known as the host and the virtual machine (VM) is the guest. A single host can support multiple guests, even of different operating systems (OS), so long as the host has sufficient hardware resources. The special software used to create and run the VMs is known as a hypervisor or a VM monitor. It distributes system resources such as memory, CPU, and storage as needed to the guest VMs according to the parameters established in the hypervisor's configuration.

From the perspective of a user, the guest VM behaves just like a physical server. As an example, imagine a server running Microsoft Windows 10 as the host OS, Microsoft Hyper-V as the hypervisor, and both Ubuntu Linux and Windows Server 2019 as guests. When interacting with the Ubuntu Linux guest, it will seem like a dedicated server.

VMware produces a number of different hypervisors for servers, and is perhaps the most widely used. In addition to their selection of hypervisors meant to run on a host OS (including Windows, Linux, and macOS), they have an enterprise hypervisor called VMware ESXi that is meant to run directly on the server hardware without a host OS. Microsoft's Hyper-V has been available on their OSs since Windows 8 and Server 2012, and is a strong player in the market as well. VirtualBox is a free and open-source hypervisor currently developed by Oracle. It is easy to use and popular for testing and development but not as well suited to enterprise production.

Cloud Computing

Given the option, many libraries are choosing to take their servers and services to the cloud. To use cloud computing is to essentially outsource a part of the infrastructure responsibilities to a service that is accessed via the internet, whether it is simply using physical servers in a vendor's data center or turning over responsibility for everything but the application itself. It is important to understand that the cloud is not something mystical that exists apart from physical reality—rather it is, in fact, a data center with physical servers provided by a vendor that the user connects to over the internet.

Cloud service providers use virtualization of servers, and so gain the benefits of that technology, but on a scale with resources that a localized data center would probably not be able to provide. Additionally, vendors may provide higher levels of support beyond just the data center maintenance, all the way up to the application, which means that libraries can redirect their resources and staff expertise from low-level systems support to the library service they are providing.

Service Models

The service models provided by cloud vendors are generally thought of as three layers, in which the infrastructure layer is closest to the actual, physical server and the software or application layer is farthest from it.

Infrastructure as a Service

In the infrastructure as a service (IaaS) model, a vendor gives direct access to a specified amount of computing resources, and it is the user's responsibility to install and configure anything on it. This is similar to having a dedicated server in a local data center where the data center is responsible for maintaining the physical infrastructure, including the hardware and network connectivity, but the library has full access to the server to manage as they please.

This is a good option if you don't want the responsibility for the hardware but do want the freedom of managing everything software-related, including the OS, database management, and applications.

Platform as a Service

Platform as a service (PaaS) is a step away from the server for the user, where the vendor will maintain the OS and provide a limited selection of applications for installation to the user. This is a common service option for those interested in providing web services without the hassle of maintaining the server or system. The Linux, Apache, MySQL, PHP (LAMP) stack is frequently offered as a base for web services, and there may be other applications available for installation, such as Drupal or Wordpress.

Although users don't have complete freedom to configure the server or OS, they will be responsible for managing the database and applications selected for installation. Command line access may be provided via SSH and there may be a web management interface with limited capabilities; two tools that can come in handy are secure file transfer protocol (SFTP) for uploading and downloading files, and phpMyAdmin to interact with the database system.

PaaS is a good option if you want control over the applications installed without the worry of maintaining the hardware or system, but it is important to note that you will not have root access to the server and probably won't have the ability to configure the OS or web server. Also be sure to check whether the service supports the specific applications and scripting languages that you want to use.

Software as a Service

The software as a service (SaaS) model is probably the most familiar to the general internet user. In this model the vendor provides a fully functional application and provides for the maintenance of the application as well as all of the underlying software and hardware. Perhaps one of the earliest well-known SaaS was web-based email. Now web applications are becoming commonplace, with one of the biggest names being Google's Workspace (formerly known as Google Apps and then G Suite)—a collection of cloud-based productivity and collaboration software that users access via a web browser or application on their computer or mobile device.

Of course the software in this model can be anything that is deliverable via the internet, and a number of library vendors are moving into this space. The responsibility to the library then becomes application administration and configuration to varying degrees, depending on the service provided, while the vendor updates the software and ensures that it has the necessary resources to perform well.

Cloud Service Providers

Although there are a number of cloud service providers of varying size, Amazon Web Services (AWS) is the largest by far. AWS offers services across all of the models previously discussed from direct access to virtual servers (EC2) to data storage (S3), and many, many more. Even many SaaS providers use AWS for their backend. Microsoft Azure and Google Cloud Platform are perhaps the next biggest players, but lag far behind AWS in market share. They each provide their own range of IaaS and PaaS offerings separate from their popular SaaS application suites Office 365 and Google Workspace. Other cloud providers include Oracle Cloud, DigitalOcean, and Rackspace.

Many major library platform vendors have either moved their offerings to the cloud or else offer a cloud version in addition to a traditional self-hosted platform. They mostly occupy the SaaS space and often have web interfaces for both the library user and library support staff. Some include application programming interfaces (APIs) for the purpose of harvesting data and interacting with other applications or services. Some examples in the library realm include library management systems (LMS) Ex Libris Alma and OCLC Worldshare Management Services, discovery layers EBSCO Discovery Service and Ex Libris Primo, and archival systems DuraCloud and ContentDM, among many others.

When evaluating a cloud service provider consider things like their reputation for security and privacy, as well as their geographic location because the data stored will be subject to their local laws. Any time a service is outsourced, there should be a service-level agreement that spells out the expectations for the level of service provided, including maintenance, updates, upgrades, security, and support response time.

OPERATIONS

Server operations refer to the overall administration and management of the servers supported and services provided. We can only touch on the topic here; entire books have been written that specialize in different areas of server operations.

System Administrator

A system administrator, also commonly referred to as a *SysAdmin*, is primarily responsible for both the physical and software-related tasks regarding the design, implementation, and maintenance of computer servers. Some of the responsibilities may include installing and replacing server hardware components, maintaining a data center, monitoring server performance and security, installing and configuring OSs and other software, writing scripts to automate tasks, and troubleshooting issues with both the server hardware and the services provided by the servers.

The role of the system administrator often overlaps with those of network administrators and database administrators, so much that smaller operations may have one team or even one person responsible for all three roles. The system administrator will also closely support the work of the web developer and the LMS administrator.

In library nomenclature, it is common to refer to the person who administers the LMS as a *systems librarian*. In the past, this was perhaps a more accurate description because the libraries often self-hosted the LMS on local servers, and so were responsible for the server's configuration and maintenance as well as that of the database the LMS used and necessary connections to other applications and networks. However, with the growing trend of libraries moving to cloud-hosted LMSs, much of the systems work for LMSs is handled by the vendor, leaving library employees to specialize in the administration of the LMS application.

Operating Systems

There are a variety of OSs that can be used on servers, including, Windows, Linux, Unix, and FreeBSD, and the administrator can run similar types of services on all of them. Also, you aren't limited to choosing just one ecosystem because, depending on the service, a server with one OS can often support clients and other servers of differing OSs. There are, however, significant differences between OSs, so it is important to become familiar with their particular compatibilities, tools, protocols, file structures, and methods for file security and user management.

Windows Server 2016 and Windows Server 2019 are the two most recent versions of Microsoft Windows Server. Mainstream support for Windows Server 2016 ends on January 11, 2022, and, although several older versions are no longer receiving mainstream support, they are still under extended support—though only for a few more years. There are many Linux OSs to choose from, with some of the popular flavors being Red Hat Enterprise Linux, Ubuntu Server, Fedora Server, and CentOS.

Server Administration

Documentation

As in all other areas of technology support, documentation is important to server administration and maintaining that documentation a key task for administrators. A runbook is a specific set of documentation particular to systems support that details various procedures for running servers and the services that they provide. It is useful both as a reference during normal operations and for troubleshooting problems.

Remote Administration

Most servers are meant to be managed remotely. For servers in a data center, physical access should be limited and, as with the cloud, it may be impossible to physically access your servers.

RSAT is a feature in Windows Servers and Windows 10 to administer servers remotely. Server Manager is a console in RSAT that gives you an overview of the servers being managed and can affect limited changes to them, which is useful when managing a large number of servers. For directly managing a single server, Remote Desktop remains an option for a graphical user interface (GUI) and PowerShell for the command line interface (CLI).

To manage Linux and other Unix-like servers, SSH remains the standard protocol for connecting with a CLI client. A VNC client can be used to connect to a server using a GUI. Additionally, hypervisors often have a web interface that administrators can use to manage their VMs.

Logs, Monitoring, and Performance Analysis

Keeping logs and monitoring performance are vital to providing reliable services and minimizing downtime caused by problems that occur. A log is the raw-text output of messages from a system, usually to a text file where it is stored until a retention period may expire. It usually consists of a list of events, with each event noting a timestamp, and perhaps a brief description, type of event, and the process name or ID number.

Some applications have monitoring systems built in; certain events can trigger notifications to administrators using email or SMS text messages about the event. They may also have graphical dashboards that visualize the data being logged, and make it easier to monitor performance. Even cloud providers may have custom dashboards that incorporate data from different applications for the administrator.

SERVER TYPES

Servers may be used for many purposes, and require different sets of software and protocols, depending on circumstances. The following are some of more common types of servers that may be supported by a library.

File and Storage Server

One of the most basic and common roles for a server is to store and serve files. File servers can be specialized for file sharing, with super-fast input/output for database access, or high-capacity drives with multiple backups and periodic snapshots for long-term storage. The main purpose of the file server drives the design and determines the amount of storage space, the backup and recovery configuration, the required access speed, and the necessary security of the server.

Using a file server provides a way for users to access their files from anywhere on the network. Using shared folders allows you to assign access permission to folders for a group of users, enabling them to store files meant to be shared with that group. Having these files in a central location gives you the ability to manage their backup schedule, but also the responsibility for their recovery should anything go wrong. Any backup and recovery system should be regularly tested to ensure that it will behave as expected when needed.

When administering a file server, there are a number of things for the SysAdmin to monitor, including backups for their success, remaining space in storage, disk health and failures, and individual use. Even as the cost of storage is forever decreasing, it is entirely possible to run out of storage space—particularly with large media files like video or digitized images—and you do not want to be caught by surprise.

Today many libraries and other organizations are turning to cloud services to provide for file sharing and storage. One of the great advantages of a cloud solution is that files can be accessed from virtually anywhere there is an internet connection—no need to connect to the home network to access files. Many people have become familiar with cloud storage options like Google Drive, Box.com, and Microsoft OneDrive. These companies can also leverage their extensive resources to ensure files are backed up regularly and with confidence. While libraries are generally moving to the cloud for these types of services, SysAdmins may still need to provide local storage for certain types of sensitive data, for local applications, because of policies regarding the storage of data, or for legacy services.

Print Server

A print server manages the print queue for attached printers, and provides access for users over the network. It can also do load balancing for high-demand locations by treating several physical printers as a single logical printer, and so distributing the jobs between them. Using a print server eliminates the need for every single computer to have an attached printer; however, when planning their distribution in a building, consider their adjacency to users as people are only willing to walk so far to retrieve their print jobs. There may be situations that justify printers for individuals, or at least in a secure location with limited access (e.g., for printing sensitive information).

Windows Server offers Print and Document Services (PDS) to manage printing and scanning on the network. Services that can be enabled in PDS are print server, distributed scan server, internet printing, and Line Printer Daemon—which is able to accommodate Linux and Unix-like OSs such as macOS.

Linux and macOS use the Common Unix Printing Service (CUPS) for a print server. CUPS uses the Internet Printing Protocol for communicating with printers and client computers, and can be managed via a web interface.

Database Server

A database server hosts and provides access to a database management system (DBMS). Sometimes it resides on the same server as the application that primarily makes use of it, although that is not always the case.

Well-known examples of DBMSs include the Oracle Database and Microsoft SQL Server, which are both proprietary, MySQL and PostgreSQL, which are both open source, and the lighter-weight but still popular Microsoft Access and FileMaker Pro. A fork of MySQL called MariaDB is also gaining in popularity. The "M" in the popular web stack LAMP is MySQL.

Data stored in a relational database is accessed using a query language known as structured query language (SQL). SQL isn't a programming language in its own right; rather, it is used either to directly query the database or in conjunction with scripting and programming languages. Many APIs have also been developed to interact between specific languages and the database, including Open Database Connection and Java Database Connection.

With regard to library management systems, it used to be the case that the database was a commercial product like Oracle Database that resided on a server in the library's data center. As library management systems have moved to the cloud, the vendor has taken responsibility for maintaining the DBMS, with library staff primarily interacting with the database through the vendor's management software (e.g., Ex Libris Alma). But there are still plenty of situations in which libraries use databases, including database-driven websites, institutional repositories, archival systems, and homegrown databases.

Web Server

Web servers host web sites. When you type a web address into a web browser, the browser issues a request to the server hosting the site, which in turn sends back the information using the hypertext transfer protocol (HTTP). For a long time, Apache HTTP Server has been the dominant web server on the market. In recent years, however, the open-source NGINX has gained significant ground. Microsoft's Internet Information Services (IIS) is a distant third.[1]

Web servers are often packaged with other software used to run websites known as a *stack*. LAMP (Linux, Apache, MySQL, PHP) is one of the most well known web stacks, but there are a wide assortment of combinations that usually include an OS (e.g., Linux), a web server (e.g., Apache), a DBMS (e.g., MySQL), and a scripting or programming language (e.g., PHP). Sometimes they also include APIs or other specialized software, and they aren't limited to including just one language.

Linux is by far the most popular OS for web servers, although there are some that use Microsoft Windows. Apache and NGINX both generally—although not exclusively—run on Linux servers, and IIS only runs on Windows. There are many DBMSs, as mentioned in the previous section. Many languages can also be used, including PHP, Perl, Python, ASP, JavaScript, and Ruby. Languages can be categorized according to their purpose, as we will see later in chapter 8, "Web Design and Development."

If you are using a web application or content management system, you will have to make sure that the underlying web server technology matches the requirements and is configured correctly. Cloud service providers can make it easy to get a website up and running because there are options where they handle as much of the underlying technology as you are willing to let go. A common situation is for the cloud provider to maintain the web stack with a selection of languages and content management systems available for installation—sometimes with a single click in a web interface. This is a great option for libraries that aren't able to or would rather not devote the staff expertise to supporting the web server. The drawbacks include limited flexibility with configurations, particularly with the underlying OS and web server itself (such as Apache).

Proxy Server

A proxy server is used as a gateway for network traffic, sitting between the sender and the receiver. It is frequently situated between a smaller network and a much larger one, such as the internet and, depending on the configuration, can have different effects on the traffic passing through. At its simplest, a proxy server receives incoming traffic, then forwards it on to the intended recipient. As traffic passes through the proxy server, it has the opportunity to change the information such as encrypting it for stronger security. As proxy servers can be set up to process outgoing web requests from a network, they are sometimes used to filter web traffic by using blacklists of web addresses and keywords.

It can also appear to the recipient that the originating IP address is that of the proxy server rather than the actual sender. This feature is frequently used for privacy purposes as the identity of the sender can be masked. From the perspective of the recipient, the traffic will appear to have originated with the proxy server—including identifying information such as the geographic location. In this way a computer user in San Francisco may send a website request through a proxy in London, which then passes the request to the intended recipient, but it appears to the recipient as if the request originated in London. The response is returned to the proxy server, which then passes it along back to the original requestor in San Francisco. This is a method that some people use to circumnavigate web censorship.

Another use is what is called a *reverse proxy*. In this case the proxy is set up to handle incoming requests, which it then forwards as appropriate—often to a web server. Because the proxy handles the incoming traffic first, it can be used to assist with load balancing for multiple web servers, for serving cached web content, and as additional security.

Mail Server

Mail servers facilitate the delivery of email from a client to another mail server. Although the likelihood of running an email server from the library today is fairly low, and many organizations are transitioning to cloud-based email services, there are still many parent organizations of libraries that host mail servers. It is also useful to have a basic understanding of how email works because the library technician may be responsible for supporting email clients on computer and mobile devices, or using applications that use email protocols.

There are actually many mail servers to choose from with varying features, but perhaps one of the most well-known for organizations is Microsoft Exchange Server. Exchange is more than a mail server; it also incorporates a calendaring service as well. Linux servers often have sendmail or postfix as mail servers, though there are other options as well.

An email may begin life in a client—whether on a desktop, a mobile device, or a web application—where a message is composed. The client (which is also described as a *mail user agent*) sends the message to the mail server the account is tied to. The mail server has a mail transfer agent, which looks up the domain of the intended recipient as specified in the email address (the part that comes after the @) and, using Simple Mail Transfer Protocol, it sends the message on. The destination mail server receives the message and, using a mail delivery agent, the message is delivered to the appropriate mailbox.

At this point, the message is still on the recipient's mail server and the recipient has to retrieve it. There are two protocols commonly used for retrieving email messages, Internet Message Access Protocol (IMAP) and Post Office Protocol (POP). Although there are many differences between the two protocols, there are a few major ones that encourage the use of IMAP for many situations. When POP checks the mail server for messages, it downloads everything from the server to the client, leaving nothing behind. This is okay if you don't want to leave the messages behind—perhaps for privacy reasons or to stay under a quota—but it is terribly inconvenient for anyone who uses the same email account with more than one device. IMAP syncs changes between the server and client, meaning that when messages are downloaded to the client a copy also remains on the server. Any changes made on the client are then synced back to the server. This allows for multiple devices to access the same account as any changes made will be synced with all of them.

Although it is easy to think of email in terms of the end user's personal situation, it is also important to note that messages can be sent and received by mailing lists and applications as well, such as automated overdue notices sent from an LMS, or an email form on a website.

SUMMARY

Servers are specialized computers used to provide many different services over a network to both local users, and via the internet. Hardware in servers are similar to desktop computers, but feature advanced RAM and redundant storage and power supplies. The configuration of storage is of particular importance to server administration using a method known as RAID. Physical servers are usually hosted in data centers that feature specialized security and environmental controls. Virtual servers are much more efficient with resources than physical servers because of their ability to dynamically scale. Even cloud service providers take advantage of virtualization in their data centers. The services provided are generally categorized into one of three models: IaaS, PaaS, and SaaS.

The SysAdmin is typically responsible for server operations, including the physical and software-related implementation, maintenance, and troubleshooting. There are a number of OSs to choose from, including Windows Server 2019 and several Linux flavors. Remote administration of servers is usually necessary, and can be accomplished using either the command line or a GUI. Among the important tasks involved with server administration are keeping logs and monitoring performance to ensure reliable services and assist with troubleshooting problems.

There are many different types of servers, with software designed to provide many different services. Some of the more common server types that a library might employ include file and storage servers, print servers, database servers, web servers, proxy servers, and mail servers.

KEY TERMS

Application programming interface (API)
Blade server
Cloud computing
Data center
Database management system (DBMS)
Database server
File and storage server
Infrastructure as a service (IaaS)
Log
Mail server
Platform as a service (PaaS)

Print server
Proxy server
Rack-mount server
Redundant array of independent disks (RAID; also redundant array of inexpensive disks)
Remote administration
Software as a service (SaaS)
System administrator
Uninterruptible power supply (UPS)
Virtual server
Web server

QUESTIONS

1. Describe server hardware and what makes it different from regular desktop computers.
2. What are the common RAID levels?
3. What are the three main server form-factors?
4. What are the pros and cons of hosting a server in a local data center versus a cloud service provider?
5. Describe the three types of cloud service models: IaaS, PaaS, and SaaS.
6. List and describe different roles that a server may fill. Are there any that you would add to what is listed in this chapter?

ACTIVITIES

1. Investigate the technology environment in a library. What services are being provided from servers or a data center located in the library? From a local data center external to the library but part of the same organization? From a vendor-hosted or a cloud service provider?

2. Set up a VM on a computer and install your choice of OS on the VM. VirtualBox (https://www.virtualbox.org/) is a free, open-source hypervisor (VM monitor) that can run on a regular OS. There are many Linux options available if you don't have access to a Windows or macOS license (e.g., Ubuntu, https://ubuntu.com/download/desktop).

FURTHER READING

Breeding, Marshall. "Up in the Air: Cloud Computing and Library Systems." *Computers in Libraries* 38, no. 10 (2018): 9–11.

Gonzales, Brighid M. "Analyzing EZproxy SPU Logs Using Python Data Analysis Tools." *Code4Lib Journal* no. 42 (2018).

Cervone, Frank. "An Overview of Virtual and Cloud Computing." *OCLC Systems and Services* 26, no. 3 (2010): 162–65.

Iles, Robert, and Emre Erturk. "Case Study on Cloud Based Library Software as a Service: Evaluating EZproxy." *Journal of Emerging Trends in Computing and Information Sciences* 6, no. 10 (2015): 545–49.

Kralicek, Eric. *The Accidental SysAdmin Handbook: A Primer for Entry Level IT Professionals*, 2nd ed. New York: Apress, 2016.

Limoncelli, Tom, Christina J. Hogan, and Strata R. Chalup. *The Practice of System and Network Administration*, 3rd ed. Upper Saddle River, NJ: Addison-Wesley, 2016.

Mitchell, Erik T. *Cloud-based Services for Your Library: A LITA Guide.* Chicago: ALA TechSource, 2013.

Negus, Christopher. *Linux Bible*, 9th ed. Indianapolis: John Wiley and Sons, 2015.

Nemeth, Evi, Garth Snyder, and Trent R. Hein. *UNIX and Linux System Administration Handbook*, 5th ed. New York: Pearson Education, 2018.

Wilson, Robert T., and Ellen Dubinsky. "Piloting a Homegrown Streaming Service with IaaS." *Code4Lib Journal* no. 42 (2018).

Syrewicze, Andy, and Richard Siddaway. *Pro Microsoft Hyper-V 2019: Practical Guidance and Hands-On Labs*. New York: Apress, 2018.

Thomas, Orin. *Inside Out: Windows Server 2016.* Microsoft, 2017.

RESOURCES

Amazon Web Services: https://aws.amazon.com/
Apache, HTTP Server: https://httpd.apache.org/
CyberDuck: https://cyberduck.io/
CUPS: https://www.cups.org/
Microsoft, SQL Server: https://www.microsoft.com/en-us/sql-server/
Microsoft, Windows Server: https://microsoft.com/windowsserver
MySQL: https://www.mysql.com/
NGINX: https://www.nginx.com/
Oracle Database: https://www.oracle.com/database/
Red Hat Linux: https://www.redhat.com
Ubuntu Linux Server: https://www.ubuntu.com/server
VirtualBox: https://www.virtualbox.org/
VMware: https://www.vmware.com/

Cloud Service Providers

Digital Ocean: https://www.digitalocean.com/
Google Cloud Platform: https://cloud.google.com/
Microsoft, Azure: https://azure.microsoft.com
Oracle Cloud: https://www.oracle.com/cloud/
Rackspace: https://www.rackspace.com/

NOTE

1. "Usage of Web Servers," W3Techs, accessed on March 26, 2019, https://w3techs.com/technologies/overview/web_server/all; "Technologies Market Share: Web Server," SimilarTech, accessed on March 26, 2019, https://www.similartech.com/categories/web-server.

7

Information Security

Libraries have an obligation to protect their technology and the data that resides on or traverses over their information systems and networks. Information security involves an awareness of potential threats and a plan to mitigate them. Malicious actors may attempt to steal data or to harm information systems, personal information may be collected by advertising agencies seeking to target potential customers, or users may otherwise be interested in circumventing censors or remaining anonymous to observers.

The information system owner has a responsibility to establish preventative measures to protect the system as well as possible, to monitor the system for problems, and to respond to and recover from any incidents that occur.

This chapter introduces many issues, threats, and preventative measures relating to information security. It first touches on some information security management concerns that help provide a big-picture view before diving into some details. Next, it introduces many of the security threats to information systems, including hacking, social engineering, and malware, as well as those specific to Wi-Fi and the internet. The chapter then moves on to a discussion of tools and tactics available to protect personal computers. Finally, it addresses network security covering firewalls, proxy servers, authentication, network security protocols, and web server security.

INFORMATION SECURITY MANAGEMENT

The regulations, policies, and procedures that an organization must comply with and undertake to protect information systems and data is collectively known as *information security management*. This requires consideration of the types of data to be protected, what risks may threaten system integrity, regulations the organization may be compelled to follow, and how to best implement security practices.

Privacy

Protecting the privacy of individuals is a major factor of information security. This includes data collected by an organization like a library, online behavior of users, and communications between a user and a system or other user. Libraries have a long tradition of protecting patron privacy, to the point of not maintaining circulation histories and anonymizing database transactions. In addition to practices regarding how the library handles patron data, there are many things to be done with information systems to protect users from malicious attacks and unscrupulous advertisers.

Personally identifiable information (PII) is a concept that appears in discussions of user privacy and information security, which describes personal data. PII need not be a single piece of data that could be used to identify a person (such as a social security number); it can also be multiple pieces of data that when used together can distinguish an individual. The protection of PII figures as a major role of information security.

Regulations and Policies

Libraries are often beholden to the information security policies of their parent organizations in addition to any state or federal regulations. Depending on the type of organization, whether a city, university, corporation, hospital, law firm, and so on, there may be additional requirements in place to protect data and patron privacy. It is a good idea to become familiar with the applicable policies and regulations, and to conduct regular audits to ensure compliance before something can go wrong. Being a victim of a data breach, particularly if you were out of compliance, is not an enjoyable experience, and can cause real harm as well as lead to a reprimand or even a lawsuit.

Federal agencies are required to comply with the Federal Information Security Modernization Act of 2014 (FISMA Reform), an update to the 2002 act, which describes information security policies and requirements.[1] To receive federal funding, educational institutions from elementary schools to universities must comply with the Family Educational Rights and Privacy Act of 1974 (FERPA), which governs access to student education records.[2] If an organization is conducting e-commerce or financial transactions electronically, it has to follow the Payment Card Industry Data Security Standard (PCI DSS).[3] This is of particular interest to libraries who conduct fines and fees collection online. The healthcare field has the Health Insurance Portability and Accountability Act of 1996 (HIPAA),[4] which includes rules that govern how personal information should be handled, particularly with regard to electronic information systems. In 2018, the European Union enacted the General Data Protection Regulation (GDPR),[5] which governs the protection and handling of personal information.

Library Application Security

For any locally installed system the library will bear responsibility for information security. Many applications, however, are moving to cloud-hosted solutions. Although vendors bear much of the responsibility for securing information on systems they host, the library also has responsibility for being aware of how data is handled and what protections are in place. This becomes more complicated when data is transferred between the vendor's system and a different vendor or a locally hosted system. An analysis of how data is handled and what protections exist or may be put in place should play a key role in the decision to acquire and use any product.

Alex Caro and Chris Markman[6] propose seven criteria by which to evaluate products: data breach policy, data encryption, data retention, terms of service "ease of use," patron privacy, secure connections, and advertising networks. It may be that the library's parent organization has a specific security assessment to follow before acquiring a product or licensing a cloud service. EDUCAUSE provides the *Higher Education Cloud Vendor Assessment Tool* as a template for evaluating products.[7]

In "Privacy and Security for Library Systems," Marshall Breeding discusses several technological issues to consider when assessing products, including secure transmissions, secure storage, server logs, and web tracking. He goes on to share data gathered from a survey of vendors who provide integrated library systems and discovery systems to evaluate "how well they defend patron privacy and handle overall security."[8] Sometimes the library may have the ability to configure security settings or develop solutions to mitigate concerns. At other times the library is wholly dependent on the vendor.

THREATS

Many people are familiar with the idea of a computer virus or a hacker breaking into a system, stealing data, and wreaking havoc. The simple truth is that anything that may gain unauthorized access or cause harm to a system is a threat. It may happen through hacking, social engineering, malicious software such as viruses and Trojans, or a combination of methods. It can occur over wired and wireless networks alike, as well as the internet. Depending on the technology in question, different methods and tools are used—including legitimate ones, but when they are used for malicious purposes they become attacks.

Hacking

Hacking can generally be thought of as altering an object or process in a way that it was not originally intended to be used. *Computer hacking* specifically refers to modifying computer hardware or software, whether to solve a problem or overcome security. Computer hacking taken at face value is not a nefarious activity, and in fact "white hat" hackers are often employed by software security companies to investigate possible vulnerabilities to identify them and then produce fixes or patches. In the IT industry, those who hack computer systems with malicious intent are known as "black hat" hackers, or *crackers*. Popular culture, however, tends not to distinguish between ethical hackers and criminals, and so the term "hacking" is often synonymous with criminal activity.

Hackers may target vulnerabilities in systems with exploits designed to take advantage of a software bug or a security hole through which they may gain unauthorized access. When a vulnerability becomes known, the software developers will create a patch to fix the vulnerability—assuming that the software is being supported. This is why it is so important to only use supported software, and to keep it up to date. A *zero-day exploit* is one that takes advantage of a vulnerability that is unknown to the producer of the software. Days are counted from when a vulnerability becomes known; therefore, a zero-day is particularly dangerous because the software producer has probably not done anything about it—if they are even aware of it.

Password Cracking

Using a password to gain access to a system or file is perhaps one of the most familiar authentication methods. When a hacker attempts to gain unauthorized access using this method, it is known as *password cracking*. The simplest way for a hacker to gain access is with a known password, perhaps one that had been stolen, but there are a number of other ways as well. Hollywood often depicts the *brute-force attack*, in which a hacker uses a program that attempts all possible characters, with numbers, letters, and symbols scrolling by until the right combination is found. This is an enormously inefficient method as the greater the number of possible characters and longer the password, the greater the number of possible passwords; therefore, the longer it will potentially take to crack. However, that is not to say hackers don't attempt this method, as the software is not difficult to obtain and hardware necessary to run the software becomes more powerful.

A more common technique is the *dictionary attack*, wherein software will attempt using commonly known passwords and ordinary words. This is one reason it is recommended to use a phrase and to mix character types when creating a strong password. *Credential stuffing* uses a set of stolen usernames and passwords that may have been obtained from a data breach. As many people reuse passwords for different accounts, this technique uses these known credentials to break into other systems and services.

Social Engineering

One method that a malicious hacker may use to obtain confidential information is *social engineering*. People are a significant security weakness, and so social engineering targets that weakness by attempting to manipulate people into sharing passwords or other private information that may aid in hacking a system. Although the attack is often technical in nature, it doesn't have to be. The attack could just as well be made via a telephone call during which the recipient of the call is tricked into divulging information. The more that the attacker knows about the target, the easier it is to crack a password or pretend to be the target to fool security systems or people into thinking that the attacker is actually the user.

Phishing

A common method of social engineering is *phishing* (pronounced "fishing") in which an attacker attempts to trick the victim into providing personal information such as passwords, social security numbers, or credit card information—or seemingly benign personal information that can be used to recover passwords. Often the phishing attempt will come in the form of an email disguised to appear to come from a familiar source. It may ask for a response to include the requested information, or may have a link to a website disguised to look like a legitimate and known site for which the victim is intended to enter the information. As the success rate of general phishing attacks is quite low, attackers cast as wide a net as possible, usually by sending spam email to long lists of email addresses that may have been harvested by bots or even purchased.

Spear phishing is a form of phishing that is highly customized for the target, in an effort to make it seem as legitimate as possible. The attack might target a set group of people, perhaps a single organization, or even an individual. The attacker uses information appropriate to the organization to make it appear legitimate, or even personal information that was discovered elsewhere, including what is publicly available on the web, on social media, or discovered through other hacks.

Malicious Software

Commonly known as *malware*, malicious software is programmed specifically to take some harmful action against a computer system. It may operate by exploiting software vulnerabilities to cause damage, steal information, or provide unauthorized access. Malware may take on a number of different forms, some of which are closely related and may describe different aspects of the same individual malware.

Virus

A virus is designed to spread to other computers when run, infecting additional networks and systems with copies of the same malicious software. It may infect a computer when the user downloads it from the internet, as an attachment in an email, or may even be purposely placed on a computer. While most files are transferred over a network these days, any possible way to access a computer is a potential attack vector—such as universal serial bus (USB) flash drives. Sometimes the virus is attached to a legitimate file or program to trick the user into running it. When the code is executed, it goes to work attempting to spread to new targets as well as accomplish whatever harmful tasks it was programmed for.

Worm

A worm is a special virus that is self-replicating. Whereas a virus can sit benignly in a system until the program is run, a worm will actively attempt to spread of its own volition.

Trojan

Trojans take their name from the ancient Greek legend. Greek warriors were hidden inside a wooden horse, which was offered as a gift to the city of Troy. When the Trojans accepted the giant horse into their fortified city, the Greek warriors snuck out, opened the gates, and allowed the Greek army into the city. Trojan malware is disguised as a legitimate program or file and delivers a payload of a virus or other malware when it is run.

Rootkit

Rootkits are designed to go after root, or administrator, access to the operating system of the computer. This type of malware can be powerful and damaging, yet is also adept at staying hidden. Once it obtains complete access and control over the system, it can dig in deep, making it difficult to detect and remove. From there it can modify the operating system or other programs as well as cause other damage, and provide remote access to the compromised system.

Spyware

Software created to track different aspects of user behavior without the user's knowledge is known as *spyware*. It may track the websites a user visits to sell the information to advertisers, it may generate targeted pop-up ads on the computer (sometimes known as *adware*), or it may watch for text entered into web forms to facilitate identity theft. A *keylogger* is a particular type of spyware that records every stroke on the keyboard. It may then "phone home" to deliver the information it has recorded, including passwords entered into forms and other personally identifiable information. Spyware isn't only used by hackers; it may be used by the police during investigations or by businesses to keep an eye on their employees. Although there are stand-alone antispyware tools (such as Malwarebytes), many antivirus tools now include the capability to handle spyware.

Ransomware

Ransomware is a particularly nasty attack that is taking place increasingly often. Ransomware is programmed to encrypt an entire hard drive. Without the decryption key, the victim cannot access files—they are unreadable and unrecoverable. The attacker will offer to provide the key for a ransom, often paid in cryptocurrency such as BitCoin. These types of attacks are becoming more common because it is possible for the attacker to remain completely anonymous throughout the process. If the system has been backed up, the victim has the option of ignoring the ransom demand and simply restoring the backup. But if not, then the victim must decide whether to cut their losses or meet the demands of the attacker.

Backdoor

Much like it sounds, a backdoor is a hidden way for someone to gain remote access to a system, bypassing normal authentication measures. It may have been intentionally set up by the software developer or it may have been installed by an attacker. Backdoors may be delivered and installed by many methods, including Trojans or viruses.

Bot

Bot comes from "robot," and is any program intended to run automated tasks. There are many examples of legitimate uses, such as a search engine spider that is used to crawl the web and provide data for a web search index. When used maliciously, a bot can be remotely controlled to accomplish many different purposes. Large armies of bots are known as a *botnet* and can be remotely directed in a coordinated attack against a single target. This is how a distributed denial of service (DDoS) attack is carried out. With many requests taking place at the same time, it is possible to overwhelm a web server (or other service) and prevent legitimate traffic from getting through. Because bots can be installed on any network-connected device, internet of things (IoT) devices such as smart light bulbs are particularly vulnerable to having a bot installed.

Wireless Threats

Wireless technology is susceptible to sniffing and man-in-the-middle attacks. As providers of publicly accessible Wi-Fi, libraries should pay keen attention to Wi-Fi threats.

Sniffing allows someone to eavesdrop on wireless traffic and is easy to accomplish on an unencrypted Wi-Fi network. Software is readily available to conduct packet sniffing, where any data on the network that is not encrypted can be viewed and logged by someone who is watching. This is also the case when a Wi-Fi network uses a captive portal for login, for example on some public Wi-Fi networks, where the login process might be secure, with the user entering a password in a pop-up browser window, but is then transferred to an unencrypted network.

As opposed to a sniffing attack in which someone is able to watch network traffic but not interfere, a *man-in-the-middle attack* involves someone intercepting communication then passing it along to its intended recipient. This gives the attacker the opportunity to not only view traffic but also to make changes. This is usually accomplished by the attacker impersonating the recipient, be it a known person or a service, and is only successful so far as it is able to fool those on either end of the communication.

Web and Internet Attacks

Aside from the internet as a source of malware, there are also threats that take advantage of the specific technologies that enable the internet and the world wide web.

Spoofing

When an attack pretends to be someone or something it is not, this is called *spoofing*. This type of attack isn't unique to the internet; spoofing is a common type of telephone scam that takes advantage of caller ID. Email spoofing is similar in that it involves the forging of the sender's identity to make it appear as though an email was sent from a legitimate email address. If an email seems to have come from a known sender, it is more likely to be opened. This is a common way to spread email viruses or conduct phishing attacks.

IP address spoofing, like email spoofing, forges the IP address on network traffic to make it appear as though the sender is a different computer system. This is sometimes used to defeat authentication systems that rely on IP addresses. It may be used in denial-of-service and other attacks, to hide the origin of the attack.

Domain name server (DNS) spoofing and DNS hijacking are related attacks that involve the redirection of a website request to a different site, which may pose as the site originally requested. A DNS server acts as a sort of traffic director, that translates a website uniform resource locator (URL) into the actual internet protocol (IP) address that will connect with the correct server through the internet. If a DNS server has been hacked and IP address entries changed to point at the wrong website, it is said to be "poisoned."

Website Vulnerabilities

Websites also have specific vulnerabilities that hackers sometimes target. Some involve injecting malicious code into a website that may cause damage to a web server, allow an attacker to hijack a website, or provide access to information in a database behind the website. *Cross-site scripting* is a common vulnerability that involves inserting a malicious script or programming code into the site. Sometimes these attacks are conducted by appending the script to a valid site URL, causing it to run when entered. A *structured query language (SQL) injection* is a specific attack that affects a SQL data-base–driven website. It could result in corrupting the database or dumping info for the attacker, and is one way that data breaches can happen through a website. Web forms are particularly vulnerable to these types of attacks.

Distributed Denial of Service Attack

A DDoS attack involves many sources sending traffic to a single service or website in an effort to overwhelm it with so many requests that legitimate traffic can't get through, possibly even crashing the server. Despite this, a DDoS attack itself does not infect computers with a virus or result in a data breach, although it may be used as part of a coordinated attack that involves other methods as well.

Because the attack sources are distributed, it is difficult to sort out the legitimate traffic from the false. In the case of botnets, the source of the attack may even come from many legitimate systems that have been compromised—often without the knowledge of the owner. A computer that has been compromised in a way that it can be remotely controlled is known as a *zombie agent* and is a common way to conduct a DDoS attack. Any internet-connected device may be used in a DDoS attack, which includes IoT devices such as light bulbs and doorbells.

PERSONAL COMPUTER SECURITY

Now that we have reviewed some of the threats to computer systems, we can discuss methods for protecting personal computers. While antivirus software may be the first thing that comes to mind there are many additional tactics an individual can use to secure data on their computer and protect their communication over networks.

Updates and Patches

One of the simplest and yet most critical things that users can do to protect their computers is to keep software up to date. It can be tempting to disable automatic updates—although they have become less intrusive than in the past, they can still be an irritation if they cause an interruption. They are crucial, however, to receive fixes for vulnerabilities to a system, and because some time may already have passed since the vulnerability was made known to the developer, each day that passes represents possible exposure to hacks, viruses, and other malicious attacks. This is particularly true of the operating system, and so it is especially urgent to install security patches and updates as soon as they become available. Fortunately, most operating systems automatically check for updates and install them for you, although users and technicians need to make sure that they do not disable them.

This is also why it is important not to use unsupported software. If an application or operating system is no longer being supported, developers will not be working to discover vulnerabilities or provide fixes. The longer a vulnerability goes uncorrected, the greater the chance it will be exploited. It is risky to use an operating system that is past its end-of-life, especially for any internet-connected computer.

Antivirus Software

Patching the operating system and software alone is not enough to protect a computer. Antivirus software is your main defense against malicious software such as viruses, Trojans, and others. The antivirus software must also be continually updated. As new malware is discovered, the dictionary of virus definitions is updated so that antivirus software can continue to defend against new threats. The landscape of malware is constantly evolving with new and improved viruses developed all of the time.

Viruses may be delivered to a system many different ways—any way that a file can be transferred, whether from physical media or over a network, is a threat. Antivirus software will keep watch on network traffic and system processes for known threats, and scan files that attempt to transfer to the computer.

Although operating systems often have built-in virus protection, it isn't always enough to rely only on it alone, instead of also using a third-party product. Even macOS and Linux, although targeted far less than Microsoft Windows, are by no means immune to viruses and should also be protected by additional antivirus software. There are many options for antivirus software, some free and some not, some from major security vendors such as Norton, McAfee, and Kaspersky, as well as other highly regarded products such as Adaware, AVG, Bitdefender, and Malwarebytes. Many technology publications provide reviews of antivirus software including CNET,[9] PC Magazine,[10] and Tom's Guide,[11] among others.

Password Managers

With an ever-increasing amount of account credentials to keep track of, the ability to create unique passwords for each account and remember them all is quite impossible. If a person uses the same password for more than one account and that password is compromised, then every site where that password was used is suddenly vulnerable. Not to mention the simple fact that a strong password is a complex one, and so difficult to remember on its own in the first place. For these reasons, password managers are highly recommended by security experts.

A password manager remembers all of your credentials for you, and if you don't have to remember them, they can be strong, complex, and unique to each account. Password managers often have the ability to recommend a strong password when creating or updating accounts. It is just up to the user to remember a single master password that will unlock access to their collection of credentials. The most secure password managers store the credentials on the local computer or device rather than in the cloud, and they are encrypted so that even if a hacker had access to the machine with the stored passwords, they would be unreadable. Often the master password is the key to decrypt the passwords as needed.

Most web browsers remember passwords for you now and, with an account, can sync these passwords across different machines. Operating systems also have built-in password managers, such as macOS Keychain Access. There is also third-party software that specializes in storing, encrypting, and syncing account credentials. LastPass, KeePass, and 1Password are all examples. This software often uses web browser plug-ins and a mobile device app.

Not all password managers are created equal, but simply using one and taking advantage of the opportunity to create unique passwords for individual accounts is a huge step in personal account security. With a single master set of credentials to remember, it becomes easier to remember a long, complex password and to take advantage of additional layers such as multifactor authentication (MFA).

File Security

Encryption is highly recommended for securing files on a computer, with whole-disk encryption perhaps the simplest method rather than encrypting individual files. Encryption works by taking a key, usually a password, and plugging it into an algorithm that transforms any data it is applied to into an unreadable code. If the data were stolen, it would be indecipherable even if the criminal knows the algorithm applied as long as he or she doesn't have the password key. Using the same key to both encrypt and decrypt something is known as a *symmetric key cipher*.

BitLocker is the encryption software included with Microsoft Windows and FileVault is macOS's native encryption program. Both can be set to encrypt the entire hard drive, with decryption taking place automatically when the user logs into his or her account. A number of third-party encryption software packages are also available that can be used instead of or in addition to the native software, including open-source software such as VeraCrypt.

File permissions are a way to control access to files that are shared with other users. Although it is possible to set permissions on personal computers, most users use cloud platforms such as Google Drive for collaborating. When sharing files, it is vitally important to pay attention to whom the settings allow access, in addition to what level of access they may have—from simply viewing the file up to editing and possibly taking ownership of it.

Unix File Permissions

Unix-based operating systems (such as Linux and macOS) have a file permission system in which various combinations of three different types of access (read, write, and execute) are applied to each of three different sets of users (the owner, a group of users, and everyone else), for each file and directory. This can be represented with either the number 0 through 7 or by using the characters *r*, *w*, and *x*, as demonstrated in table 7.1. When numbers are used to describe a file's permission settings, they are written with three digits, with the first place representing the owner of the file (also *u* for "user"), the second place for members of the file's group (also *g*), and the third place for everyone else (also *o* for "others").

You will most commonly run into Unix file permissions while administering or accessing a server.

Table 7.1. Unix File Permissions

Digit	Text	Permissions Granted
0	---	All access is denied
1	--x	Execute only
2	-w-	Write only
3	-wx	Write and execute
4	r--	Read only
5	r-x	Read and execute
6	rw-	Read and write
7	rwx	Read, write, and execute

Secure Communications

There are a number of measures that can be taken to keep communications over networks secure and private—by both the organization and the private individual. Certain web browser add-ons can help improve security, including two produced by the Electronic Frontier Foundation: *HTTPS Everywhere* causes website connections to default to HTTPS whenever possible and *Privacy Badger* blocks trackers on websites. There are also mobile messaging apps (e.g., Signal) and email services (e.g., ProtonMail) that specialize in private and secure communication.

HTTPS

HTTPS is different from regular HTTP, with the s meaning "secure" as it uses transport layer security (TLS) to encrypt traffic between a user and the web server. It is frequently used on websites that handle sensitive information such as banking, but is increasingly being used by other websites as well to protect user privacy. If a website does not use HTTPS, then you can assume that someone could eavesdrop on the data transmitted if they wanted to. Current web browsers tend to show a padlock in the address bar to indicate whether the connection is secure.

Virtual Private Network

Although a secure connection protects the content of transmissions, other information about the connection is exposed—such as your IP address or what website you are connected to. A virtual private network (VPN) is a tool that can provide additional privacy and security. It operates by encrypting and routing all traffic through intermediary servers, thus obscuring both the original source and destination of the traffic to any observers. VPNs are also useful for making communications private when using an unsecure network such as a public Wi-Fi connection. Many commercial VPN services are available, and it is recommended to use one whenever connected to open, public Wi-Fi to protect against sniffing and other eavesdropping attacks.

Public-key Encryption

Public-key encryption is a type of asymmetric key cipher that uses a pair of keys—one to encrypt and the second to decrypt—rather than a single key as in a symmetric key cipher. This method is often used to secure communications between two people or to create a verifiable digital signature. If person A wants to send an encrypted message to person B, they will use person B's public key to encrypt the message—a key that is publicly available to anyone who may wish to use it. However, the encrypted message can only be decrypted by the second key of the pair, a private key known only to person B.

TOR

TOR (formerly known as The Onion Router) is a specific software package that takes advantage of several technologies for the purpose of anonymizing the user and concealing online activities. It basically works on a principle similar to a VPN, only on a much larger scale, where instead of the traffic being routed through a single server, it moves through a number of relays, further obscuring the source. It was originally developed by the United States Naval Research Laboratory and is now supported by the nonprofit TOR Project. It is likewise used by people interested in protecting their privacy and avoiding censors as well as for illicit activities.

Windows Security

Windows Defender Security Center is the central control panel for several security-related applications in Microsoft Windows 10. It includes access to Windows Defender Antivirus, a full-fledged, built-in antivirus application; Windows Defender Firewall, a personal, software-based firewall; and Family Options, which is similar to what you might expect to find in a parental controls application. Windows also has other options for providing security such as user account settings, automatic updates, BitLocker for drive encryption, and file sharing permissions.

MacOS Security

Like other operating systems, macOS has a number of built-in security features. Some of these are accessible via the System Preferences, including Users & Groups, for user account settings; Parental Controls; Security & Privacy, through which you can access FileVault, which provides disk encryption; Gatekeeper, which restricts from where applications can be downloaded and installed; Firewall settings; and Privacy settings. You can also set up two-factor authentication (2FA) through the iCloud settings, and use a local password manager called Keychain.

NETWORK SECURITY

Aside from implementing security practices for individual computers, many security measures can be taken at the network level. Libraries may not have direct access to some of these methods, but they can insist on certain practices with those who do and use applications and services that use secure methods. However, if the library is able to administer the network, then the library does have responsibility for its integrity and security.

Firewalls

Firewalls are an important element of network security, and are designed to act as a barrier between an external and internal network that applies a set of rules to determine whether to allow network transmissions to pass through. They can be used in many different locations and with a variety of configurations on a network. A firewall may be placed between a local area network and the internet, between internal networks, or at the connections between a server and a network. They can exist in layers that accomplish different sorts of filtering, sectioning off specific resources on a network. Libraries should have a keen interest in using firewalls, both to protect the internal network from malicious traffic and to protect user data that resides in databases and on servers.

A network administrator sets the rules by which a firewall determines whether to allow traffic to pass. It considers the port through which the traffic is attempting to travel, the associated IP address of the sender, the protocol used, and the type of application making the connection, among other things. If something attempts to make a connection that is not allowed, the connection request will be rejected or ignored.

Packet filtering and network address translation (NAT) are two methods used by firewalls to examine traffic. Packet filtering works by examining individual data packets as they attempt to pass through the firewall. Both incoming and outgoing traffic are checked for their protocol, port number, and both the source and intended destination. NAT is used to hide the true network addresses of computers on a network. This is where the difference between a public and private IP address can come into play. The NAT has a directory that can be used to redirect incoming traffic to the correct address. It is useful from a security standpoint because it can prevent a malicious actor from discovering the actual IP address of a sensitive server.

Proxy Servers

A proxy server acts as an intermediary between two computers, receiving traffic from one computer then passing it along to the destination. Then, when a response goes back, it travels through the proxy server again. This most basic type of proxy server is known as an *open proxy*, and simply forwards requests from a user. As the destination server sees the traffic as coming from the proxy server and not the user, it can be used to hide the IP address of the source. This is one way to obscure someone's identity when accessing websites. On the edge of a network, where internal users send traffic out through it to the internet, it can be used to keep the internal network structure secret. In a similar manner it can also be used to bypass filters or IP address–based restrictions if the proxy is external to where the restrictions are enforced.

Reverse proxies are more commonly used in security applications than open proxies. In a local network environment where outside traffic accesses a locally hosted web server, for example, a reverse proxy will receive the incoming requests and forward them along to the destination server. Then the response will go back out to the user through the reverse proxy, appearing to have come from the proxy server without identifying the web server itself. It also separates incoming requests from directly accessing the server in question. This is useful not just for security but also for load balancing servers. That is, a website may have duplicate copies on multiple servers to distribute traffic and not overload any one server, but the user does not need to know which specific server to connect to; it needs only the ability to connect to the reverse proxy.

EZproxy

EZproxy is a well-established product in the library world that was designed to give a library's patrons who are not currently on the official library network access to online resources such as subscription databases. It currently has several components, including the ability to authenticate users with the home institution's preferred authentication method. The *proxy* part of EZproxy involves the user connecting to the EZproxy server, which then connects to the online resource on their behalf. The online resource recognizes the EZproxy server as being covered by the library's subscription and so allows access.

Authentication

Authentication is the method by which a user is verified as someone allowed access to a system or resource. Typically, a username and password will be used to verify the identity of a user. Systems may have their own native authentication method built in, perhaps as a simple login, but increasingly they are able to check an external database of users such as Lightweight Directory Access Protocol (LDAP). This centralizes the work of maintaining a user directory rather than each resource having to maintain its own user list.

Several different systems are often working in concert to authenticate and provide access to resources. Sometimes a resource looks to an external source to authenticate a user before providing access. Single sign-on (SSO) is a technology whereby a user may authenticate a single time, then use a variety of unrelated resources without reauthenticating because the verification is handled in the background between the resource and the SSO service.

There is a veritable alphabet soup of protocols and standards used for authentication. The following are some of the more common:

- Kerberos is an authentication protocol that uses secure "tickets" to communicate between two parties. The tickets prove the user's identity. Microsoft Windows operating systems use Kerberos as the protocol for authentication services.
- Simple authentication and security layer (SASL) is a method of connecting an authentication service to an external application.
- LDAP is a common protocol used as a centralized directory of users and their associated passwords. Other resources on a network or system might check with the LDAP server to validate a user. Active Directory is Microsoft's implementation of LDAP for Windows-based networks.
- Security assertion markup language (SAML) is an XML-based standard for securely exchanging authentication data. It is often used as the foundation for web-based SSO.

- Central authentication service (CAS) is a protocol for web-based SSO that connects a web resource that makes a request for authentication with a service such as LDAP, Active Directory, or Kerberos.
- Shibboleth is an SSO system that grew out of Internet2 and is based on the SAML framework. It is commonly used by educational and research institutions.
- OpenID Connect (OIDC) is another popular web-based authentication system. It uses the OAuth 2.0 protocol.

Single Sign-On

SSO is frequently used as a way to simplify access to web-based resources. SSO allows a user to initially authenticate with their user ID and password; then the credentials are stored while the session is active so that other resources may check a user's identity without forcing them to enter a username and password again. Some of the benefits include the fact that the user doesn't have to maintain multiple sets of credentials (such as a password for each resource) and the resource is not responsible for maintaining a directory of user credentials—it is relying on the SSO service for that. Of course a risk here is that if a malicious actor has access to a user's SSO credentials, they now have access to every resource or service that uses that SSO service.

Biometric Authentication

Usernames and passwords are not the only set of credentials that can be used to identify a user. Biometric authentication methods use the unique physical characteristics of a person, such as a fingerprint, facial recognition, retina scanning, or voice recognition. It is becoming more widespread in consumer devices, with its introduction in mobile phones and tablet computers. Obvious advantages to biometric authentication are that the user will not need to remember a password, and it is far harder to crack or duplicate a user's fingerprint, for example. There are some privacy concerns, however, as the authentication system needs to have a copy of that fingerprint (or iris pattern, etc.) stored to verify a login. This means the user is putting trust in a system that stores information about their body. Beyond the possibility of a data breach, some also argue about the potential of misuse by the organization storing the data.

Multifactor Authentication

MFA and a common implementation of it is 2FA, which involves the use of two or more pieces of information, such as a password and a pin number, to verify a user. This is inherently more secure than just a user ID and a password, because a malicious actor needs that second piece of information in addition to the password to gain unauthorized access to a resource or system.

The second factor can be a piece of information like a pin number, a one-time password, or an answer to a security question, or it can take a physical form like a bank card, USB key, or radiofrequency identification tag. Many web services are now offering 2FA to further secure their login process, and it is highly recommended that users take advantage of it. They often use a one-time use code that is entered along with the regular credentials. The code may be sent to an email address, a phone number via SMS, or by using an automatically generated code incorporated into a physical device such as a key fob with an LCD display or a mobile phone app. Authy, LastPass Authenticator, and Google Authenticator are examples of such apps for mobile phones.

Network Security Protocols

On an unsecure Wi-Fi network, it is a simple matter to eavesdrop on the traffic of anyone using that network. Many library patrons use the provided Wi-Fi, so securing the wireless network is an important action a library can take to protect the privacy of local patrons.

Wi-Fi protected access II (WPA2) has been the foremost wireless security protocol since 2004, when it replaced WPA and wired equivalent privacy (WEP). The third generation of WPA was announced in 2018 and has slowly started appearing on devices. WPA3 promises to be even more secure and harder to crack than the previous standard.

Secure Wi-Fi, however, only encrypts traffic over the Wi-Fi network. Once it travels beyond the Wi-Fi network, say to a website, it is no longer protected by the Wi-Fi security protocol. This is where other technologies working in conjunction can continue to protect the patron's privacy. Wherever possible, HTTPS should be enabled on services and websites that the library provides or subscribes to.

HTTPS uses TLS to encrypt traffic between a user and the destination website. This is particularly important when a user might enter data into a webform—like a catalog search, authentication credentials when logging into a service, or accessing any personal information. Even if the resource is hosted by a vendor, and not directly configurable by the library, it is still incumbent upon the library to request HTTPS to protect their patrons' privacy.

Web Server Security

A website that is secure will have a digital certificate installed on the server that verifies who the owner of the website is. Certificates are issued by a third-party organization known as a *certificate authority*, which does the work of verifying websites. Web browsers contain a list of known and trusted certificate authorities, and if something looks amiss, the browser may present you with a warning. Users can check for information about the certificate themselves, in some browsers by clicking the padlock icon in the address bar, and look for information such as the owner of the site, the organization that issued the certificate, and the expiration date of the certificate.

Obtaining and installing a certificate on a server is not a difficult process. There are a number of certificate authorities to obtain the certificate from, including GeoTrust, VeriSign, InCommon, and DigiCert, among others. Installing a certificate makes it possible to provide a secure HTTPS connection.

SUMMARY

Given how much library patrons use our information systems and networks, and the amount of personal data available on them, it is integral that we do our best to secure our systems and protect our users' privacy as well as the integrity of our systems. In addition to our ethical concerns for patron privacy, there are a number of regulations and policies to adhere to. Libraries also have a particular interest in the security of library-specific applications, in how vendors handle data in cloud-hosted solutions, and how data may be transferred between and among various technologies.

Having an awareness of the myriad threats a system faces will aid in assessing risk and establishing preventative measures. Threats may take the form of hacking, password cracking, social engineering, phishing, or any of a variety of different types of malware. Wireless networks are susceptible to certain threats, and both the web and internet present risks that must be managed.

Modern operating systems have a number of security tools, and there are many additional steps a user may take to protect their personal computer. First among these steps is to maintain up-to-date software and operating systems and ensure that patches and updates are applied as soon as they are available. Antivirus software is also key to protecting a computer. Other steps involve the use of a password manager, using file security options such as permissions and encryption, and taking steps to secure communications over networks and the web.

It is incumbent upon the system administrator to utilize methods to protect the network and the systems and services that are on it. Firewalls and proxy servers are two network components that play a key role in protecting network resources. Authentication is important for authorizing access to resources, and is of particular interest to libraries with regard to the many systems and databases we provide.

KEY TERMS

Antivirus software	Malware
Distributed denial of service (DDoS) attack	Multifactor authentication (MFA)
Encryption	Personally identifiable information (PII)
EZproxy	Phishing
File permissions	Privacy
Firewall	Proxy server
Hacking	Social engineering
HTTPS	Single sign-on (SSO)
Information security	Virtual private network (VPN)

QUESTIONS

1. Explain the concept of information security.
2. Choose a regulation introduced in this chapter (e.g., FISMA Reform, FERPA, PCI DSS, HIPAA, or GDPR). Describe it and how it may apply to libraries.
3. What security criteria should libraries consider when evaluating a product or service?
4. List and describe information security threats.
5. Is there a particular threat that libraries may be vulnerable to? Why?
6. What are some of the measures that individuals can take to protect themselves from threats?
7. What are some of the measures that can be taken to secure a network?

ACTIVITIES

1. Investigate a library—what information security measures are they using with the network, employee computers, public computers, and servers? What kind of data do they collect about patrons, and how do they ensure the security of the data?
2. Select several measures to implement that will improve your personal information security (e.g., install antivirus software, install some browser plugins, or use a password manager). Write about your experience. Was it difficult to implement? What recommendations do you have for others who may want to do something similar?

FURTHER READING

"Information Security Guide: Effective Practices and Solutions for Higher Education." Higher Education Information Security Council. Accessed August 11, 2019. https://www.educause.edu/focus-areas-and-initiatives/policy-and-security/cybersecurity-program/resources/information-security-guide.

Breeding, Marshall. "Privacy and Security for Library Systems." *Library Technology Reports* 52, no. 4 (2016).

Ciampa, Mark D. *Security+ Guide to Network Security Fundamentals*, 5th ed. Boston: Cengage Learning, 2015.

Clark, Ian. "The Digital Divide in the Post-Snowden Era." *Journal of Radical Librarianship* 2 (2016): 1–32.

Cunningham, Andrew. "The Best Password Managers." *Wirecutter*, July 17, 2019. https://thewirecutter.com/reviews/best-password-managers/.

Hennig, Nicole. "Privacy and Security Online: Best Practices for Cybersecurity." *Library Technology Reports* 54, no. 3 (April 2018).

Jones, Meg Leta. *Ctrl+Z: The Right to Be Forgotten*. New York: New York University Press, 2016.

Kralicek, Eric. "Antivirus, Spyware, Windows Updates, Spam Protection, Security and Disaster Recovery." In *The Accidental SysAdmin Handbook: A Primer for Entry Level IT Professionals*, 2nd ed. New York: Apress, 2016.

Negus, Christopher. "Learning Linux Security Techniques." In *Linux Bible*, 9th ed. Indianapolis: John Wiley and Sons, 2015.

Nemeth, Evi, Garth Snyder, and Trent R. Hein. "Security." In *UNIX and Linux System Administration Handbook*, 5th ed. New York: Pearson Education, 2018.

Parker, Carey. *Firewalls Don't Stop Dragons: A Step-by-step Guide to Computer Security for Non-techies*, 3rd ed. New York: Apress, 2018.

Pogue, David. "Accounts, Security and Gatekeeper." In *macOS Mojave: The Missing Manual*. Sebastopol, CA: O'Reilly Media, 2018.

———. "Security and Privacy." In *Windows 10: The Missing Manual*, 2nd ed. Sebastopol, CA: O'Reilly Media, 2018.

Stokes, Jeff, Richard Diver, and Manuel Singer. "Windows 10 Security." In *Windows 10 for Enterprise Administrators: Modern Administrators' Guide*. Birmingham, UK: Packt, 2017.

Stokes, Jeff, Richard Diver, and Manuel Singer. "Windows Defender Advanced Threat Protection." In *Windows 10 for Enterprise Administrators: Modern Administrators' Guide*. Birmingham, UK: Packt, 2017.

Thomchick, Richard, and Tonia San Nicolas-Rocca. "Application Level Security in a Public Library: A Case Study." *Information Technology and Libraries* 37, no. 4 (2018), 107–18. https://doi.org/10.6017/ital.v37i4.10405.

RESOURCES

Apple, FileVault: https://support.apple.com/en-us/HT204837

California State University, Information Security Policy: https://calstate.edu/icsuam/documents/Section8000.pdf

EDUCAUSE Cybersecurity Program: https://www.educause.edu/focus-areas-and-initiatives/policy-and-security/cybersecurity-program

EDUCAUSE, Higher Education Cloud Vendor Assessment Tool: https://library.educause.edu/resources/2016/10/higher-education-cloud-vendor-assessment-tool

EDUCAUSE, National Cybersecurity Awareness Month: https://www.educause.edu/focus-areas-and-initiatives/policy-and-security/cybersecurity-program/awareness-campaigns

EDUCAUSE, Security Matters Blog: https://er.educause.edu/columns/security-matters

Have I Been Pwned (Check data breaches): https://haveibeenpwned.com/

How to Geek, Bitlocker: https://www.howtogeek.com/192894/how-to-set-up-bitlocker-encryption-on-windows/

LITA, Patron Privacy Technologies Interest Group: http://www.ala.org/lita/about/igs/public/lit-Pp

National Cyber Security Alliance, Stay Safe Online: https://staysafeonline.org/

Objective-See, Free Mac Security Tools: https://objective-see.com/products.html

OCLC, EZproxy: https://www.oclc.org/en/ezproxy.html

Privacy Tools: https://www.privacytools.io/

Antivirus and Antimalware Tools

McAfee: https://us.mcafeestore.com/
Malwarebytes: https://www.malwarebytes.com/mwb-download/
Norton: https://us.norton.com/antivirus

Password Managers

1password: https://1password.com/
KeePass: https://keepass.info/
LastPass: https://www.lastpass.com

Secure Communications Tools

HTTPS Everywhere: https://www.eff.org/https-everywhere
Privacy Badger: https://privacybadger.org/
ProtonMail: https://protonmail.com/
Signal: https://www.signal.org/
TOR: https://www.torproject.org/

NOTES

1. "S.2521—Federal Information Security Modernization Act of 2014," United States Congress, December 18, 2014, https://www.congress.gov/bill/113th-congress/senate-bill/2521.
2. "Protecting Student Information," U.S. Department of Education, accessed on August 25, 2019, https://studentprivacy.ed.gov/.
3. "PCI Security Standards Council," PCI Security Standards Council, accessed on August 25, 2019, https://www.pcisecuritystandards.org/.
4. "Summary of the HIPAA Privacy Rule." US Department of Health and Human Services, accessed on August 25, 2019, https://www.hhs.gov/hipaa/for-professionals/privacy/laws-regulations/index.html.
5. "EU Data Protection Rules." European Commission, accessed on August 25, 2019, https://ec.europa.eu/commission/priorities/justice-and-fundamental-rights/data-protection/2018-reform-eu-data-protection-rules_en.
6. Alex Caro and Chris Markman, "Measuring Library Vendor Cyber Security: Seven Easy Questions Every Librarian Can Ask," *Code4Lib Journal* 32 (2016), https://journal.code4lib.org/articles/11413.
7. "Higher Education Cloud Vendor Assessment Tool," EDUCAUSE, May 24, 2019, https://library.educause.edu/resources/2016/10/higher-education-cloud-vendor-assessment-tool.
8. Marshall Breeding, "Privacy and Security for Library Systems," *Library Technology Reports* 52, no. 4 (2016): 13.
9. Clifford Colby, "The Best Antivirus Protection of 2019 for Windows 10," CNET, August 25, 2019, https://www.cnet.com/news/the-best-antivirus-protection-of-2019-for-windows-10/.
10. Neil J. Rubenking, "The Best Antivirus Protection for 2019," PCMag, August 21, 2019, https://www.pcmag.com/roundup/256703/the-best-antivirus-protection.
11. Paul Wagenseil, "Best Antivirus Software and Apps 2019," Tom's Guide, August 23, 2019, https://www.tomsguide.com/us/best-antivirus,review-2588.html.

8

Web Design and Development

The library website is crucial to the modern library. It is used to provide access to many electronic resources and tools, including the library catalog or search feature, online databases, digital libraries, interlibrary loan services, and other electronic resources. It is also used to provide information about the library; contact information and operating hours; policies regarding circulation and usage of resources; and information about collections, events, and special programs. For some patrons, it is the primary way in which they interact with the library.

Although libraries have had a presence on the World Wide Web for a long time, the rapid development of web technologies have also changed user expectations of a library website, and the resources that it takes to maintain one. Whereas one librarian used to maintain a simple Hypertext Markup Language (HTML) site in his or her spare time, specialized roles have emerged to handle the different aspects of web development. It is helpful for everyone to have a basic understanding because many library functions have a web-related element to them.

This chapter begins with a high-level overview of website architecture, describing the anatomy of a webpage, the basics of web server architecture, an introduction to content management systems (CMSs) and programming languages, and an overview of web developer tools. Next it focuses on the practicalities of web development, including the specialized roles on a web team, the web design process, and a selection of design strategies. The chapter finishes by introducing a few web development topics: the semantic web, web application programming interfaces (APIs), web analytics, and web accessibility.

WEBSITE ARCHITECTURE

A webpage is a visual presentation of the *source code*, as written using languages such as HTML and Cascading Style Sheets (CSS). This code is provided by a network connected web server. As an alternative to directly coding individual webpages, a CMS is a platform that provides many advantages, such as a simple way for content editors to update webpages without using HTML. There are a number of different languages beyond HTML that have additional capabilities, and can be used in concert to create dynamic websites. There are also a number of tools that can be used to aid the web developer, from text editors to development platforms.

Anatomy of a Webpage

A webpage is transmitted as code from a server to a web browser that translates it into a visual presentation of graphics, text, and layout as seen by the user. Although best practices for web design are continually evolving as technologies advance and different fields of study investigate user behavior, certain conventions have emerged.

Layout

Some common elements of a webpage's layout are a banner, footer, navigation menus, and the content area. A horizontal banner usually occupies the top of a webpage, often a graphic that serves as the main branding for the entire website and appears as a way to inform the user as they navigate throughout the site that they have not left the website.

Navigation menus are a common and important feature of many sites. The main menu serves as the top-level navigation for a website, with submenus displayed as navigation within different portions of a website. The main navigation is usually found in one of two places—either as a horizontal menu of links, usually immediately below the main banner; or as a vertical menu on the far left of the page. Sometimes a secondary menu may appear as a dropdown list when the pointer hovers over a link, or a link is clicked on.

The footer is a horizontal area at the bottom of the webpage. For a long time it was used to present just a few pieces of information such as contact information, copyright, and the date the page was last updated. But recent trends are making greater use of the footer as an extended navigation menu with links to many areas of the site.

The content area is essentially any space not taken up by menus and banners. Content areas can be subdivided into blocks or columns, but they essentially exist to present the information that the page is meant to convey.

Source Code

Behind the visual presentation of the webpage is what is known as the *source code*. This is the programming—sometimes using multiple coding languages—that tells the web browser what content to display and how to display it. Many web browsers have a *view source* menu option that displays the code behind the page, although if the page is dynamically generated, you may only see the function calls.

A static webpage (also known as a *flat webpage*) presents an individual webpage as it is coded, in contrast with a dynamic webpage, which may have interactive features or vary based on changes in content pulled from a server. Static webpages are usually programmed in HTML and stored as a single file. They are able to load faster because of their simplicity; however, any dynamic content must be processed on the user's computer (described as "client-side") and each page must be individually edited by the web developer to introduce any changes. Even though this is how websites were often managed in the early days of the World Wide Web, it quickly becomes cumbersome to maintain.

A dynamic webpage might be database driven, and often uses a server-side scripting language such as PHP, Perl, or ColdFusion to generate pages. Resources can be reused among multiple webpages, and the content can be generated dynamically from a source external to the page such as a database. It can also take on interactive functionality, in which a user might provide some input and the webpage dynamically changes to reflect the input. An example of dynamic interactivity is the filtering option commonly found in web store search results. The processing is done on the server's side, then loaded in the user's web browser.

An important concept in web design is the separation of content and presentation. This is the idea that the visual presentation of a webpage is considered apart from the content and structure. The visual presentation refers to the graphical design, colors, font styles—anything that affects the appearance—and is often coded using CSS. The content is both the information conveyed, such as text or data, and the structure of the document, and may be coded in HTML.

Web Server Architecture

The code, graphics, and other parts that make up the website live on a server that is network accessible. In chapter 6, "Server Administration," we introduced the web server and the database server, and covered different cloud service models. A decision must be made regarding where the website will be hosted—locally or in the cloud? If it is hosted locally, you will need the expertise to manage the web server. If it is hosted by a cloud service, the level of control can vary from full server access to almost none.

In chapter 6 we also talked about the web stack, a set of software packaged together that makes it possible to serve up a website. Depending on the particular functionality wanted, different applications are required. The Linux, Apache, MySQL, PHP (LAMP) stack is just one of many different solutions available.

For the purpose of web development, it is a recommended practice to have multiple servers used as part of the workflow. A basic workflow might involve three servers, supporting three iterations of the website. The production server hosts the live, public website in its final published form. Any changes to this site either in content or functionality should already have been tested and vetted before "going live" on the production site. Editorial access to the production site should be very limited.

The staging server is identical to the production server in the way it is set up, including any software applications or modules. The website hosted on the staging server is nearly identical to the production website, and its purpose is to test any new functionality in an environment identical to the production site, as well as to prepare content before final editorial review and subsequently pushing it over to the live site.

The development server is similar but not necessarily identical to the production server, and the content of the development website may not be up to date with the production website. Content on the development site may include filler, such as the common placeholder text that begins, "Lorem ipsum." The main purpose of the development server and site is to function as a working environment where new settings, plug-ins, and functionality, as well as major layout or graphic changes, can be tested. If a portion of a website is undergoing a redesign or entirely new pages are being designed, they may begin their life on this server.

Other servers might be used beyond the three previously explained, and could function as experimental servers for testing major server software changes such as major version upgrades or for initial development of new functionality. Keeping these sites on separate servers helps to control access, and also protects other servers from unintentional changes that result in breaking functionality on the website. Servers that mirror the production server can also be used to assist with high traffic volume through load balancing.

Content Management Systems

An option for serving up a website is to use a web CMS. With a CMS, you can add content to the website without any knowledge of programming or HTML. The web developer can focus on developing the functionality and presentation of the site, using templates and stylesheets to enforce the appearance while leaving content creation to the content experts. Templates add presentation consistency, navigation menus can be reused throughout a site, and modules add functionality. An entire content workflow can be established by assigning permissions that control access to specific areas of the site as well as the ability to create, edit, or publish content.

A CMS is a way to bring a lot of functionality to your site without needing the skills to program scripts or web applications from scratch. Different CMSs have varying ability for customization and all have specific software requirements for the web server. Again, a hosting decision needs to be made, with the greatest flexibility afforded to those who maintain their own web server—but doing so also requires expertise. Fully hosted CMSs can be user-friendly, but may have many constraints in terms of functionality and presentation.

A CMS often needs a server-side scripting language and database management system installed on the web server. Some of the most popular CMSs are open source, and freely available for download and installation. Wordpress, Joomla!, and Drupal are just three of many products available. When considering an open source CMS, it is vital to look for an active user community that serves as both a source of support and continued development. Paid support can also be an option for some CMSs, including open-source products.

Markup, Scripting, and Programming Languages

Although HTML is often thought of as the programming language that makes websites what they are, there are actually many different languages used that have different capabilities and can be used in concert to produce a final web product. Although some languages can fit into multiple categorizations, used in the context of websites you can generally describe them as either a *markup language*, a *scripting language*, or a full-fledged *programming language*.

The World Wide Web Consortium (W3C) is an international standards organization that develops and maintains many standards for web technologies, including web-specific languages, and for many years maintained the HTML standard. In May 2019, responsibility for publishing the HTML standard passed to the Web Hypertext Application Technology Working Group, a partnership of browser vendors Apple, Google, Microsoft, and Mozilla.

A *validator* is a program that examines code for basic standards compliance, and is particularly useful for determining that it is "well-formed"—that the document uses correct structure and syntax. It could be thought of as a spell and grammar checker for source code. However, just as a spell checker can't tell you whether a story has a good narrative, a code validator does not see the big picture of the website, only whether the code is being used correctly. The W3C maintains a code validator service for markup languages like HTML and XHTML, as well as other content such as CSS. Many development tools such as text editors have code validation built in, and may be able to check many different programming languages.

Hypertext Markup Language

HTML is a document markup language widely used to create webpages. A markup language uses document tags that describe the structure of the document and the content using structural elements. Used in conjunction with a stylesheet, content can be formatted in a consistent manner by defining the format and layout. Scripting languages can also be embedded to provide dynamic functionality to the webpage.

HTML was originally created by Tim Berners-Lee in 1990 as a way for researchers to share documents using the internet, and included a feature called the *hyperlink* that allowed users to navigate from one document to another. The web browser was the client-side software application invented to retrieve and present HTML-formatted documents. The HTML Living Standard is the current version in use, and has many enhancements, including the ability to embed video elements into an HTML document.

Extensible Markup Language

Extensible Markup Language (XML) describes content, conveying meaning for what is found within the tags. XML is a flexible language that is both machine- and human-readable and makes it possible for data to be manipulated and interchanged between web services. MARCXML is an XML schema developed by the Library of Congress specifically for use with machine-readable cataloging (MARC) data.

Cascading Style Sheets and Extensible Stylesheet Language

Style sheet languages define the presentation of a document, and so enable the separation of content from presentation. They focus on the appearance of webpage elements such as background colors, spacing, and the formatting of text.

CSS is perhaps the most well-known style sheet language and is frequently used in conjunction with HTML. They are so called because of the hierarchical manner in which styles can be inherited by HTML elements. CSS styles can be defined within an element tag, and only refer to the content contained within the tag. As elements can be nested in other elements, styles can be inherited from parent elements as long as the specific property has not already been defined. Styles can also be defined on a global level for an entire document—outside of any elements, and in completely separate documents known as *external stylesheets*, which the HTML document can reference. These external stylesheets can be referenced by multiple webpages, ensuring uniform styling across an entire site. Then, if the designer wants to override the style of a particular property for a specific webpage, or even a specific element, the definition can be made at the appropriate level.

Extensible Stylesheet Language (XSL) is not a specific defined language; rather, it is used in reference to multiple languages that are used to style and transform XML documents. Some of the XSL languages include XSLT, XQuery, XPath, and XSL-FO, and they serve different functions, from presentation formatting of XML documents to transforming XML documents to PDF files.

JavaScript and Asynchronous Java Script and XML

JavaScript is a language generally embedded in webpages as small programs meant to run in the user's web browser. As such, it is often described as a client-side scripting language. Along with HTML and CSS, web browsers are built with the capability to execute JavaScript, incorporating dynamic functionality of a limited manner into websites.

Asynchronous JavaScript and XML (AJAX) is web development practice that combines several languages to create web applications. It enables a webpage to have content that changes without the need for the entire webpage to reload. JavaScript Object Notification (JSON) can be used in place of XML for data retrieval and exchange.

PHP, Perl, and ColdFusion

Server-side scripting languages are able to use the storage and processing power of the server before rendering the results in the user's web browser. Because the processing takes place on the server, the appropriate applications and libraries have to be installed. PHP, Perl, and ColdFusion Markup Language are examples of languages that are widely used to create dynamic websites and web applications. They often interact with external data sources such as a database.

Java, Python, Ruby

Most programming languages don't exist in just one category, as they may have multiple uses. Java, Python, and Ruby may be considered alongside other server-side scripting languages, but can also be considered separately because they were created as more general-purpose programming languages. In a web development context, they are primarily used for building web applications.

Developer Tools

A large variety of web development tools can aid in the design and maintenance of websites. From web browser plugins to full-featured development platforms, there are many options depending on the task to be accomplished and the skill of the user.

Text editors can assist with writing code and often have helpful features such as spell checker, syntax highlighting (coloring text according to type of code), automatic formatting, and code completion (suggestions for syntax and code elements). These features are all language dependent, so a particular text editor may or may not support a particular language. The capability of a text editor can range from a simple, no-frills text editor such as TextEdit for macOS or Notepad for Microsoft Windows, to full web development applications that include an editable graphical preview of the webpage. A wide range of text editors are available, with some of the notable names being Adobe Dreamweaver, BBedit, BlueGriffon, Komodo Edit, Microsoft Visual Studio, and Notepad++.

A What You See Is What You Get (WYSIWYG) editor, often pronounced wiz-ee-wig, is a graphical editor that hides the code from the user, instead making it possible to edit content or a document as it should appear in the final product. A lightweight WYSIWYG editor is often included with CMSs, allowing for content editors to create and format content without having to use HTML, CSS, or any other programming.

All of the major web browsers now have integrated developer tools that can be used for debugging, testing, or simply examining both the source code and graphical elements of a webpage. Browser plugins and extensions can provide additional functionality. Some of these tools might verify hyperlinks or check the accessibility of a page.

Graphics editing applications are also important to web design. They might be used during the design process, to create draft versions of a webpage as well as creating and editing images and other graphics for the website. Adobe Photoshop and Adobe Illustrator are well known commercial options, while GNU Image Manipulation Program (GIMP) is an open-source alternative.

WEB DEVELOPMENT

Web development is the actual practice of designing, creating, implementing, and maintaining a website. There are several sets of skills required to develop a website so, depending on the size of the organization, the personnel involved may range from a team of dedicated employees to those with additional library roles. There are several steps in the design process noteworthy to web design, including information architecture, content planning, and interface design. Several strategies to consider are responsive web design (RWD), user-centered design (UCD), and user experience (UX) design. Usability testing helps ensure a user-friendly design.

Team Roles

A library web team might discuss and review decisions that affect the website, conduct planning for site development and enhancements, and review content for publishing. Many libraries don't have a team of employees dedicated full-time to web development. Often these roles are distributed to employees who have other functional duties in the library, with the team lead possibly filling several roles. This depends on the size of the library as well as the particular skills that employees have.

If there is a web governance body at the parent institution level, it is strongly recommended to have someone from the library participate. The decisions that are made there regarding design, templates, content policies, and branding may greatly affect the library site.

Web Administrator

The web administrator, also known as the *web master* or perhaps *web librarian*, is the lead person with regard to the coordination of website-related planning, development, and maintenance. If there is a web team or department, the web administrator is the chair or head. He or she is responsible for web operations and project management, and are point-of-contact for library administration, stakeholders, and vendors.

Web Designer

The web designer is proficient with graphic design and web styles, and has responsibility for the visual layout and presentation of the website. He or she has a knowledge of user interface design, web accessibility standards, and usability. The web designer does not necessarily need to be a programmer because he or she does not create web applications or manage a server. A web designer employs usability testing to improve and refine designs.

Web Developer

The web developer is familiar with web programming languages such as HTML, CSS, JavaScript, and scripting languages to create code for the website. he or she should have some database design skills to aid in web application development, and some basic server and network administration knowledge.

Content Editor and Content Creators

The primary role of the content creators is to develop content for the website. They write the text, provide appropriate multimedia, and review website content to keep it fresh and up to date. The content editor plays a role in the publishing workflow, ensuring a consistent voice, and reviewing content prior to publication on the website. He or she may also need to encourage content creators to keep the content that they are responsible for fresh. Content editors provide training for web content creators, or anyone else who will contribute to the website. Neither the editor nor creators necessarily need to know anything about web design or programming—in fact, they might be working with WYSIWYG editors in a CMS, and not ever see any code.

Web Librarian

A web librarian doesn't have a specific role on a web team, per se. The web librarian may either play a leadership role such as a lightweight web administrator and coordinate the work of the web team, or he or she may have sole responsibility for everything on the website from the library's perspective, perhaps in a situation in which the majority of responsibility for developing the website is outsourced. In any case, a web librarian probably has additional duties to the library that are not web related.

Other Specialized Roles

Only the largest libraries will have the resources for dedicated Web Application Programmers. These employees can customize applications and develop innovative new solutions. In a small or medium-sized institution, the accessibility officer might be a secondary role assigned to a library employee, while a large institution might have a dedicated accessibility officer or even an entire team with the responsibility to review pages and ensure that they meet accessibility requirements. This is an ongoing task that is never complete. Other specialized roles include backend developer, information architect, and trainer.

Design Process

The development of a website should be iterative so that it will continue to evolve and improve, as informed by usability testing. It is unusual these days to be in a position to design a website where none existed before, and it can be tempting to start completely from scratch even when a site already exists. When approaching a redesign, a decision must be made whether to take an iterative approach and incrementally improve the existing site, or to design something completely new. Even when starting over, there is still much that can be learned from the existing site.

Analysis and Planning

When starting the design process, a decision needs to be made regarding the scope of the project to help manage resources and avoid scope creep, which can lead to overspent budgets, missed deadlines, and confusion about project goals. There may also be institutional policies that constrain design decisions such as branding, color schemes, required templates or navigation menus.

Whether the project is part of an iterative cycle or beginning something entirely new, take stock of the opportunities and constraints that will affect the final product. Are you required to use a specific platform, or is there an opportunity to move to a new platform, like a CMS? Is there an opportunity for customization, or a need to upgrade old software? Are there limits to the software packages that can be installed on the web server? Would this be a good time to consider a move to a cloud-hosted solution? Will the site design and implementation be handled in house, or will any work be outsourced? Are there constraints of budget, staffing, or expertise?

Spend some time analyzing the current site. Web analytics and server logs can be mined for data about users and their behavior. Usability testing can be highly informative, confirming good design decisions, exposing problems that you were unaware of, and suggesting possible solutions based on user expectations. If it works, you may not want to change it. On the other hand, you may discover users have trouble accomplishing certain tasks, so you may want to consider changing the method for completing them.

Gather requirements for the design. As library websites are highly integrated with other services over which the library may have limited control, think about how things like the item search function, access to personal accounts, and other linked or embedded services will fit in. Create a communication plan for eliciting input from stakeholders from the very beginning, and informing them with the appropriate amount of information during the design and implementation process. Different stakeholder groups may have different needs for the library website, and will be able to provide useful feedback about draft designs. Conduct an environmental scan. Examine other websites and think critically about their design and functionality.

Information Architecture

The organization of content throughout the website, their relationships, and structure are what is known as the *information architecture* of a website. The purpose of a well-designed information architecture is to present information throughout the site in a logical and consistent manner that aids in the intuitive navigation of content by users. The ultimate goal is for users to find their way quickly and painlessly, and be able to repeat the task on subsequent visits.

Logical groupings of information for a website may not necessarily reflect their physical-world counterparts, or the way that certain library systems are designed. Users may not be familiar with the organizational structure of library departments and personnel, so the main content groupings of the website shouldn't match the organization chart. Instead, content might be organized into related services or tasks that are meaningful to the user. The top levels of organization often form the basis for the main navigational menu, and inform navigation throughout the site. It is important to note, however, that navigational menus don't need to be direct copies of the site's hierarchical structure and in fact pages can be linked from multiple locations if it makes sense and isn't overdone.

Card sorting is an exercise that can be used to ascertain how best to group content and what labels to apply to the groupings. To conduct a card-sorting exercise, write content titles or descriptions onto index cards or sticky notes and ask the participants to sort them into related groups. You can choose whether to provide labels to categorize the content under or let the participants create the labels. It is also possible to conduct the exercise using web applications such as Optimal Sort.

Card sorting can be conducted with different stakeholders, and then the results can be analyzed to see how users categorize and label content. Of particular interest are where there is a high level of agreement between different stakeholder groups; this can inform an organization scheme that will work for a large percentage of the website's users. Content that has a low level of agreement is interesting as well because it can give you insight into how different types of stakeholders seek information, or it might call into question the content itself.

Content Planning

Creating a strategy for the site's information architecture will help determine in large part what subjects need to be covered by the content presented. Reviewing websites from similar institutions may provide some ideas. Also consider the interactions that take place at service points inside the library— what types of questions are asked at circulation and reference desks? What type of information and what tasks are patrons seeking to accomplish? What services or collections should be highlighted? Think about all of these things from the perspective of the user.

Some general categories of information commonly found on library websites include contact information for service points, departments, and individual staff; policy information with regard to borrowing, computing, or special services; and access to various research tools such as the library catalog or electronic databases.

In the results of a survey of library websites, Anthony S. Chow, Michelle Bridges, and Patricia Commander[1] list the most common types of library website content. Some of the content most commonly found includes operating hours, general contact information, location information, access to electronic resources, access to the library catalog, circulation information, library news and events, description of library services, access to personal accounts, information about interlibrary loan, information about services for children and teens (public libraries), and course reserves (academic libraries).

In *Technology and the School Library: A Comprehensive Guide for Media Specialists and Other Educators*, Odin L. Jurkowski[2] specifically addresses features and content commonly found on school library websites.

When it comes to creating the content and writing the text, it is important to involve the content experts. It can alleviate the web team of having to write content for the entire website, while also putting the responsibility into the hands of the people who are most knowledgeable. Establishing a workflow that involves a content reviewer helps maintain a consistent voice throughout the website and ensures minimal quality standards. Currency of content is also important. In addition to regular reviews of all website content, some areas may need more frequent attention.

Interface Design

The interface design of a website takes into account the visual presentation of the site and includes layout, graphical design, colors, and interactive elements such as menus and links. All of this together has a profound effect on the user experience.

Wireframes are a useful design tool that can be thought of as a skeleton of a webpage, before content and graphical elements are added. A wireframe can start off as a simple pen and paper sketch, with boxes and labels describing content areas, graphics, and navigation. As you work through drafts, you can then move on to mock-ups using prototyping software or page images created in graphic editing software. Starting off your design with wireframes allows for iterative prototyping without the time investment of coding all of the functionality, and the flexibility to make rapid changes based on feedback. By keeping the draft designs lightweight and allowing user input to guide the process, the user experience becomes the driving factor—not the technical functionality or preferences of the web designers.

The amount of freedom the web designer has varies based on previous decisions for the current site as well as institutional requirements for branding, styles, templates, and software platform. Institutional logos often go through an approval process, and there may be a required color scheme and text font. These decisions are made to brand and unify webpages throughout a website. This can become problematic if large banners or navigation menus that are not specific to the library are required that take up significant screen real estate. Although this can be frustrating, we need to do our best to create a good user experience even within those limitations.

Rene J. Erlandson and Rachel A. Erb state succinctly, "Following standard graphic design principles—contrast, repetition, alignment, and proximity—will help you create an attractive, engaging virtual library environment."[3] Color contrast is important to web accessibility, making the text on a webpage more readable. White space can be used to separate and highlight content within a page. Using a standard font and repeating navigational and graphical elements throughout a site improves the usability and makes for a consistent experience.

External stylesheets may be used to create consistent fonts, colors, and styles throughout a site. A template can be designed to be reused that will incorporate standard navigation and page layouts. Using stylesheets and templates not only help to unify a website, but have the added benefit of greatly reducing the time investment and upkeep involved in coding and updating individual pages.

Implementation and Maintenance

Bring all of the elements of the site together in a complete, functioning, test website before "going live." This is a good time to do a final round of usability testing, to discover if the new site will behave as expected and if users are able to accomplish desired tasks. Provide sneak peeks of the new design and begin educating users about the forthcoming changes. Expect it to take time for them to adjust to anything that requires users to change how they interact with the site. If possible, try to plan a launch for a time when it will be minimally disruptive. An academic library would do well to avoid a major overhaul during midterm exams, for example.

After a website goes live, it is time to begin the maintenance phase. Content should be kept fresh and up to date, both to ensure currency and to prevent the site from becoming stale. Regular accessibility checks should be conducted. Carry out scans for broken links that need to be updated.

It may be tempting to just let the site design be, occasionally updating some content but leaving the design and functionality alone until years pass and it desperately needs a complete overhaul. Instead, iterate improvements to the website, as informed by usability testing. Making incremental improvements serves to continually refine the site and make it easier for users to adapt to changes.

Design Strategies

Mobile Web Design

As mobile devices have become commonplace, it has also been accepted that web design has to take this into account. The number of people accessing websites, including library websites on their mobile phones and tablets, cannot be ignored. There are several approaches to developing a solution for mobile access. Early on, recommended practice was to develop an entirely separate website, with its own URL. It would have been a lightweight site with minimal graphics and pictures—if not entirely text-based, as well as reduced content and functionality when compared with the main, desktop-oriented site. Part of the thinking was that people wouldn't spend much time using their mobile device with the website, and they were only looking for quick access to basic information. The mobile site was designed to fit a much smaller-resolution screen than a typical desktop or laptop monitor. An advantage of this approach was the ability to design a site to maximize compatibility with mobile devices; however, this necessitated the maintenance of an additional site to the main website, and could lead to problems if information on one site did not match the other.

Adaptive web design was the next stage in mobile design. As the variety of mobile devices increased, so did the variety of screen sizes. Web designers created multiple versions of a website for several different, common sizes—which led to five or six websites needing to be maintained. There are some shortcuts, such as using different stylesheets for different screen resolutions rather than entirely different websites and using a script to detect the device screen resolution to apply the best fit. Although some websites still use this approach, the proliferation of an endless variety of screen sizes and resolutions has made it difficult to recommend. Advances in web design have led to other options, such as RWD or the option to create an application that users may install on their mobile devices.

Responsive Web Design

RWD has become the preferred method for mobile web design in large part because of the ability for the site to fit nearly any resolution. Instead of relying on fixed-width designs, in which layouts are created for predefined screen sizes, RWD automatically adapts to whatever screen size or orientation a device might use. By moving away from dedicated mobile sites to a single, responsively designed site, users have access to the same content and functionality regardless of whether they are using a desktop computer, laptop, tablet, or mobile phone. This is particularly important for multidevice users who move from one device to another, expecting to have a similar experience. There are also obvious advantages in terms of the work required to maintain a single site.

RWD works by using a flexible (also called *fluid*) grid layout, in which content areas are defined using relative measurements, such as percentages, instead of fixed measurements, like pixels. Images and font styles are dynamically resized as defined in their CSS style. Beyond simply shrinking elements to fit a smaller screen, content areas might move around—for example a page that has three columns when viewed on a desktop computer monitor might reduce to a two-column or even one-column layout. In-page navigation becomes more important in some of these cases, to help alleviate endless scrolling when content that might be easily navigable on a laptop computer is combined into a single, lengthy column.

Another trick frequently used is to hide the main navigation menu shown on the full-width version, and use a floating icon to dynamically display or hide a menu. It is typically identified by three horizontal, parallel lines that, when selected, will pop-up the menu. Selecting a second time causes the menu to disappear. By "floating" over the content, the option to open the menu is always easily available no matter where on the page the user might have scrolled to.

A number of frameworks that use HTML, CSS, and JavaScript are available to make it easier to implement a responsively designed site. Bootstrap, Foundation, and Cascade are three such frameworks. Additionally, many CMSs have implemented RWD either natively, or through modules and plugins that can be added.

Mobile Applications

A basic mobile app is a website in an app container that is installed on a mobile device. Of course, a mobile app can bring a lot more functionality than a straight website and can tie into many of the technologies found in devices, such as the camera, Bluetooth, or GPS. This affords the opportunity for a greatly enhanced tool, beyond that of a website. However, the resource cost to program and maintain a mobile app separate from a website, and a different version for each mobile operating system, is more than many libraries can afford. Although there are frameworks and platforms that make it easier to get into mobile app development, the responsibility usually falls to staff who are application programmers and developers, as opposed to web design and development staff.

User-centered Design

UCD is a philosophy and set of practices wherein the needs, behavior, and expectations of the user guides decisions made at every step of the design process. There are a number of ways to obtain this information, including usability testing and analytics, but the point is to incorporate frequent input from users.

A couple of tools that can be used to assist UCD are personas and scenarios. Very early in the design process, create personas to represent typical users. If there are disparate user groups, create personas representative of each. Consider their motivations and needs, the context in which they will engage with the design, their skills and experience, and some personal details to make it easier to imagine the persona as a "real" person.

Next, create a scenario for each persona that describes a real-life situation or event that the persona might experience. In it, detail how the persona would go about accomplishing tasks, how he or she would come to use the website, how he or she would interact with it, and what kind of success the persona might have.

By keeping a design process user-centered, the expectation is to create a design with a high degree of usability for the user.

User Experience Design

UX design can be thought of as a big-picture, holistic approach to design thinking. It incorporates a number of disciplines, including human-computer interface design, UCD, graphic design, information architecture, usability, and accessibility. UX is concerned with the user's entire experience while interacting with the product. As applied to web design, the goal is for a meaningful and user-friendly website that leads to a good user experience—one in which the user feels competent and satisfied, having accomplished their task.

Usability Testing

It is a recommended practice to conduct usability tests regularly. They need not be large, expansive efforts; instead frequent, focused usability tests can result in targeted feedback and improvements on a relatively short timeframe. The point being to evaluate the website, or specific features of it, by testing it on actual users. By observing how real users interact with the website to accomplish tasks, designers can determine how usable the site is and make informed improvements.

There are many methods for conducting usability tests. A basic example might go something like this: a small group of people are recruited to participate individually in the test. The scope of the test is small, with a short list of tasks identified for the participant to complete. The participant sits at a computer in a room along with the person who administers the test. The person administering the test reads a script that introduces the participant to the test, and then asks the participant to complete the predetermined tasks. The participant is asked to talk out loud about steps he or she is taking and thoughts while doing so. Often, screen recording software such as Camtasia is used to record the participant's actions for later analysis. There may be additional team members present to observe and take notes about the participant's behavior.

Other methods of usability testing include the use of paper prototypes instead of a functioning website, eye-tracking to analyze where users focus their attention, A/B testing in which two designs are tested and the results are compared; and heuristic evaluation in which experts examine a design against a set of principles.

WEB DEVELOPMENT TOPICS

Semantic Web

The semantic web is a collection of standards and frameworks that aim to make the web machine-readable. Using technologies such as Resource Description Framework, data can be described, shared, and reused across the web. Linked data Is closely related and describes the structured data that can be interchanged using semantic web and internet technologies. BIBFRAME is a linked-data model developed by the Library of Congress as an alternative to the MARC standards.

Web APIs

An API is a method through which data can be requested from a system to be used by another. Web APIs in particular set out the rules of communication for the data exchange to take place over the web. A mashup often relies on web APIs to pull in information from external servers to be displayed in a custom manner on a website. They can greatly enhance the capabilities of a website by introducing additional functionality, or creating interactive features that use data from external sites. Many web services expose data through web APIs. Many social media services provide APIs that allow data to be extracted, for example.

Simple Object Access Protocol and Representational State Transfer are the two primary software frameworks used for web APIs. Typically, a script (written in a language such as PHP or Python) will make an API call for data to a server using HTTP and JSON or XML, providing parameters for the data as described by the particular API. An API key may also be required, which authenticates the requestor as being approved to use the API and make requests of the server.

Web Analytics

Web analytics is a method of collecting and measuring usage of a website. A lot of information can be collected about users, where they come from, and what they do on the website. It is possible to ascertain the geographic location visitors are located in based on IP address, the operating system, screen resolution, and web browser in use. You can learn how much traffic individual pages receive, how much time is spent on a page, what page they were on previously, and where they went next. Some of the questions this information can answer are which pages receive the most traffic, which the least, how users got there, and from where they leave the website. If it turns out a page that you expect to be heavily visited is not, you might consider making it more prominent on the site or changing terminology used to guide visitors to it.

Analytics software often has reporting tools that aid in analyzing all of the data collected, including spreadsheets and graphs that can be manipulated to incorporate different data sets at varying levels of granularity. Because analytics software is written from the perspective of e-commerce and marketing, some of the data—such as conversion rates—is not so useful for libraries. Nonetheless, there is still a lot of helpful information to be learned about the way a web site is (or is not) used.

Google Analytics is the most popular web analytics tool,[4] and it is free to create an account and use. It generates a script that includes an account number, and must be embedded into each page that will be tracked. After it is live, Google begins tracking traffic on the pages. The account interface includes a dashboard that can generate reports about all of the information that is being tracked.

Web Accessibility

Web accessibility is the practice of web design so that everyone can access and use a website regardless of ability or disability. Libraries have both an ethical and legal responsibility to ensure that the resources they provide are accessible to all users. Section B.2.1.21 of the American Library Association Policy Manual, "Services to Persons with Disabilities," states, "The library has the responsibility to provide materials 'for the interest, information, and enlightenment of all people of the community the library serves.' (See also the Library Bill of Rights.) When information in libraries is not presented in formats that are accessible to all users, discriminatory barriers are created."[5]

In chapter 2, "Technology Management and Support," we discussed accessibility with regard to technology, the legal requirements as established by Section 508 of the Rehabilitation Act (29 US Code § 794d),[6] and various assistive technologies. The United States Access Board published the *Section 508 Standards for Electronic and Information Technology* in which one section, 1194.22 "Web-based Intranet and Internet Information and Applications," describes specific guidelines for web accessibility such as, "A text equivalent for every non-text element shall be provided."[7]

The Web Content Accessibility Guidelines (WCAG) are the official standards published by the W3C Web Accessibility Initiative (WAI). These guidelines explain specific technical practices to follow and, as the different elements are testable, it is often used as a tool when conducting audits for accessibility. A few of the elements include providing alternate text for images, using high-contrast colors, and including captions with video content. There are also particular ways to structure your content and tables so that a screen reader can navigate the page correctly. The Association of Research Libraries provides a Web Accessibility Toolkit (https://accessibility.arl.org/), which includes a lot of useful information and best practices for web accessibility as well as links to additional resources.

A number of tools can test a webpage to see if it meets accessibility standards, ranging from browser plugins, to text editors with built-in testing and free site-testing tools, to full-featured commercial services. There is the WAVE Web Accessibility Evaluation Tool, Functional Accessibility Evaluator, Compliance Sheriff by Cyxtera, and Siteimprove, just to name a few options.

SUMMARY

Many factors go into web design and development, and the field continues to evolve as technologies progress. The library website is an essential part of the overall library program, so it is important to have an understanding of what is involved to provide a quality service.

The website programming is known as the *source code*, and it determines the content, functionality, and visual presentation as translated by a web browser. Several elements are common to a webpage's layout, including a banner, footer, navigation menus, and the content area. The web server stores the website files, and is network accessible whether hosted locally on in the cloud. An example of a web server workflow involves three servers: a production server, a staging server, and a development server. CMSs can bring a lot of functionality to a site without needing the skills to program scripts or web applications from scratch. HTML and CSS are common markup and stylesheet languages, whereas client-side scripting languages like JavaScript and server-side scripting languages such as

PHP can add dynamic functionality to a website. There are a number of tools to aid in web design and development, with the text editor being a key tool in the developer's toolset.

Because of the specialized nature of the different aspect of a web development, it is useful to have a team on which the members take on different roles. Some of the roles involved include the web administrator, web designer, web developer, content editor, and content creator. The design process should be iterative and informed by usability testing. The different stages involve analysis and planning, information architecture, content planning, interface design, implementation, and finally maintenance. RWD is the recommended strategy to take into account mobile devices. UCD, UX design, and usability testing are all valuable strategies to consider as well.

The semantic web is a collection of standards and frameworks that aim to make the web machine-readable. Web APIs make it possible to pull in information from external servers and enhance the functionality of a website. Analytics is a method of collecting and measuring usage of a website to examine user behavior and apply the lessons to improve the site design and architecture. Libraries have both an ethical and legal responsibility to build accessible websites, following the WCAG published by the W3C WAI. Regular accessibility audits should be conducted to ensure compliance; fortunately, a number of tools and services exist to aid in testing.

KEY TERMS

Client-side
Content management system
Cascading Style Sheet (CSS)
Dynamic webpage
Extensible Markup Language (XML)
Hypertext Markup Language (HTML)
Information architecture
JavaScript
Markup language
Responsive web design (RWD)
Scripting language

Server-side
Source code
Text editor
Usability testing
User experience (UX) design
Web accessibility
Web application programming interface (API)
Web development
Web server
What You See Is What You Get (WYSIWYG)
Wireframe

QUESTIONS

1. What are the common layout elements of a webpage?
2. What is source code?
3. In a three-server web development workflow, what is the purpose of each server?
4. List and describe different roles people might hold on a web team.
5. Describe the web design process.
6. What is usability? What strategies can be taken to improve web usability?
7. What is web accessibility and why is it important?

ACTIVITIES

1. Investigate a library. Who has the ability to make changes to the website? What are the different roles held by staff with regard to web services? Is there a governance group or editorial review?
2. Conduct a card-sorting exercise for an imaginary library website that you are designing. Are you surprised by any of the results? If you were to conduct the same exercise with a different group of participants—perhaps of a different stakeholder group—might the results differ?

FURTHER READING

Adams Jr., Richard M. "Overcoming Disintermediation: A Call for Librarians to Learn to Use Web Service APIs." *Library Hi Tech* 36, no. 1 (2018): 180–90. https://doi.org/10.1108/LHT-03-2017-0056.

Azadbakht, Elena, John Blair, and Lisa Jones. "Everyone's Invited: A Website Usability Study Involving Multiple Library Stakeholders." *Information Technology and Libraries* 36, no. 4 (2017): 34–45. https://doi.org/10.6017/ital.v36i4.9959.

Blakiston, Rebecca. *Usability Testing: A Practical Guide for Librarians.* Practical Guides for Librarians, no. 11. Lanham, MD: Rowman & Littlefield, 2015.

Chow, Anthony S., Michelle Bridges, and Patricia Commander. "The Website Design and Usability of US Academic and Public Libraries." *Reference and User Services Quarterly* 53, no. 3 (Spring 2014): 253–65. https://doi.org/10.5860/rusq.53n3.253.

Comeaux, David J. "Web Design Trends in Academic Libraries—A Longitudinal Study." *Journal of Web Librarianship* 11, no. 1 (2017): 1–15. https://doi.org/10.1080/19322909.2016.1230031.

Hardesty, Juliet L. "Transitioning from XML to RDF: Considerations for an Effective Move towards Linked Data and the Semantic Web." *Information Technology and Libraries* 35, no. 1 (2016): 51–64. https://doi.org/10.6017/ital.v35i1.9182.

Krug, Steve. *Don't Make Me Think, Revisited: A Common Sense Approach to Web Usability*, 3rd ed. Berkeley: New Riders, 2014.

Maloney, Krisellen, and Paul J. Bracke. "Beyond Information Architecture: A Systems Integration Approach to Web-Site Design." *Information Technology and Libraries* 23, no. 4 (2004): 145–52. https://doi.org/10.6017/ital.v23i4.9656.

Mitchell, Erik. "The Organizational Role of Web Services." *Journal of Web Librarianship* 5, no. 2 (2011): 146–51. https://doi.org/10.1080/19322909.2011.572448.

Potnis, Devendra Dilip, Reynard Regenstreif-Harms, and Edwin Cortez. "Identifying Key Steps for Developing Mobile Applications and Mobile Websites for Libraries." *Information Technology and Libraries* 35, no. 3 (2016): 43–62. https://doi.org/10.6017/ital.v35i3.8652.

Schmidt, Aaron, and Amanda Etches. *User Experience (UX) Design for Libraries.* Chicago: ALA TechSource, 2012.

Smith-Yoshimura, Karen. "Analysis of 2018 International Linked Data Survey for Implementers." *Code4Lib Journal* 42 (2018). https://journal.code4lib.org/articles/13867.

Sundt, Alex, and Teagan Eastman. "Informing Website Navigation Design with Team-Based Card Sorting." *Journal of Web Librarianship* 13, no. 1 (2019): 37–60. https://doi.org/10.1080/19322909.2018.1544873.

Tidal, Junior. "One Site to Rule Them All, Redux: The Second Round of Usability Testing of a Responsively Designed Web Site." *Journal of Web Librarianship* 11, no. 1 (2017): 16–34. https://doi.org/10.1080/19322909.2016.1243458.

RESOURCES

A List Apart: https://alistapart.com/
HTML Living Standard: https://html.spec.whatwg.org/
Journal of Web Librarianship: https://www.tandfonline.com/loi/wjwl20
W3C, CSS Validation Service: https://jigsaw.w3.org/css-validator/
W3C, Markup Validation Service: https://validator.w3.org/
W3C, Semantic Web: https://www.w3.org/standards/semanticweb/
W3C, XML: https://www.w3.org/XML/
Web4Lib Electronic Discussion: http://web4lib.org/

Content Management Systems

Drupal: https://www.drupal.org/
Joomla!: https://www.joomla.org/
Wordpress: https://wordpress.com/

Web Development Tools

Adobe Dreamweaver: https://www.adobe.com/products/dreamweaver.html
BBedit: https://www.barebones.com/products/bbedit/
BlueGriffon: http://bluegriffon.org/
Komodo Edit: https://www.activestate.com/products/komodo-edit/
Microsoft Visual Studio: https://visualstudio.microsoft.com/
Notepad++: https://notepad.plus/

Responsive Web Design

Bootstrap: https://getbootstrap.com/
Cascade: https://jslegers.github.io/cascadeframework/
Foundation: https://foundation.zurb.com/

Usability

Google Analytics: https://analytics.google.com/
OptimalSort: https://www.optimalworkshop.com/optimalsort
Techsmith Morae: https://www.techsmith.com/morae.html
Usability.gov: https://www.usability.gov/

Accessibility

ARL, Web Accessibility Toolkit: http://accessibility.arl.org/
Compliance Sheriff: https://www.compliancesheriff.com/
Functional Accessibility Evaluator (FAE): https://fae.disability.illinois.edu/
Siteimprove: https://siteimprove.com/en-us/accessibility/
W3C, Web Content Accessibility Guidelines (WCAG): https://www.w3.org/WAI/standards-guide-lines/wcag/
W3C, Web Accessibility Evaluation Tools List: https://www.w3.org/WAI/ER/tools/
WAVE Web Accessibility Evaluation Tool: https://wave.webaim.org/

NOTES

1. Anthony S. Chow, Michelle Bridges, and Patricia Commander. "The Website Design and Usability of US Academic and Public Libraries." *Reference and User Services Quarterly* 53, no. 3 (Spring 2014): 253-65. https://doi.org/10.5860/rusq.53n3.253.
2. Odin L. Jurkowski, *Technology and the School Library: A Comprehensive Guide for Media Specialists and Other Educators*, 3rd ed, 84-90. Lanham, MD: Rowman & Littlefield, 2017.
3. Rene J. Erlandson and Rachel A. Erb, *Technology for Small and One-Person Libraries: A LITA Guide.* New York: American Library Association, 2013.
4. "Usage of Traffic Analysis Tools for Websites." W3Techs: Web Technology Surveys, accessed January 4, 2020, https://w3techs.com/technologies/overview/traffic_analysis.

5. "B.2 Intellectual Freedom (Old Number 53)," *ALA Policy Manual*, American Library Association, accessed January 4, 2020, http://www.ala.org/aboutala/governance/policymanual/updatedpolicymanual/section2/53intellfreedom#B.2.1.21.
6. "29 U.S. Code § 794d. Electronic and Information Technology," Legal Information Institute, Cornell Law School, accessed January 4, 2020, https://www.law.cornell.edu/uscode/text/29/794d.
7. "Section 508 Standards for Electronic and Information Technology," US Access Board, accessed on January 4, 2020, https://www.access-board.gov/guidelines-and-standards/communications-and-it/about-the-section-508-standards/section-508-standards.

9

Software and Systems Development

Although the wholesale development of a new system from scratch may not be commonplace in libraries, librarians often find themselves involved in the development process from the perspective of the customer, creating requirements and contributing expert feedback to vendors as they design and improve systems.

The software and systems development realm is not the sole purview of expert programmers, however. Many library employees are involved in maintaining databases and websites and discover that through coding they can make more efficient and powerful use of information systems. By coding—or writing scripts and programs—it is possible to manipulate data found in databases or websites, combine data from different sources, conduct complex data manipulation, pull data and display it on websites, and conduct analysis. Even at a beginner's level, the ability to create scripts can make it easier to perform repetitive tasks and design custom solutions.

This chapter examines several aspects of software and systems development, and introduces many concepts that a seasoned developer will be familiar with. The first section addresses the development process: describing software development as a project from a library perspective, the steps inherent to the development life cycle, and a quick review of alternate development methods. Next, the chapter gives an introduction to programming, including some code examples, and an overview of common programming languages. As databases are an integral part of much library work, the chapter presents an introduction to database design, as well as an introduction to structured query language (SQL) programming. Finally, the chapter addresses two development-related topics: application programming interfaces (APIs) and open-source software.

THE DEVELOPMENT PROCESS

Software Development

Many libraries today do not have the resources in-house to embark on large development projects. Nonetheless, an understanding of the software development process is certainly worthwhile—even if development is not undertaken in-house—as libraries often work closely with organizational partners and vendors to develop and improve software products. Being able to work with software developers, and to communicate library needs, concerns, and philosophy, is critical to developing solutions that are successful.

Understanding software development is also useful for projects that are small in scope. The lone developer may not dive so deeply into every aspect, but most projects will at least touch on each area.

Although every library won't have a dedicated developer, the role may be a part of someone's responsibilities, or there may be several library employees who contribute part of their time to developing scripts, web apps, or integrated library system (ILS) improvements, to name a few things.

Initiating a Project

There are many reasons that a library might choose to embark on a project that involves software development: improving a library service, getting better performance from an existing system, implementing stronger controls into a system, reducing cost, responding to a change in business procedures, or supporting a new product or service.

Any project is affected by factors both within and without the organization. Hopefully a strategic plan will help set the direction and priority for projects. Sometimes the impetus comes from desired features or problems identified by library staff. Sometimes managers have a vision for a new service that they would like to implement. Sometimes technology staff recognize improvements that can be made to the system. Usability studies can be helpful in getting input from library patrons about how an existing system performs, and can be used to initiate a project.

External factors may also exert an influence. Technology changes quickly, and systems that interconnect may require adjustments. Government regulations or a reduced budget may introduce constraints. A vendor may not offer all of the services a library may need (or can afford), or else may change their service model, and so initiate a software development project by the library.

Business Analysis

For any system to be successful, it is critically important to understand the business case for the system. Start with a high-level understanding of the library's mission, functions, organization, and services. This understanding might be second nature to a library employee but will need to be communicated to an external developer. Then you can drill down into the specific problem you are attempting to solve by investigating existing processes, workflows, transactions, and expected results. Be sure to involve users and listen carefully while developing a plan. Use project management tools and remain flexible.

Conduct a feasibility study to determine whether or not a project is worthwhile. Consider how the solution will fit into the current user environment. Determine what resources are needed to complete the project, and whether they are available. Keep in mind that resources can take many forms—finances, employee time, computer hardware, and software. Are there scheduling constraints and is it possible to complete the project in the available time? What are the costs of postponing the project, or not doing it at all?

The preliminary investigation should result in a project proposal. Depending on the scope of the project, this step may be accomplished very quickly or may take some extensive research. It is important to understand the problem or opportunity at hand—research the cause, the context, and the environment. Define the project scope and any constraints. Perform fact-finding to inform the investigation and analyze the project usability, cost, and benefit. Ultimately evaluate the feasibility of the project and create a document with this information. Projects that require

---

TEXTBOX 9.1

Project Proposal Outline

- Project title
- Team members
- Introduction and summary
- Preliminary investigation findings
  - Scope and constraints
  - Feasibility
  - Other findings
- Cost estimates
- Expected benefits
- Recommendations

resources and approval will benefit from a formalized project proposal that presents the findings and recommendations.

Strategies

Traditional software solutions are influenced by compatibility issues with existing hardware and software, such as the operating system. Traditional software is designed to be run on individual computer workstations or over local area networks. Web-based features are considered enhancements and scalability is greatly affected by local server and network limitations. Security, however, is easier to control because of the limited scope. There are still many relevant reasons to pursue a more traditional development setting, but in recent years much software development has shifted to the cloud.

Cloud-based software solutions are delivered over an internet-based framework. The web is the platform (as opposed to the operating system), and as a result the software solution is hardware and software agnostic—from the end user's perspective. The backend, of course, may still be built on a specific hardware and software platform. Cloud-based solutions are easily scalable and less dependent on desktop computing power because servers do at least some of the heavy lifting. They may require less local support because the infrastructure is likely provided as a service by the cloud provider, although they often require middleware to communicate with legacy systems. With cloud computing, the focus shifts away from which devices can store data and run applications to which devices provide the easiest access to the data and applications.

A decision must be made about whether to build an entirely new solution or to acquire something someone else has produced, then customize it. Even when a developer is starting from scratch, however, chances are that he or she is using software libraries and bits of code someone else developed as a foundation.

Who will develop the software? One option is to acquire a solution and use it as-is, straight out of the box. It may be that the vendor will provide limited customization during implementation. Another option is to acquire the solution but customize it locally or hire consultants to do the work. This is commonly done with open-source software systems, which are frequently easier to modify because of their exposed code, as opposed to proprietary software that is often closed-source and essentially a black box. A solution developed entirely in house may not have the same upfront financial obligations but will instead require staff expertise to create and maintain. Any in-house solutions should be carefully considered for future viability and support because you don't want to find yourself in a situation where the only person capable of maintaining the custom solution is not available.

Systems Development Life Cycle

There are many models for the software or systems development life cycle, such as the waterfall model, agile software development, rapid application development, and iterative development. They each have particular strengths that make them suited to certain situations or philosophies. What follows in this section is a more approachable life cycle called the *systems development life cycle* (SDLC), which also has a lot in common with other models.

Planning

During the planning phase, the initial project analysis takes place and documentation is produced. A planning document is well-defined, uncluttered by unnecessary details, and serves as a touchstone to keep the design process on target. Each objective listed should identify a particular task that the system must support. Identify the scope and boundary of the system to help prevent unnecessary growth of the project. Describe the reasons or justification for the project. What is the purpose? How

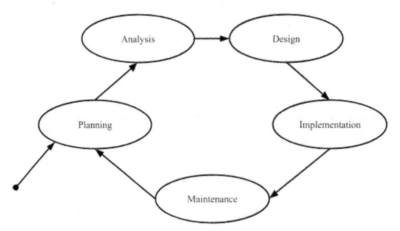

Figure 9.1 The Systems Development Life Cycle

much will it cost and how long will it take? What are the risks of doing the project? What will be the effect during the transition (e.g., during an ILS migration)? How will the project be assessed when it is complete?

Analysis

Requirements collection and *analysis* form the process of collecting and analyzing information about the organization to be supported by the system and uses this information to identify the requirements for the new system. Information can be collected by gathering documentation, conducting interviews, direct observation, and surveying users. Depending on the system in question, you may need to analyze the data and transaction requirements. Fact-finding can lead into information about the user requirements. Using that information, a logical model of the system can be created.

Object-oriented analysis is a specialized method that translates very well to object-oriented programming languages such as C++ and Java. It is a different paradigm that uses an abstract way of thinking, in which everything is an object.

Design

At the end of the analysis phase, a logical model is produced. The logical model then needs to be converted into a physical model and then implemented. The design phase creates the blueprint for implementation—although if the system can be purchased off the shelf, little design is needed. Then the only designing to do is within the constraints of the system and may involve enhancements or customizations.

The design phase can be broken down into several parts—a logical design phase during which you construct a model of the system to show the data and relationships, a physical design phase during which decisions are made about how to physically implement the logical design into the target platform, and the application design phase during which the user interface and application programs that use and process data are designed in detail. Data flow diagrams, decision trees, and entity-relationship (E-R) diagrams are tools that can be used to describe the processes and data that make up the new application. The system architecture translates the system's logical design into a physical structure that includes hardware, software, and processing methods.

Implementation

Implementation is the physical realization of the design in the target environment. Testing is a crucial part of the implementation phase to discover errors. Conduct usability testing to improve system performance and better meet the requirements of the users. The tasks that make up implementation include application development, documentation, testing, training, data conversion, and system changeover.

During application development, the designs prepared in the previous phase are used to begin the process of turning design logic into specific instructions that the computer system can execute. This is where any actual coding takes place.

As the system is developed, it is important to produce documentation. Program documentation describes the application for other programmers in terms that they will understand. Documentation is within the code, often as comments, that describe blocks or lines of code. Additional documentation, which describes the system's functions and implementation, configuration, and inputs and outputs, might be intended for system administrators and other IT staff. User documentation is meant for the end users, and includes help screens, tutorials, context help, user manuals, and FAQs.

During implementation, it is important to test the system—no matter how small the project might be. Try to break the system, use correct as well as incorrect data to try and expose any problems, and get independent users to test as well. The test environment should always be separate from the operational environment.

Finally, the day will come when it is time to go live with the finished product. Existing data is loaded into the new system. Automate as much as possible for efficiency, and check for any errors or missing data. A direct cutover will be the least expensive in terms of resources needed to maintain the system but can also be risky. If something goes wrong, a decision will have to be made whether to try and adjust on the fly or to roll back to the old system—if that is even possible. The least risky changeover is to run the old system in parallel with the new system. You can work out any bugs in the new system and make the changeover when everyone is comfortable with how it performs. However, this can introduce data inconsistencies if data is entered into one system and not the other. Other changeover options include running a small pilot with a select

> **TEXTBOX 9.2**
>
> **System Changeover Options**
>
> : Direct cutover
> - Parallel
> - Phased
> - Pilot

group of users before rolling the system out to everyone, or to conduct a phased changeover with the system implemented in stages.

Maintenance

The final phase of the system development life cycle is maintenance. It begins after the system has been fully implemented and the project has concluded. The maintenance phase involves monitoring the performance of the system, conducting maintenance and fine-tuning, and regular upgrades. User support is part of this phase, and can involve training, producing additional documentation, troubleshooting, and responding to user requests.

Development Methods

Aside from the previously mentioned SDLC, a number of other methods can be followed, with many shared characteristics but also particular strengths.

Joint Application Development

Rather than having the software team develop a system in isolation, joint application development (JAD) involves the users in the development process. The team represents a cross-section of stakeholders so that different perspectives inform the fact-finding process. They meet for a certain period to collect information and analyze the requirements for the new system. This method can be expensive, but the key users participate directly, and can result in more accurate requirements and a better understanding of project goals.

Rapid Application Development

Rapid application development (RAD) is another team-based technique; however, it goes beyond requirements modeling to parallel the entire SDLC process. A requirements planning phase combines the planning and analysis phases of the SDLC. Users interact with the systems analysts to develop prototypes that will eventually meet their needs. Users continue to participate during the program and application development. This method results in systems that are developed quickly and can save costs, but there is less time to develop quality.

Agile Methods

There are a number of agile methods for development, such as Scrum and Kanban, that share a number of things in common. Agile methods emphasize continuous feedback as prototypes are developed incrementally. They are flexible and efficient with frequent deliverables, although a high level of skill is required and a lack of structure can introduce risk.

PROGRAMMING

Programming is increasingly a common skill in many library roles. The depth of programming use may range from writing SQL queries while working with databases to writing short scripts that manipulate data to coding custom web applications. The development of full software suites in house does not happen often in libraries, but a basic understanding of programming can go a long way to help communicate with vendors and IT professionals as well as to improve your own workflows.

   Hello World is often the first program that many learn to write, regardless of the language used. In it, a variable is defined as the character string "Hello World" and a command is issued to print the variable, with the end result that "Hello World" is displayed on the screen. As you venture into the world of programming, there is a good chance that you will start with "Hello World."

Introduction to Programming

Block Coding

Visual programming languages (VPL) are a popular way to introduce programming concepts, particularly in K–12 educational settings. They use a graphical interface with blocks and symbols that represent commands and other elements of a program. The user can click and drag graphical elements to manipulate the program, and they are often based on actual programming languages. Blockly is a VPL developed by Google that can output code as JavaScript, PHP, Python, Lua, and Dart.[1] It is open source, and can be used as the foundation for other VPLs. The MIT Media Lab developed the block-based VPL, Scratch, primarily for use in childhood education. It can be used to create programs or animations, as well as with physical computing products such as Lego EV3, Makey Makey, and the BBC micro:bit.[2]

mBlock is a block-based VPL built on Scratch for use with Makeblock robots and Arduino boards, and can output code in Python.[3]

Software developers won't be using these block-based platforms to program library systems, but they are an approachable way to learn programming concepts and may also feature in library services that involve STEM activities.

Programming Basics

Pseudocode is often used as an intermediary step between the design logic and actual programming of code when planning a program. There isn't a strictly defined language for pseudocode; instead, it is a method to describe the different portions of a program, following the general structure of a program and describing the actions or processes that will take place. It can be thought of as a rough draft of a program, intended for the human programmers to work out what is needed without following the strict syntax and correct text a computer would need to process the program.

When writing a program, it is important to think about how the computer will proceed through the lines of code. When reading the code, the computer will start at the first line and continue line by line to the end. While executing, the program will also read line by line, but there may be times when it repeats an instruction or skips over some. For clarity, it is good practice to put each new instruction on a line of its own. We are going to use pseudocode to introduce some basic programming statements.

The WHILE command is a type of loop that is preceded by a condition. While the condition is met, the program will repeat the instructions. This will continue until the condition is no longer met.

```
WHILE (condition is met)
     Do this thing
```

REPEAT-UNTIL is similar to the WHILE loop but with an important distinction—the condition test for continuing the loop takes place after the instruction.

```
REPEAT
     Do this thing
UNTIL (condition is met)
```

IF-THEN-ELSE is a method for checking whether a condition is met before proceeding with an instruction. If the condition is met, then the program will proceed to the next line where the instruction is. Otherwise, the program will go on to the ELSE, and follow that instruction. It is also possible to nest IF-THEN statements within IF-THEN statements, increasing the complexity.

```
IF (condition is met)
Do this thing
ELSE
Do this other thing
```

Comments are documentation within the programming code. Different languages have their own specific ways to signify comments, usually with a particular character that tells the program to ignore the text that follows. Two ways that comments might be indicated use //, or /*, and */:

```
// ignore this entire line
/* ignore these several lines
you could
```

```
put a whole
paragraph here
*/
```

Some programming terminology follows:

- The *syntax* of a programming language refers to the rules, characters, and structure as strictly defined for that particular language. For example, there may be a specific way to signify the end of a line of code—perhaps with a semicolon.
- A *function* is a group of code within a program, often that receives some input, performs a task, then produces an output. Programs are made up of functions, which can be thought of as mini-programs within the larger program. It is also possible to call on functions that are frequently used and have been stored in an external *library* to save the programmer the time of rewriting a function that has already been created.
- A *variable* in a computer program is not unlike a variable in a mathematical formula. However, it isn't necessary to use a single character to signify the variable—variables can also be named, making their purpose more apparent. If a variable is declared within a function, it can only be used within that specific function. However, if it is declared outside of any functions, it is known as a *global variable* and can be used throughout the program.
- A *compiler* is used to translate a program written in a language understood by the human programmer into the language used by the platform that the program is to run on. For example, a program written in C++ needs to be compiled for a Windows desktop computer to execute it.
- An *integrated development environment* (IDE) is a program that a software developer can use to write code. It includes many helpful tools such as error detection, syntax hints, highlighted code, and version control.

Scripting

Scripts are small programs used to automate tasks. They are often written to make life easier and may range from scripts written by an individual user for their own personal needs, to those widely shared to help with complex or repetitive tasks. Many people have used scripting as an entry to point to programming. With a specific issue to solve that has a small scope, it is a great way to begin to learn a programming language.

In "Coding for Librarians: Learning by Example," Andromeda Yelton states:

> Unless you're aiming to be in a pure development role, it's not practical to learn all the software topics that might be of interest; by contrast, mastering the fundamentals of programming and learning how to make one language do a few useful things is an achievable goal that will give you powerful, flexible new ways to approach your everyday librarian work.[4]

A shell script can be used to automate tasks that you would do at the command line. If you work regularly with databases, SQL queries can be written as scripts so that they can be reused when needed. Scripts can be used to add dynamic functionality to web pages by using a language such as JavaScript. Python is a general-purpose programming language that can also be used for scripting.

Object-oriented Programming

Object-oriented programming is the standard method of software development when using current programming languages. The basic premise is that software is coded in chunks that are self-contained and meant to accomplish bits of the overall program. As a result of being self-contained, the objects have defined boundaries and are less likely to conflict. This also affords modularity of the code, as the self-contained objects can be reused or even copied for use in other programs. Another aspect of object-oriented programming is inheritance. Objects can contain other objects in a hierarchical structure, with the *child* inheriting the attributes of the *parent*.

Command Line Interface

An important thing to become comfortable with as a programmer is the command line. A command line interface (CLI) is a text-based interface in which the user types text commands to interact with the computer system, as opposed to the graphical user interface with images and graphics, which is commonly used with a mouse or touchscreen. MS-DOS is an example of an operating system in which the primary user interface is the command line. Modern operating systems also have a CLI, but it is a little hidden from the casual user.

The Microsoft Windows CLI is called Command Prompt. In macOS and Linux the CLI is Terminal. Once in the CLI, you can navigate the computer, issue commands, change configuration settings, run programs and scripts, and write to files.

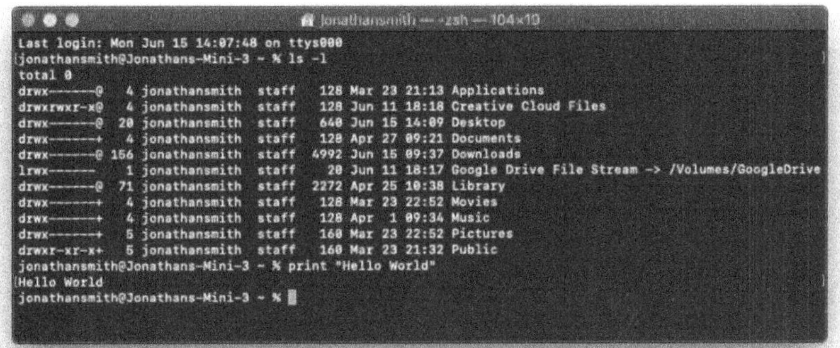

Figure 9.2 Screenshot of Terminal in macOS
macOS is a registered trademark of Apple Inc.

Programming Languages

There are far too many programming languages to list here without turning this book into a glossary. There are also many types of languages that may be classified according to their purpose or shared characteristics, such as how they are constructed. When a new language is developed, it is often built on the foundations of another language, borrowing concepts and making improvements, and so we have what may be considered "families" of programming languages. Some languages are closer to "natural language," and so are easier for humans to read, whereas others may appear more cryptic but allow the programmer to be more efficient in coding. What follows is a sampling of programming languages, including some of the more common languages that a programmer working in a library is likely to see.

C, C++, C#

C, C++, and C# are closely related. C is a general-purpose, procedural language, and was developed in the 1970s. C++ (pronounced: "see plus plus") was introduced in the late 1980s as an improvement

Software and Systems Development

to C and continues to be widely used in everything from embedded systems to computer games. C# (pronounced: "see sharp") is the most recent variation, and shares much in common with Java.

Java

Not to be confused with JavaScript, Java is an object-oriented language that can run on any operating system using Java Virtual Machine. It is used to program both desktop applications and web applications.

JavaScript

Considered one of the more readable and easier to learn languages, JavaScript is widely used for web scripting, and runs in the web browser on a client computer. It is the *J* in AJAX (asynchronous JavaScript and XML) and, along with Hypertext Markup Language and Cascading Style Sheets, is a good language to learn for web development.

Ruby

Ruby is also one of the more readable and easier to learn languages, and is often used for scripting. When used with Rails (also described as *Ruby on Rails*) it can be used for writing web applications. It shares many features with Python.

Perl

Perl originated as a scripting language for Unix and was influenced by C. It is often used for server-side scripting and forms the foundation of many websites. It is also used in cases similar to that of Python.

PHP

PHP is a web language used to create dynamic web pages and is often used in conjunction with SQL databases. It is a server-side scripting language, and the "P" in the popular web server stack Linux, Apache, MySQL, PHP.

Python

Python is popular and is widely considered an easy-to-learn language. It is a general-purpose language used for application development as well as scripting.

Structured Query Language

SQL is used specifically to interact with databases.

DATABASE DESIGN

Databases underlie many of the information systems that we interact with on a daily basis. They consist of structured sets of data, and are used by websites, search engines, and library-related information retrieval systems such as library catalogs, discovery interfaces, and e-journal collections. A database is a collection of related data, stored in tables. A database management system (DBMS) provides an interface between a database and the user or system who needs to access or manipulate the data. An application program is often the front end that a user interacts with—be it a library management system or a website. The application program sends requests to the DBMS, which obtains the appropriate data from the database and returns it to the application for the user.

The design process for a database is similar to that of other information systems in that it begins with a logical design, then the physical design, and finally the application design. The most common type of database used today is the relational database. In a relational model, associated data are linked, forming individual relationships and allowing data to be stored and retrieved according to their relationships. SQL is the most common programming language used to manage the data in relational databases.

Relational Database Design

The Relational Model

A file processing system stores data in one or more separate files. Some matching data are inevitably found in multiple files, requiring more space than if there was no redundant data. Data integrity problems can occur if updates are not applied to the appropriate data in every relevant file. In a relational database, data is stored in tables that are connected by common fields. These common fields are known as *keys*.

There are a number of advantages to using a database over a file-processing system. With a database, you can reduce redundancy and enforce consistency, and so have less chance for conflicting values. Security, such as access permissions, can be enforced to prevent certain users from viewing or manipulating specific parts of the database. The data exists independent of the way it is physically stored. As long as users are familiar with the relationships among the tables, they can access the data in an almost unlimited number of ways. You can even work with data from multiple tables simultaneously.

Entity-Relationship Modeling

E-R modeling is a top-down approach to database design. Start by identifying important data and the relationships between the data. Then add more details, such as the information you want to hold and any constraints on the data

Entities are sets of objects with the same properties, and can be physical or conceptual. Attributes are the properties of an entity or a relationship. They hold the values that describe each occurrence of an entity or relationship. The end result is an abstract model that displays the relationships between entities. After creating the E-R model, the next step is to translate it into a set of tables that represent the data. Then, you normalize the tables to eliminate data redundancy and anomalies.

Normalization

There are two goals to the normalization process: eliminating redundant data and ensuring data dependencies make sense. This is accomplished through an iterative series of refinements to the table structures until they meet criteria called *normal forms.* First normal form (1NF) is critical for a relational database, although it is common to take normalization as far as the third normal form (3NF). A table is in 1NF when the intersection of every column and record contains only one value. You must eliminate multiple values from each field and eliminate duplicate columns from the table. This is accomplished by creating separate tables for each group of related data and identifying each row with a primary key.

A table that meets the second normal form (2NF) is also in 1NF. 2NF applies to tables with composite primary keys; that is, the values in each non–primary-key column can be worked out from the values in all of the columns that make up the primary key. To achieve 2NF, remove subsets of data and place them in separate tables. Then create relationships between tables using foreign keys.

A table in 3NF must also be in 2NF (and 1NF). The values in all non–primary-key columns can be worked out from only the primary key column or columns and no other columns. To achieve 3NF, remove all columns that are not dependent on the primary key.

Establishing Table Structures

Every table contains at least one column known as the *primary key*, which uniquely identifies each record. A superkey is a column or set of columns that uniquely identifies a record within a table. A candidate key is a superkey that contains only the minimum number of columns necessary to have a unique identifier for each record. A primary key is the candidate key selected to identify each record uniquely. The use of a primary key enforces table-level integrity because each is unique, and so ensures that there are no duplicate records. The primary key is also used to establish relationships with records in other tables. Every table in a database should have a primary key column. The candidate keys not chosen to be the primary key are called *alternate keys.* A foreign key is data within a table that matches a primary key from a different table. This helps ensure relationship-level integrity, as the foreign key values must match existing primary key values from a different table.

Introduction to Structured Query Language

SQL is the standard data manipulation language used for relational databases. SQL can be used to create the database and table structures, for basic data management, and to perform both simple and complex queries. The following section gives you a brief taste of how to code in SQL.

The SELECT statement is the basis of every query you pose to the database. Of the following options that can be included in a query, only SELECT and FROM are required. WHERE is used to filter the results of the query, GROUP BY is used to summarize, HAVING is used to filter groups, and ORDER BY sorts the table. By default, the table is sorted in ascending order—although this can be overridden.

```
SELECT     columnName
FROM       tableName
WHERE      condition
GROUP BY   columnName
HAVING     condition
ORDER BY   columnName
```

Using a hypothetical database of library items, if you wanted a simple list of monograph titles you would write the query as:

SELECT title FROM Monographs;

The SELECT statement can accommodate multiple columns in a single request, so if you were interested in additional data the query might look like:

```
SELECT title, authorLastName, authorFirstName, ISBN, publicationYear
      FROM Monographs;
```

If you would like to see all of the data in a table, there is a shortcut to save the time of listing every single column:

```
SELECT *
FROM Monographs;
```

To sort the table first by author's last name in descending order, then by title in ascending order it would look like:

```
SELECT title, authorLastName, authorFirstName, ISBN, publicationYear
      FROM Monographs
ORDER BY authorLastName DESC, title ASC;
```

WHERE is used to filter the table and can be used with a number of different factors such as comparisons (=, < >, <, >, <=, >=), a range (BETWEEN), membership (IN), pattern matching (LIKE), and empty records (IS NULL). The operators NOT, AND, and OR can also be used. Building on the previous examples, if we only wanted books by authors with the last name of "Smith" we would write:

```
SELECT title, authorLastName, authorFirstName, ISBN, publicationYear
      FROM Monographs
      WHERE authorLastName = 'Smith';
```

This just gives you an idea of SQL commands; of course many more advanced queries can be made, and they can include mathematical calculations, pattern matching, aggregate functions, and nested subqueries.

SOFTWARE DEVELOPMENT TOPICS

Application Programming Interfaces

Increasingly, systems are including APIs that allow programmers to write custom scripts or programs that extract data from or directly interact with the system. An API is a defined method or protocol for communicating with a system and may be created for a web-based system, a database, an operating system, or any other software system. Documentation is critical for describing how a script or program can interact with the system.

Sometimes an API key is necessary for a program or script to use an API. This is a unique string of characters used to identify an application or project to the API, which does a check to ensure that the user of the key has been granted access.

APIs present an opportunity to developers. Many systems, including library-centric systems and databases, provide APIs as a way to access data. As an example, the cloud-hosted library management system Ex Libris Alma makes an API available to customers to access data and workflows.[5] Harvard Library[6] and the Library of Congress[7] both make collection data freely available via APIs. It isn't necessary to write a long, complex program to take advantage of APIs; frequently, a short script is enough to accomplish a simple task to extract and manipulate data that has been made accessible.

Open Source Software

Open-source software (OSS) is created with the intent that anyone can view the source code, modify it, and create derivatives. It is also often freely available. The Linux operating system is a famous example of OSS. OSS is often developed by a collaborative user community that may be spread around the world. They use a public repository with version control to share code and documentation, and to coordinate work. GitHub, GitLab, SourceForge, and Bitbucket are all popular code repositories used by open source software projects.

OSS is usually free; the business model is built around offering services to customers. These services may include hosting, implementation, customization, and user support. Often the companies providing these services are also active participants in developing the software.

On its face, "free software" may sound appealing to the user, although anyone considering the adoption of OSS should consider the total cost of ownership. The price tag may be negligible, but other costs may include customization to the software or system, whether in house or by a vendor, and the cost of maintenance, again by using in-house resources, which would require time and training, or by an external vendor. It is also important to make sure that the OSS is under active development, releasing regular updates and fixes. If you will be supporting the software locally, good documentation and an active user community will be critical.

Aside from the many famous OSS examples available, there are also a number of products that have been developed by or for the library community. Koha and Evergreen are open-source integrated library systems. LibLime is a company that provides cloud hosting and support for Koha. SubjectsPlus is a library-centric website platform, and Zotero is a popular citation management tool. In the digital library and institutional repository space, Dspace, Eprints, and Omeka are open source solutions.

SUMMARY

Libraries are often participants in software and systems development from the customer perspective, providing design requirements, feedback and input, and feature requests. Development also takes place in libraries, often on a smaller scale, that involves in-house projects. Individuals also take on development projects to improve systems, add features, or create solutions that make their life easier.

The development process should be approached as a project to manage, with an analysis conducted that examines points such as the scope and constraints, the feasibility of the project, the estimated cost, and the expected benefits. The SDLC is a well-known process that incorporates five phases: planning, analysis, design, implementation, and maintenance. There are many other methods as well, including JAD, RAD, and agile methods such as Scrum and Kanban.

The ability to write programs or scripts is a useful skill for library employees whether improving a system used in the library, creating a widget for the website, or conducting data analysis. Programming languages share basic elements, and pseudocode can be generally applied to describe the different parts of a program when used to plan a program out in easy to understand language. There are many different languages, with a variety of purposes, strengths, and ranges of difficulty.

Database design is an important topic for library employees to understand, because databases are ubiquitous in libraries. The relational model involves matching data using *keys* and E-R modeling. SQL is the standard data manipulation language used for relational databases.

KEY TERMS

Application programming interface (API)
Business analysis
Coding

Command line interface (CLI)
Comments
Database design

Database management system (DBMS)
Entity-relationship (E-R) model
Normal forms
Open-source software (OSS)
Programming language
Project proposal
Proprietary software
Pseudocode

Relational database
Script
Software development
Structured Query Language (SQL)
System changeover
Systems development life cycle (SDLC)
Total cost of ownership

QUESTIONS

1. What are some of the things that can be accomplished through writing code?
2. What are some of the reasons that a library might embark on a software or systems development project?
3. List and describe the five phases of the SDLC.
4. Define the following programming terms: *pseudocode, syntax, function, variable, compiler*, and *IDE*.
5. Describe the relational model of a database system.
6. What should factor into the total cost of ownership for a new system?
7. What are some of the things to consider when evaluating OSS?

ACTIVITIES

1. Identify a software or systems development need for a real or imaginary library. Create a project proposal to solve this need. Use the project proposal outline from this chapter to structure the document.
2. Complete a programming tutorial or workshop in the coding language of your choice. See the chapter resources for some suggested sites (e.g., Code.org, Codeacademy, LinkedIn Learning, and Treehouse).

FURTHER READING

Engard, Nicole C., Kara Mia Jalkowski, Denise M. Erickson, and Scott Bacon. *More Library Mashups: Exploring New Ways to Deliver Library Data.* Medford, NJ: Information Today, 2015.

Nemeth, Evi, Garth Snyder, and Trent R. Hein. "Scripting and the Shell." In *UNIX and Linux System Administration Handbook*, 5th ed. New York: Pearson Education, 2018.

Thomsett-Scott, Beth, ed. *The Librarian's Introduction to Programming Languages (A LITA Guide).* Lanham, MD: Rowman & Littlefield, 2016.

Tilley, Scott R., and Henry Rosenblatt. *Systems Analysis and Design*, 11th ed. Boston: Cengage Learning, 2016.

Viescas, John L. *SQL Queries for Mere Mortals: A Hands-on Guide to Data Manipulation in SQL*, 4th ed. Boston: Addison-Wesley, 2018.

Weisman, John. "Developing Applications in the Era of Cloud-based SaaS Library Systems." *Code4Lib Journal* 26 (2014). Accessed on February 29, 2020. https://journal.code4lib.org/articles/10029.

Yelton, Andromeda. "Coding for Librarians: Learning by Example." *Library Technology Reports* 51, no. 6 (2015).

API Case Studies

Germann, Jonathan E. "Approaching the Largest 'API': Extracting Information from the Internet with Python." *Code4Lib Journal* 39 (2018). Accessed on February 29, 2020. https://journal.code4lib.org/articles/13197.

Hodges, David W., and Kevin Schlottmann. "Reporting from the Archives: Better Archival Migration Outcomes with Python and the Google Sheets API." *Code4Lib Journal* 46. (2019). Accessed on February 29, 2020. https://journal.code4lib.org/articles/14871.

Neumann, Mandy, Jan Steinberg, and Philipp Schaer. "Web-Scraping for Non-Programmers: Introducing OXPath for Digital Library Metadata Harvesting." *Code4Lib Journal* 38. (2017). Accessed on February 29, 2020. https://journal.code4lib.org/articles/13007.

Ramshaw, Veronica, Véronique Lecat, and Thomas Hodge. "WMS, APIs and LibGuides: Building a Better Database A-Z List." *Code4Lib Journal* 41 (2018). Accessed on February 29, 2020. https://journal.code4lib.org/articles/13688.

Suranofsky, Michelle, and Lisa McColl. "MatchMarc: A Google Sheets Add-on That Uses the WorldCat Search API." *Code4Lib Journal* 46 (2019). Accessed on February 29, 2020. https://journal.code4lib.org/articles/14813.

Zweibel, Stephen. "Scraping BePress: Downloading Dissertations for Preservation." *Code4Lib Journal* 47 (2020). Accessed on February 29, 2020. https://journal.code4lib.org/articles/15016.

RESOURCES

Blockly: https://developers.google.com/blockly
Code.org: https://code.org/
Code4Lib—Libraries Sharing Code: https://wiki.code4lib.org/Libraries_Sharing_Code
Codeacademy: https://www.codecademy.com/
Library Carpentry: https://librarycarpentry.org/
LinkedIn Learning: https://www.lynda.com/
mBlock: https://www.mblock.cc/
Scratch: https://scratch.mit.edu/
Stack Overflow: https://stackoverflow.com/
Treehouse: https://teamtreehouse.com/

Code Repositories

BitBucket: https://bitbucket.org/
GitHub: https://github.com/
GitLab: https://about.gitlab.com/
SourceForge: https://sourceforge.net/

Language Specific MARC Resources

PHP: File_MARC https://pear.php.net/package/File_MARC/
Python: pymarc https://pypi.org/project/pymarc/
Ruby: ruby-marc https://github.com/ruby-marc/ruby-marc/

Open Source Library Software

Dspace: https://duraspace.org/dspace/
Eprints: https://www.eprints.org/

Evergreen: https://evergreen-ils.org/
Koha: https://koha.org/
LibLime: https://liblime.com/
Omeka: https://omeka.org/
SubjectsPlus: http://www.subjectsplus.com/
Zotero: https://www.zotero.org/

NOTES

1. "Blockly," Google Developers, accessed on March 9, 2020, https://developers.google.com/blockly.
2. "Scratch," MIT Media Lab, accessed on March 9, 2020, https://scratch.mit.edu/.
3. "mBlock," Makeblock Co., accessed on March 9, 2020, https://www.mblock.cc/.
4. Andromeda Yelton, "Coding for Librarians: Learning by Example," *Library Technology Reports* 51, no. 6 (2015).
5. "REST APIs," *Ex Libris*, accessed on March 9, 2020, https://developers.exlibrisgroup.com/alma/apis/.
6. "Harvard Library APIs and Datasets," Harvard Library, accessed on March 9, 2020, https://library.harvard.edu/services-tools/harvard-library-apls-datasets.
7. "About the loc.gov JSON API," Library of Congress, accessed on March 9, 2020, https://libraryofcongress.github.io/data-exploration/.

10

Specialized and Emerging Technology Services

Libraries serve an important function for patrons when providing equitable access to specialized and emerging technology. A number of different services have developed around emerging technologies, thanks in part to libraries adapting their culture to support content and knowledge creation in addition to content consumption. These new services tend to be specialized, depending on the activities supported. Digital media labs use high-performance computers and specialized software for audio, video, and graphical production. Makerspaces involve a variety of equipment and tools for the fabrication of physical objects, often (but not always) with a digital component to the creation process. Immersive learning labs are emerging as educational spaces that incorporate augmented and virtual reality.

This chapter discusses the creative and innovative potential for these specialized services. It then describes several types of spaces and services, including 3-D printing, 3-D scanning, and extended reality, among others. Finally, the chapter reviews a few trends that have been identified as future possibilities.

CREATIVE AND INNOVATIVE SPACES

Libraries offer a variety of spaces for patrons, from quiet spaces for focus and reflection to noisy, collaborative spaces. The addition of creative and innovative spaces enable a variety of learning activities and events, and can serve as a lab for experimentation, learning, and knowledge creation. They empower patrons with equitable access to emerging technologies that support experiential and active learning, creativity, and innovation.

Creative spaces are an opportunity to form partnerships—with industrial or community organizations, or for academic libraries to collaborate with other departments and disciplinary schools. These collaborations can bring in expertise that may help guide programs or even hands-on help working with patrons and conducting workshops.

The mission statement of the Sonoma State University Library Makerspace exemplifies the aim of many creative spaces:

> The SSU Makerspace is a place to dream, make, and innovate. SSU students, faculty, and staff are invited to explore digital fabrication, prototyping, and a wide range of technology to transform idea to reality. All disciplines and skill sets can experience new technologies through workshops, experimentation, and free-play. By providing the tools and ingredients, we encourage creativity and inquiry, and facilitate cross-disciplinary collaboration.[1]

Creative spaces have the potential to encourage knowledge creation and sharing, innovation, and invention, while providing a comfortable working environment for patrons with a variety of skill sets and backgrounds. Whether through direct instruction or self-directed learning, patrons may gain the ability to:

- Assess and select appropriate technologies for the planned project.
- Gain familiarity with the design and creation process.
- Apply principles of problem solving and iterative design.
- Function collegially in an interdisciplinary environment.
- Evaluate methodology and techniques for effectiveness and usability.
- Engage in self-directed improvement.

The physical space used can take a variety of forms, depending on purpose and constraints. Pop-up or mobile experiences in the form of a cart with supplies and equipment can bring a makerspace or virtual reality (VR) to a multipurpose space or classroom. Some activities benefit from smaller rooms, such as audio production, where the environment can be controlled and interruptions are minimal. Other activities may need space to spread out, with a lot of surface workspace and an assortment of tools at hand, as in a makerspace. Certain activities might produce a significant amount of noise, or have particular infrastructure requirements—so it is important to be thoughtful when planning the location of a creative space.

LIBRARY SERVICES

Digital Media Labs

Digital media labs are not new to libraries, but have been continually evolving as technologies change. They tend to support creative digital endeavors that might involve activities such as audio-video production, graphic design, video game design, animation, and conversion of analog formats to digital formats. They typically have specific computer requirements, along with additional equipment and specialized software. The space used could be a lab with a set of computer workstations, small rooms (or studios) with a computer and special equipment, and storage for equipment lending.

Hardware and Equipment

Some of the activities that take place in digital media labs require computers with generous amounts of memory, processing power, and hefty graphics processing capabilities. Video production, animation, and game design are among the most demanding. In addition to a good computer with a good-size monitor, there can be quite a bit of specialized equipment. For audio production, you may want microphones, a mixing console, a midi keyboard, and to consider soundproofing a room for audio recording. For video production you may want cameras, lighting kits, and possibly a green-screen setup. Conversion of analog media to digital requires specialized equipment appropriate to the media being digitized (e.g., a VHS player). Some libraries have specialized equipment like cameras and lighting kits available for patrons to borrow. Most other creative activities in digital media labs can be accomplished simply with a good computer and the right software.

Software

An assortment of software is available for various creative digital activities, ranging from free and open-source (FOSS) to proprietary software. A sample list of software for various creative activities appears in Table 10.1.

Table 10.1. Digital Media Software

Software	Activity	URL
Autodesk Maya	3-D computer animation	https://www.autodesk.com/products/maya/
Blender (FOSS)	3-D computer animation	https://www.blender.org/
Audacity (FOSS)	audio production	https://www.audacityteam.org/
Apple GarageBand	audio production	https://www.apple.com/mac/garageband/
Unity	game development	https://unity.com/
Avid Pro Tools	music production	https://www.avid.com/pro-tools
Adobe Photoshop	raster graphics	https://www.adobe.com/products/photoshop.html
GIMP (FOSS)	raster graphics	https://www.gimp.org/
Adobe Illustrator	vector graphics	https://www.adobe.com/products/illustrator.html
CorelDRAW	vector graphics	https://www.coreldraw.com/
Inkscape (FOSS)	vector graphics	https://inkscape.org/
Adobe Premiere Pro	video production	https://www.adobe.com/products/premiere.html
Apple iMovie	video production	https://www.apple.com/imovie/
Apple Final Cut Pro	video production	https://www.apple.com/final-cut-pro/

3-D Printing

Perhaps one of the more familiar digital fabrication technologies, 3-D printing is exemplified by its recent, widespread adoption in libraries. When a library has a makerspace, the 3-D printer is often located there, although many libraries that do not have makerspaces yet offer 3-D printing as a service.

Starting with a computer file of a 3-D model, the user loads the 3-D model into software known as a *slicer*. This software "slices" the model into layers, determining the literal pathway that the 3-D printer will follow to create the printed object. This is output as g-code, a file that the printer controller software interprets and uses to operate the 3-D printer.

In fused-filament fabrication (FFF), the 3-D printer melts plastic filament, which it deposits onto a flat surface known as the *build plate*, similar to the way a crafting glue gun extrudes a line of melted glue. The print head or print bed moves around on an X- and Y-axis, while the print head extrudes a single layer of plastic. Then the print head moves up a tiny bit on the Z-axis to create space for another layer of plastic, which it deposits on top of the previous layer. This process repeats until the 3-D printer finishes creating the objects.

Although not nearly as common in consumer or hobbyist applications as FFF printers, it is also possible to obtain stereolithography apparatus (SLA) printers. In this case, the printer begins with a reservoir full of resin. The build plate sits just inside the resin, and a laser is used to cure the resin in layers. SLA printers aren't as common as FFF printers because there are far fewer models available in the consumer market. They can also be messy and smelly, but make very detailed prints.

3-D printing uses a process known as *additive manufacturing*, so called simply because an object is created by adding material to material. The material cannot be deposited into midair; it must build

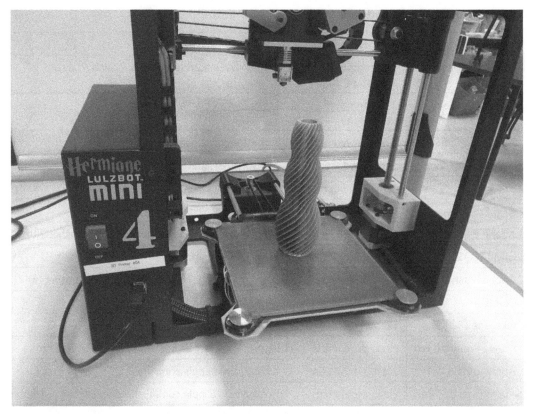

Figure 10.1 LulzBot Mini FFF 3D printer

upon a surface, whether the build plate or other material. For parts of a model that need to be printed in midair, say the midpoint of an arch, lightweight supports need to be created. Often this is a simple matter of checking a box in the slicer software, which then automatically adds the supports in the appropriate locations. After the print is complete, the user cuts or breaks off the supports, and perhaps finishes the surface by sanding. Another option is available, however, for printers with multiple print heads that can work with more than one material at the same time. Polyvinyl alcohol (PVA) is a water-soluble material that 3-D printers can use. If the supports are printed using PVA, upon completion the object can be placed in water for a few hours while the PVA dissolves. This affords the ability to print highly detailed or hollow objects that would otherwise be difficult or impossible to remove the supports from.

> TEXTBOX 10.1
>
> **List of FFF Plastic Filament Types**
>
> - acrylonitrile butadiene styrene (ABS)
> - polylactic acid (PLA)
> - polyethylene terephthalate, glycol-modified (PETG)

A number of consumer-level 3-D printers are available on the market that will sit comfortably on a desktop. LulzBot, Prusa, and Ultimaker are manufacturers of highly rated and popular desktop 3-D printers. Many websites publish reviews of 3-D printers and *Make:* publishes an annual guide to digital fabrication that is full of reviews and specifications.[2]

3-D Scanning

Digitization has greatly increased the availability of unique and rare items, although more commonly it is accomplished through scanning or photographing flat items in the form of papers, photographs, or maps. Scanning in 3-D affords the ability to digitize three-dimensional objects such as realia, artwork, and historical artifacts. Using a 3-D scanner results in a digital object that is a 3-D model, which might

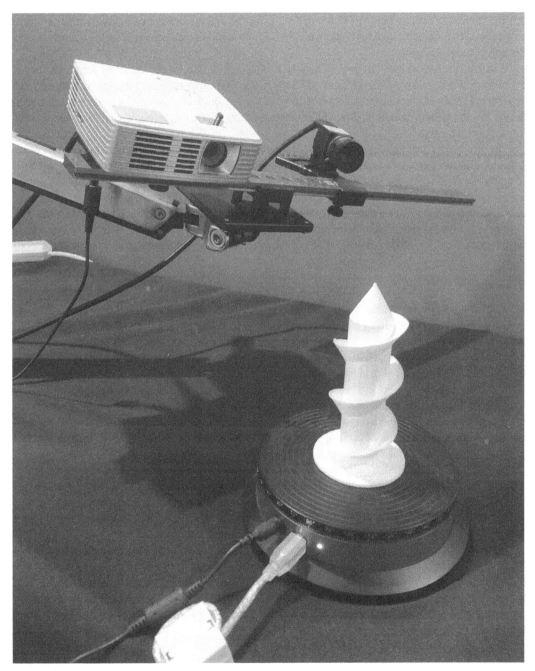

Figure 10.2 David SLS-2 3D scanner

then be made available in an online repository or gallery. An architect or video game designer might use a scanned object as an asset in the virtual environment. Others might study the 3-D model, or import it into 3-D modeling software to edit the 3-D model. In a makerspace, a user might 3-D print the 3-D model, thus copying a physical item.

Three different methods are commonly used for 3-D scanning: photogrammetry, laser triangulation, and structured light scanning (SLS). In photogrammetry, a camera is used to take multiple images at different angles in relation to the object. Software then examines the images and looks for common visual structures from which to form a 3-D model. The equipment can range from a common smartphone that has a camera to multiple expensive high-definition cameras set up in an array around the object to be scanned.

Laser triangulation involves projecting a laser dot or line onto an object, while a camera that is offset from the laser observes the position. Software is then able to determine the distance to the laser image on the surface of the object and construct a 3-D model following multiple measurements. Relatively inexpensive desktop 3-D scanners that use laser triangulation are available on the market for use by hobbyists.

SLS involves a projector and one or two cameras offset from the position of the projector. Black and white patterns of light are projected onto the object while the camera watches. Software is able to discern how the patterns have been deformed by the object, and construct a 3-D model. Multiple scans are taken from a variety of angles, and the software will stitch the models together by matching points that have similar three-dimensional features. The final 3-D model can be full color; however, SLS does have a weakness when scanning transparent or shiny surfaces. SLS scanners come in a variety of form factors, from handheld scanners that can be taken into the field to desktop varieties.

Makerspaces

Much of the equipment found in library makerspaces relate to digital fabrication, using computer-aided design and computer-controlled equipment to produce physical objects. As hobbyist and consumer-level equipment have become more reliable and easier to use, it has become easier for users to rapidly prototype ideas, iterating improvements to product designs with a variety of tools at their fingertips. Not everything in a makerspace is related to digital fabrication, however. Textiles, arts and crafts, and electronics are just as common in library makerspaces. Other maker realms not usually found in libraries include woodworking, metalworking, and studio art such as ceramics. While library makerspaces will usually have hand tools and perhaps a selection of small power tools, the type of equipment and materials found in workshops and studios tend to be of a sort that create an amount of noise or mess that is not welcome in many libraries.

The equipment found in a makerspaces requires infrastructure considerations as well. An abundance of power is needed to run all of the equipment, and sufficient networking will be necessary for the computers used in design or for operating the equipment. Depending on the types of material and equipment used, ventilation might be a concern. Certain activities, like soldering, laser cutting, and 3-D printing may have air filtration or ventilation requirements.

Safety must also be planned for. Makerspaces may include equipment and tools that can seriously injure someone or start a fire if used improperly. A first aid kit should be in an obvious location, and a fire extinguisher is a must if there is a laser cutter. Patrons should be taught how to operate tools and equipment in a safe manner. There are many examples of library makerspaces requiring patrons to prove their ability to operate equipment safely or to complete a training course before being given free access to equipment.

Makerspace Equipment

Libraries should expect to be hands-on providing technical support for makerspace equipment. A significant amount of maintenance can be involved, but it is certainly doable. A lot of hobbyist and consumer maker equipment was originally developed with a DIY approach by enthusiasts. They often have limited warranties, and the amount of support provided is mixed. Look for products that have robust user communities as they will often be the main source of documentation and support.

There is now a list of equipment required for a makerspace to be successful. The tools and technologies selected often reflect the interests of the users, as well as the infrastructure and resource constraints of the library. Different library makerspaces may choose to focus in one direction or another, or may form partnerships with external organizations to support activities that may not be practical in the library. A library makerspace might have a selection of technologies from the following list. This doesn't include hand tools or other tools used in conjunction with the following equipment:

- 3-D printer
- 3-D scanner
- Computer numerical control (CNC) mill
- Computers
- Electronic components and kits
- Embroidery machine
- Extended reality (XR) technology
- Laser cutter and engraver
- Microcontrollers (e.g., Arduino)
- Printed circuit board (PCB) mill
- Robotics kits
- Serger
- Sewing machine
- Single-board computers (e.g., Raspberry Pi)
- Vinyl cutter

3-D Modeling

The workflow for a number of different digital technologies incorporate 3-D modeling at some point. CNC milling, 3-D printing, 3-D scanning, and VR can all touch on 3-D modeling. For beginners, Autodesk Tinkercad is a web browser–based 3-D modeling application that is approachable, and can import and export the popular file formats STL and OBJ. Autodesk Fusion 360, Autodesk Meshmixer, Blender, and Trimble SketchUp are all 3-D modeling applications for more advanced users.

Computer Numerical Control Milling, Engraving, and Cutting

CNC equipment involves milling, engraving, or cutting raw materials according to a 2-D or 3-D design on a computer. A variety of machines use the CNC method to work with a variety of materials, including wood, soft metals, blank circuit boards, plastic, and vinyl. Whereas 3-D printing is an additive manufacturing process, CNC milling is a subtractive manufacturing process because it involves the removal of material until the desired shape is finished. A CNC mill uses a bit—very similar to a drill bit—for cutting and carving away the raw material. Some CNC mills can work with copper circuit board blanks to create PCBs by engraving pathways and drilling through-holes for components. Vinyl cutters and CNC machines for crafting work strictly in two dimensions to cut designs out of adhesive vinyl, heat-transfer vinyl, paper, and cardstock using a sharp blade.

Figure 10.3 Inventables Carvey CNC mill

An important note for libraries is that CNC mills can be quite noisy, depending on the material being milled. Some mills also have enclosures that keep the mess of shavings contained until the job is done; then the user can vacuum it out with a shop vac.

Electronics

Activities involving electronics may range from kits and toys that teach basic electronics to using breadboards for prototyping ideas to soldering components onto circuit boards. Microcontrollers such as the Arduino Uno are circuit boards that work with sensors, buttons, lights, and motors, and can

Table 10.2. Selected CNC Milling Machines

Vendor	Model	Cutting area	Notes
Bantam Tools	PCB Milling Machine	14 × 11.4 × 4.1 cm (5.5 × 4.5 × 1.6 in)	enclosed
Carbide 3-D	Nomad 883 Pro	20.3 × 20.3 × 7.6 cm (8 × 8 × 3 in)	enclosed
Inventables	X-Carve	75 × 75 × 6.5 cm (29.5 × 29.5 × 2.5 in)	open

Figure 10.4 Adafruit Circuit Playground Express and Arduino Uno

add interactivity to many projects. They can be used to create robots, flying drones, weather stations, and wearable, light-up costumes, among many other creations. Single-board computers such as the Raspberry Pi include all of the circuitry and processors of a computer on a single board. They usually employ a flavor of Linux for their operating system and have input/output ports for attaching peripherals such as a monitor, keyboard, and mouse.

Adafruit and SparkFun are vendors that specialize in microcontrollers and associated kits. Digi-Key Electronics and Jameco Electronics are vendors that provide more general electronic components and parts. Guides that list specifications and help in selecting the appropriate board are published online by Adafruit,[3] SparkFun,[4] and *Make:*.[5]

Table 10. 3. Selected Circuit Boards

Vendor	Model	Notes
Adafruit	Circuit Playground Express (CPX)	Small entry-level board with features for learning Arduino.
Arduino	Uno R3	Versatile board with many features.
Arduino	Nano	Compact version of the Uno.
BBC	micro:bit	Low-cost educational board.
Raspberry Pi	4 Model B	Popular single-board computer.
Raspberry Pi	Zero	Small Raspberry Pi with limited features
SparkFun	LilyPad Arduino	Intended for e-textiles and wearable technology
SparkFun	RedBoard Artemis	Arduino Uno clone with Bluetooth

Specialized and Emerging Technology Services　　　　　　　**153**

Laser Cutting and Engraving

Laser cutters are enclosed machines that use a carbon dioxide laser to cut through or engrave material with a high degree of precision. Depending on the power of the laser (measured in watts), it can be used to engrave and cut entirely through material such as wood, acrylic, leather, cardboard, and cloth. It can also engrave—but not cut—material such as glass, anodized aluminum, ceramic, and coated metals. It is important to note that certain plastics containing chloride, such as PVC, release a highly toxic chlorine gas and should never be used in a laser cutter. As a matter of course, the vinyl cutter needs to be ventilated during operation to remove smoke and fumes, and so will need to either expel fumes outside of the building or use a dedicated filter to scrub the air.

Figure 10.5 Epilog Zing 60-watt laser cutter

Robotics

The robotics found in library makerspaces often match those used for educational purposes. Lego Mindstorms EV3 is a system produced by Lego that includes a programmable computer brick that works with a variety of sensors and motors and is also compatible with regular Lego bricks. Makeblock produces a number of educational robotics kits, including the mBot, an Arduino-based platform that can be programmed using a drag-and-drop block programming interface. There are many other Arduino-based robot kits and platforms that range in skill level from those appropriate for young children to college engineering students.

Textiles

Many makerspaces include technology for working with textiles. Sewing machines, embroidery machines, and sergers are all tools commonly employed. Software that works with digital embroidery is capable of taking an image file and converting it into a pattern that will work with an embroidery machine. The result is a colorful embroidered representation of the image file. Wearable technology marries electronics to textiles. Some microcontrollers are designed to be sewn into clothing, and can use conductive thread to incorporate sensors, lights, and other electronics.

Extended Reality

XR describes the spectrum of digitally enhanced realities, from augmented reality (AR) to full VR, and mixed reality (MR) between. They use at minimum a headset through which the user views the extended reality and sensors that track movement of the headset, allowing the user to "look around." Google Cardboard is an example that uses a mobile phone that is placed into a cardboard headset. Some examples, such as the Oculus Rift S, use handheld controllers with movements that are tracked by sensors on the headset, or set up in the room. Other products, such as the Microsoft HoloLens 2 watch the user's hand and finger movements to control and interact with virtual elements. Some products are required to be wired to a computer to take advantage of increased graphic processing power, while others are not tethered to a machine.

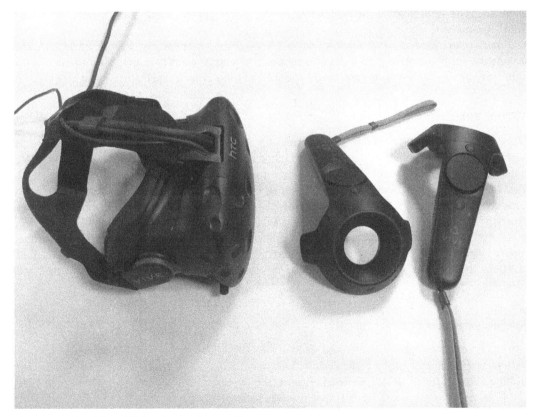

Figure 10.6 HTC Vive VR headset and controllers

VR is meant to be immersive, with the visual experience fully computer-generated. Using a headset and handheld motion controllers add to the experience. AR involves the ability for the user to see the physical world around them, with computer-generated elements projected into their field of vision. With MR, the user can also see the physical world, but the computer-generated elements are affected by the real physical environment—for example, by being aware of the size of a room or physical objects that are present.

XR headsets include:

- Google Glass 2
- HTC Vive
- Microsoft HoloLens 2
- Oculus Rift S
- Samsung HMD Odyssey+
- Valve Index

XR is used in a variety of recreational, educational, and industrial applications. Video gaming has helped bring XR to the mainstream, from VR video games on high-end gaming machines, to AR mobile games such as Pokémon GO that can be played on a cellular phone. XR can also be used by an architect to conduct a virtual walkthrough of a building, a biology student might use it to study anatomy by conducting a virtual dissection, an artist can "paint" in three dimensions using a program like Google TiltBrush, and an engineer can use it to "view" hidden infrastructure such as pipes while standing inside a building. Immersive learning is an emerging practice that applies XR to an educational environment.

Aside from the educational applications for XR, specific uses for libraries and cultural institutions include the ability to view digitized three-dimensional objects, the ability to virtually visit cultural institutions such as museums, and the ability to experience live or recorded cultural events.

FUTURE TRENDS

Trying to predict the future is a difficult task. However, keeping an eye on emerging trends in industry, society, and in education, as well as watching technological developments in general, can help signal potential trends that will affect libraries. Keeping current with library literature is certainly one way to keep tabs. There are also a few organizations in particular worth watching. The American Library Association (ALA) Annual and Midwinter conferences normally include a panel of experts who discuss emerging technology issues and applications in a session titled "Top Technology Trends." EDUCAUSE, a nonprofit association that focuses on IT in higher education publishes a well-researched annual report called the *Horizon Report*. The Pew Research Center also conducts research into the internet and other technologies. An ALA initiative called the "Library of the Future" publishes newsletters and identifies trends, as well.

Artificial Intelligence

Artificial intelligence appears as a future trend in the 2018 Midwinter[6] and 2019 Midwinter[7] editions of the Library and Information Technology Association (LITA) Top Technology Trends, the 2018[8] and 2019[9] editions of the EDUCAUSE Horizon Report, and the last edition of the New Media Consortium (NMC) Horizon Report: Library Edition,[10] which was published in 2017.

According to †he Center for the Future of Libraries:

Artificial intelligence seeks to create "intelligent" machines that work and react more like humans. AI developments rely on deep learning, machine learning, and natural language processing that help computers accomplish specific tasks by processing large amounts of training data to help the system recognize patterns, input data to drive predictions, and feedback data for improving accuracy over time.

People already interact with systems developed using artificial intelligence on a regular basis, whether they realize it or not. Personalization features of Facebook, Amazon, and Google use algorithms designed to learn from user behavior. Facial recognition, driverless cars, chatbots, voice assistants, location-based services, and recommender engines all feature the work of artificial intelligence.

The 2019 EDUCAUSE Horizon Report predicts a time-to-adoption horizon for institutes of higher education of two to three years. Aside from general uses like recommender engines and personalization, possible library applications might include automated processing of digitized collections, such as in automatic metadata creation. Libraries are also positioned to keep an eye on how artificial intelligence is used at large, and to advocate for user privacy and other ethical concerns.

Blockchain

Blockchain was noted at the 2018 ALA Annual conference during the LITA Top Technology Trends session.[11] It was also highlighted in the 2019 EDUCAUSE Horizon Report as an "important development in educational technology" with a "time-to-adoption" of four to five years.[12]

Bitcoin and other cryptocurrencies are perhaps the most well-known applications of blockchain technology. A blockchain is a list of linked records—each containing information about transactions, a digital signature, and cryptologically linked to other records. It avoids the need for a centralized authority to maintain and verify its authenticity, as blockchains are decentralized—with copies of the blockchain distributed over a trusted network. The result is a secure, authoritative digital ledger that is auditable and transparent.

As noted in the time-to-adoption by EDUCAUSE, this technology is still a number of years from widespread practical application. Nonetheless, library technologists are paying attention as there are many potential uses. Possible library applications include transaction logs, patron records, bibliographic metadata, resource sharing records, and identity management.

Internet of Things

The Internet of Things (IoT) was noted at the 2019 ALA Annual conference during the LITA Top Technology trends session,[13] and in the last edition of the NMC Horizon Report: Library Edition (2017),[14] with a "time-to-adoption" of four to five years.

We introduced the concept of the IoT in chapter 5, "Networking." IoT devices may take the form of low-tech household items or high-tech, sensor-rich objects. They are able to communicate with each other and with a network using wireless technologies like Wi-Fi, Bluetooth low energy, radiofrequency identification, and near-field communication. They may include sensors to record and transmit data, may operate the functionality of equipment, may be connected to the internet, and may control or be controlled by other IoT devices.

IoT devices have recently become prevalent in the consumer market as "smart home" devices, and include devices such as light bulbs, thermostats, and door bells, all of which can be operated remotely or programmed to respond to specific environmental stimuli. Many other applications are emerging, including smart traffic sensors, wearable technologies like smart watches, implanted medical devices, and sensors used to transmit data about urban infrastructure.

Library applications for IoT are still emerging, but there are many possibilities: environmental monitoring for special collections or archival materials, assessment of physical spaces and patron behavior, smart inventory tracking and auditing, wayfinding apps, and self-checkout and return. There are privacy and security concerns to be aware of, so libraries will need to protect the transmission and storage of data, as well as consider how secure IoT technologies are.

SUMMARY

Libraries are uniquely positioned in their communities to provide equitable access to specialized and emerging technology. They also have a role to support content and knowledge creation, an activity that is increasingly taking place in creative and innovative spaces. The physical space used for these services can take a variety of forms, depending on the purpose and constraints.

Digital media labs support the creation and production of digital products—audio, video, graphical, animation, and video game design. Sometimes the products are born digital, using specialized software. Other products may begin in a physical or analog state, and require specialized equipment like video cameras or musical instruments.

Makerspaces encompass a large variety of activities that focus on producing a physical product. Digital fabrication describes computer-controlled equipment such as 3-D printers, CNC mills, and laser cutters. Other activities may involve equipment such as sewing machines or hand tools. Arts and crafts are just as at home in a makerspace as robotics. Exploration, iteration, and cross-disciplinary collaboration are supported by makerspaces.

Some future trends as identified by LITA and EDUCAUSE include artificial intelligence, blockchain, and the IoT. It is yet to be seen how these technologies will be implemented in a widespread manner, but some libraries are already experimenting with them.

KEY TERMS

3-D modeling

3-D printer

3-D scanner

Artificial intelligence

Augmented reality (AR)

Blockchain

Computer numerical control (CNC) mill

Creative space

Digital media lab

Extended reality (XR)

Fused-filament fabrication (FFF)

Internet of Things (IoT)

Laser cutter

Makerspace

Microcontroller

Single-board computer

Virtual reality (VR)

Wearable technology

QUESTIONS

1. What role do libraries play in supporting creativity and innovation?
2. What are some of the specialized and emerging technology services that you have seen in libraries? Are there any topics or technologies that you would add to those covered in this chapter?
3. Describe 3-D printing.
4. What are the three common methods used for 3-D scanning?
5. What are some of the safety considerations for a makerspace?
6. What are some relevant sources for watching emerging trends? Are there sources that you would add to those listed in this chapter?
7. Select an emerging trend and discuss the latest developments with it.

ACTIVITIES

1. Select an emerging technology and write a tutorial for a first-time user.
2. Write an elevator pitch to implement a specialized or emerging technology service in a library. What would be the benefits and costs of this service? How would it fit into current library operations? Think about how you would justify it to administration or management.

FURTHER READING

Adams-Becker, S., M. Cummins, A. Davis, A. Freeman, et al. *NMC Horizon Report: 2017 Library Edition.* Austin, TX: The New Media Consortium, 2017. Accessed February 15, 2020, https://library.edu cause.edu/~/media/files/library/2017/12/2017nmchorizonreportlibraryEN.pdf.

Alexander, Bryan, Kevin Ashford-Rowe, Noreen Barajas-Murphy, et al. *EDUCAUSE Horizon Report: 2019 Higher Education Edition.* Louisville, CO: EDUCAUSE, 2019. Accessed February 15, 2020, https://library.educause.edu/~/media/files/library/2019/4/2019horizonreport.pdf.

Fernandez, Peter D., and Kelley Tilton, eds. *Applying Library Values to Emerging Technology: Decision-making in the Age of Open Access, Maker Spaces, and the Ever-changing Library*, ACRL Publications in Librarianship, no. 72. Chicago: Association of College and Research Libraries, 2018.

Goodman, Amanda L. "Digital Media Labs in Libraries." *Library Technology Reports* 50, no. 6 (2014).

Kemp, Adam. *The Makerspace Workbench.* Sebastopol, CA: Maker Media, 2013.

Kroski, Elyssa, ed. *The Makerspace Librarian's Sourcebook.* Chicago: ALA Editions, 2017.

Michalak, R., and M. Rysavy. "Academic Libraries in 2018: A Comparison of Makerspaces within Academic Research Libraries," *Supporting Entrepreneurship and Innovation: Advances in Library Administration and Organization* 40 (2019): 67–88. https://doi.org/10.1108/S0732-067120190000040008.

Smith, Jonathan M. and Rob Dumas. "Tried and True Makerspace Tools and Technologies." In E. Kroski (ed.), *Makerspaces in Practice: Successful Models for Implementation.* Chicago: ALA Editions/ Neal-Schuman, 2020.

Torta, Stephanie, and Jonathan Torta. *3D Printing: An Introduction.* Dulles, VA: Mercury Learning and Information, 2019.

Webb, Katy Kavanagh. *Development of Creative Spaces in Academic Libraries: A Decision Maker's Guide.* San Diego: Elsevier Science and Technology, 2018.

Willingham, Theresa. *Library Makerspaces: The Complete Guide.* Lanham, MD: Rowman and Littlefield, 2018.

RESOURCES

3D Printing

LulzBot: https://www.lulzbot.com/
Prusa: https://www.prusa3d.com/
Ultimaker: https://ultimaker.com/

3D Modeling Software

Autodesk Fusion 360: https://www.autodesk.com/products/fusion-360/
Autodesk Meshmixer: http://www.meshmixer.com/
Autodesk Tinkercad: https://www.tinkercad.com/
Trimble SketchUp: https://www.sketchup.com/

CNC Milling

Bantam Tools: https://www.bantamtools.com/
Carbide 3D: https://carbide3d.com/
Inventables: https://www.inventables.com/

Electronics

Adafruit: https://www.adafruit.com/
Arduino: https://www.arduino.cc/
Digi-Key Electronics: https://www.digikey.com/
Jameco Electronics: https://www.jameco.com/
Raspberry Pi: https://www.raspberrypi.org/
SparkFun: https://www.sparkfun.com/

Robotics

Lego Mindstorms: https://www.lego.com/en-us/themes/mindstorms/about
Makeblock mBot: https://www.makeblock.com/mbot

Extended Reality

Google Glass: https://www.google.com/glass/start/
HTC Vive: https://www.vive.com/
Microsoft HoloLens: https://www.microsoft.com/en-us/hololens/
Oculus: https://www.oculus.com/
Windows Mixed Reality: https://www.microsoft.com/en-us/windows/windows-mixed-reality
Valve Index: https://store.steampowered.com/valveindex

Future Trends

EDUCAUSE Horizon Report: https://www.educause.edu/horizonreport
Library of the Future: http://www.ala.org/tools/future
LITA Top Technology Trends: http://www.ala.org/lita/ttt
Pew Research, Internet and Technology: https://www.pewresearch.org/internet/

NOTES

1. "About the Space," Sonoma State University, SSU Makerspace, accessed February 15, 2020, https://library.sonoma.edu/makerspace/about-the-space.
2. "2019 Ultimate Guide to Digital Fabrication," *Make:* 66 (December 2018/January 2019).
3. "Adafruit Arduino Selection Guide," Adafruit, accessed February 9, 2020, https://learn.adafruit.com/adafruit-arduino-selection-guide/selecting-an-arduino.
4. "Choosing an Arduino for Your Project," SparkFun, accessed February 9, 2020, https://learn.sparkfun.com/tutorials/choosing-an-arduino-for-your-project.
5. "Makers' Guide to Boards," *Make:* Community, accessed February 9, 2020, https://makezine.com/comparison/boards/.
6. "Top Tech Trends—2018 Midwinter," ALA, LITA, accessed February 15, 2020, http://www.ala.org/lita/ttt/2018midwinter.

7. "Top Tech Trends—2019 Midwinter," ALA, LITA, accessed February 15, 2020, http://www.ala.org/lita/ttt/2019midwinter.

8. Samantha Adams-Becker, Malcolm Brown, Eden Dahlstrom, et al. *NMC Horizon Report: 2018 Higher Education Edition*, Louisville, CO: EDUCAUSE, 2018, accessed February 15, 2020, https://library.educause.edu/~/media/files/library/2018/8/2018horizonrepo.rt.pdf.

9. Bryan Alexander, Kevin Ashford-Rowe, Noreen Barajas-Murphy, et al, *EDUCAUSE Horizon Report: 2019 Higher Education Edition*, Louisville, CO: EDUCAUSE, 2019, accessed February 15, 2020, https://library.educause.edu/~/media/files/library/2019/4/2019horizonreport.pdf.

10. S. Adams-Becker, M. Cummins, A. Davis, A. Freeman, et al., *NMC Horizon Report: 2017 Library Edition*, Austin, TX: The New Media Consortium, 2017. Accessed February 15, 2020, https://library.educause.edu/~/media/files/library/2017/12/2017nmchorizonreportlibraryEN.pdf.

11. "Top Tech Trends—2018 Annual," ALA, LITA, accessed February 15, 2020, http://www.ala.org/lita/ttt/2018annual.

12. *EDUCAUSE Horizon Report 2019*.

13. "Top Tech Trends—2019 Annual," ALA, LITA, accessed February 15, 2020, http://www.ala.org/lita/ttt/2019annual.

14. *NMC Horizon Report: 2017 Library Edition*.

11

Library Management Technologies

Although all technology in a library might be thought of as "library technology," there are certainly technologies that have developed specifically to provide solutions for libraries. The library management system (LMS), digital libraries, and electronic resources such as article databases are all examples of technologies of varying maturity that have evolved for the purpose of improving library management and services. Other technologies have been adapted from industry applications to fill a specific need in libraries. Electromagnetic security systems, radio frequency identification (RFID) inventory tracking systems, and automated storage and retrieval systems (ASRS) are all examples of industrial systems particularly suited for application in libraries.

Entire books and university courses are dedicated to some of these technologies. Indeed, many library professionals specialize in these systems as they are designed specifically for the work that they do. This chapter introduces some of these technologies, taking the perspective of the technologist who is supporting these specialized systems and in turn the work of library employees.

THE LIBRARY MANAGEMENT SYSTEM

The LMS is the main enterprise system for a library. It comprises several parts, which are intended to support different functional activities in the library organization. These activities were traditionally handled separately and were tied to the life cycle of physical items in the library collection. Larger libraries may have dedicated departments for each activity, such as separate acquisitions and cataloging departments, whereas smaller libraries may have employees filling several roles. As some library work became automated, vendors developed software that was dedicated to each role. These disparate and siloed software programs were gradually brought together as an integrated library system (ILS), with interoperability built in that greatly improved efficiency as data could be shared between the systems. The programs that supported each function came to be known as *modules*. Over time, additional modules were developed and could be added to a library's ILS for a fee charged by the ILS vendor.

Evolution of the ILS to a more tightly integrated solution led some to use different terminology when referring to the primary enterprise software used by libraries—the *library management system*. In an LMS, the different roles are no longer wholly discrete, with only limited data transfer, but rather are multiple parts of a tightly unified, overarching system. Users within the system may have different roles that allow them to accomplish the different traditional tasks with the system but, thanks to a unified architecture, roles and permissions have become more granular, allowing for greater flexibility of employee roles. As such, workflows can be customized to suit the particular needs of a local institution, and not be limited to traditionally inflexible roles.

To add to the terminology mix, some vendors are now marketing their products as *library services platforms* to reflect the move to cloud-hosted solutions (a platform as a service model). On a library services platform, the walls between traditional functions have nearly disappeared, with new workflows and roles emerging that are no longer tied to a preautomation paradigm. Nonetheless, this is a time of transition for libraries and the LMS marketplace. Despite the greater flexibility of newer systems, some functional roles are still organized around traditional activities such as acquisitions, cataloging, circulation, serials management, and discovery—although tight integration means that actions taken in one area affect the others.

On a practical level, many library employees use the terminology for *ILS*, *LMS*, and *library services platform* interchangeably to refer to the main system used in the library for collection management and discovery. *Automation* is an old term that is still used occasionally and refers to the original "computerization" of manual library tasks.

Functional Roles

The traditional activities that the LMS has to support are conducted by library employees who have training and expertise in each of these areas. What follows is an extreme simplification of what are, in actuality, deep and often complex topics.

Acquisitions

Acquisitions refers to the process of acquiring new resources for the library, traditionally the purchasing and receiving of books. It is primarily concerned with the selection, ordering, receiving, and financial aspects of acquiring resources. Acquisitions support in the LMS may be tied to the institution's financial systems, as fund management is an important element, as is the processing of payments. When a new item arrives, whether print or electronic, the acquisitions staff often handles it first, receiving the item in the system and creating a record for it before passing it along for cataloging.

Cataloging

Cataloging is the description and classification of items, and the creation of the metadata that will be associated with the item to aid in discovery. With increasing frequency, the cataloging step for most resources is accomplished automatically by simply importing premade records and may occur as part of the acquisitions workflow. The Library of Congress and many other libraries contribute cataloging records to a central service such as OCLC. In this way, work does not have to be duplicated. As a consequence, original cataloging at many institutions has shifted to focus on unique items and special collections.

Circulation

After an item has been cataloged, it is ready to be accessed by patrons. The circulation functions of an LMS are concerned with inventory tracking, conducting transactions such as checking out resources, and maintaining accurate patron records. It can notify patrons when items are overdue for return or notify them when requested items (otherwise known as a *hold*) are available. The circulation system may receive patron information from outside systems, such as a university library receiving patron loads from university registrar or human resources systems. The circulation system also updates the availability of an item in the system so that the status in the discovery service is current.

Discovery

Before the library system was automated, patrons located resources by manually searching the card catalog. After the process became computerized, the interface for searching the item database came to be known as the online public access catalog (OPAC). The OPAC displays the current availability status of items and their location in the library. Items can be discovered through searching a database of the metadata associated with individual resources. The OPAC was the first part of the ILS to be brought to the web, although the functionality remained largely the same as the pre-web OPAC.

The advent of web search interfaces like Google led to a change in user expectations for the information searching experience. In addition, the rapid adoption of electronic resources by libraries greatly strained the capabilities of the traditional OPAC, and so the web-based discovery interface was born. The discovery interface features relevancy ranking, faceted searching, and the ability to combine multiple sources of information into a single, searchable index.

Supporting the Library Management System

From a technology support perspective, originally the only option for running an LMS was hosting it on a local server. An advantage of this model is direct access to the server, but it also requires a knowledgeable server administrator. Some vendors also provide a turnkey solution in which the LMS is provided on a server to the customer as a black box, to be hosted locally but without server access for the customer. In the turnkey model, the vendor is contracted to provide all support and maintenance. Of course, the advantage here is that the library does not need to have the expertise locally to support the server. As many LMS solutions have moved to cloud-hosted platforms, the full control option has disappeared while vendors take on complete systems support, affording library staff more time to focus on library-specific tasks. The exception is open-source solutions that still afford local control if desired, although there are fully cloud-hosted solutions as well.

Under the hood, the LMS uses a complex relational database to manage item records, bibliographic entries, library patrons, and much more. It is capable of globally updating records, and features powerful search capabilities and robust reporting. The reporting in particular is important for activities such as collection analysis. At first only the public discovery interface (catalog) had a web-based interface, but more recently a "back-end" web interface allows library employees to work within the system using a web browser. The LMS may also offer application programming interfaces that allow direct access to some data.

In many cases, administration of the LMS is handled by a systems librarian or other staff in the technical services unit of the library who are closely aligned with the collections life cycle or electronic resources management. With the move to cloud-hosted solutions, the need for in-house technology support has been greatly reduced as there are no longer servers to maintain or databases to manage. With user interfaces on the web, the configuration and support of LMS desktop clients is no longer common. Instead, the major concerns of technology support revolve around connection issues such as user authentication, data transfer between the LMS and external systems (such as loading patrons from an external database), and the user interface design of the patron-facing discovery interface. The library technologist also plays an important role as a liaison to the vendor who is providing technical support because the technologist is familiar with both the IT and library worlds.

ELECTRONIC RESOURCES

Electronic resource management (ERM) refers to the collection management practices for digital resources, including e-books, journal articles, streaming media, and subscription databases. Electronic resources are managed differently from other library resources as they are often licensed rather than purchased outright. To gain access to the resources, the library usually pays an annual subscription fee. Periodical databases are web accessible and have a dedicated search interface provided by the vendor with records that include metadata and abstracts. They also often provide metadata for inclusion in the discovery layer search index so that articles and e-books show up alongside the print resources owned by the library.

Full text of the resource might be accessible in a variety of combinations including being viewable in the browser, printable, and downloadable, depending on restrictions determined by the license. Streaming media services may require a browser plugin to play, and it is rare that audio or video media are downloadable by the patron.

E-books may be included in packages along with periodicals or they may be provided as a stand-alone e-book service. Restrictions are used by the vendor to control the amount of printing that can be done, and if an e-book can be downloaded, it is often controlled by digital rights management (DRM) software that requires a specialized reader program and limits what can be done with the e-book. DRM software can also cause an e-book loan to expire, so that a library patron will only be able to access the downloaded e-book for a set period, much like a borrowed print book.

Licensing agreements with vendors usually require institutions to limit access to electronic resources. A common way to handle this for onsite users is to provide an IP address range for the location—such as a university campus—that automatically grants access to the resource. This greatly simplifies the process for onsite users, who do not have to do anything to use the resource. Offsite users in this scenario need to be authenticated, and this is commonly handled with a proxy server. As discussed in chapter 7, "Information Security," the proxy server authenticates the user, then connects to the resource on the user's behalf. OCLC EZproxy is a proxy service that is widely used among libraries. In recent years, some vendors are moving to single sign-on authentication services such as Shibboleth, which negate the need for a proxy service.

DIGITAL COLLECTIONS

Many libraries, archives, and museums are actively pursuing some level of digitization to build digital libraries, digital archives, or online exhibits from their collections. These collections can be built from both physical and born-digital resources, but the process of *digitization* refers to the creation of a digital object from a physical item. Nearly any item found in a collection can be digitized, whether the original format is a text document, photograph, audio, video, or, with the advent of 3-D scanning, cultural artifacts. Institutional repositories differ in that they focus on collecting documents that pertain to a particular institution, such as academic libraries that collect papers, books, and dissertations that were produced in affiliation with the university.

Within libraries, the digitization of collections usually falls to the special collections or archives unit as the responsible party, and subject experts for the particular collections. Aside from the technological aspects of digitizing collections and managing the digital objects, of significant importance is the creation of metadata and finding aids to describe and assist in the discovery of the digital objects. One of the decisions to be made is what metadata standard to use. Other issues of concern are copyright, digital preservation, user authentication, and discovery.

The selection of items to digitize drives a digitization project. The correct equipment must be obtained if the library does not already possess it and may involve the use of hard-to-find legacy equipment for obsolete formats. The intended purpose of the project needs to be considered as well—whether the objective is to provide greater access to collections, to create long-term preservation copies of decaying media, to create a short-term digital exhibit, or else a combination of objectives. This helps determine the work that must be done, such as the extent of metadata description, the appropriate software platforms for presentation and management, and the storage solution.

When it comes to preservation the choice of storage solution is critical. Digital preservation copies tend to be very large files, particularly in the case of video. Backups are important in case the storage solution fails or suffers corrupt data. At some point in the future, the preservation copy must be migrated to a new storage solution or a new digital format. Ironically, some physical formats have proven to have greater longevity than digital ones.

Equipment

The equipment that used to digitize items depends on the format and the fragility of the item. Often, items that are visual in nature (e.g., photographs or documents) involve some type of scanner or camera system.

A flatbed scanner is generally good for single-sheet print documents, photographs, and artwork, provided the dimensions of the item fit within the dimensions of the scanner. Loose sheets that can withstand physical handling can be scanned much faster using a sheet feeder than if an operator were to physically handle each page one at a time. Transparent media such as film or slides requires either an adapter for the flatbed scanner or specialized scanner.

Overhead scanners featuring a digital camera system are used with fragile materials, oversize flat items, and bound items such as books. Overhead systems for books usually have the book placed in a V-shaped cradle with the camera and light source overhead, so that the book does not have to be placed facedown, damaging the page and the spine. More complex digital camera and lighting systems may be arranged depending on the size and format of the item, with vacuum easels used to "hang" flat items like aerial photographs or maps or spread out on a large table with a camera suspended above.

For a long time, the best that could be done to digitize three-dimensional objects was to take a photograph. Now, 3-D scanning is a new frontier in digitization for libraries and museums. The scanning process captures physical data such as detailed measurements and surface textures as well as a visual representation from multiple angles. Scanning for three-dimensional digital display and preservation by cultural institutions is in its infancy, with a number of approaches and techniques, and little agreement in the way of best practices so far.

Audio and video digitization depend on having equipment that can play back the original format. The original storage format for audiovisual resources vary widely and includes cassette tapes, vinyl records, VHS tapes, compact discs, 35-mm film reels, and many, many more. Independent of the storage medium, original recordings may be either analog or digital. An analog recording needs to be converted into a digital format, whereas a digital recording needs to be ripped and perhaps converted to a different digital format.

An audiovisual digitization setup involves a playback machine for the original format, an analog-to-digital converter, and a computer with processing software. It is possible to get equipment for popular analog formats that have an integrated analog-to-digital converter, such as record players, cassette players, and VHS machines. In other situations, the converter needs to be positioned in-line, to process the signal from the playback machine to the computer. Processing video can be demanding for the computer, so it is important to ensure that it has sufficient memory and processing power—not to mention storage for large file sizes.

Digitization

Multiple digital objects are often produced from the digitization of a single item. Best practice prescribes that at the least one preservation file and one derivative file are created. The preservation file should be of a high resolution, having captured as much data as is feasible, with the intention of preserving the most accurate digital representation possible. Preservation files tend to be quite large in size and unsuitable for general access or publishing on the web. A master derivative file is made from the preservation file for the purpose of creating additional derivatives for manipulation and access. The derivative file may be compressed to save storage space or bandwidth and in a different file format from the preservation copy as appropriate for the platform that will be used to provide access.

During postprocessing of a digital object, audio might be cleaned, a damaged image might be enhanced, or optical character recognition (OCR) might be used to make a text document full-text searchable. Although OCR software continues to improve, it is not foolproof, so the output will need to be reviewed for corrections by a human. Accessibility is also a concern and, in the case of text documents, may require things such as heading tags, image descriptions, and special formatting for tables.

File Formats

The long-term preservation file should be an uncompressed file that includes all of the data originally captured when the item was digitized. Derivative files may use compression to create smaller file sizes with the understanding that some data will be lost and unrecoverable. Lossless compression reduces the file size somewhat by discarding only unused data. Portable Network Graphics (PNG) and Free Lossless Audio Codec (FLAC) are examples of file formats that use lossless compression. Lossy compression can significantly reduce the file size, depending on the level of compression, by discarding data and using approximations to represent the discarded data. The greater the compression, the more data is discarded, and consequently the lower the quality of the file. JPEG (named after the group that created it, the Joint Photographic Experts Group) and MP3 (named after the Moving Picture Experts Group) are examples of file formats that use lossy compression.

Tagged Image File Format (TIFF) is generally accepted as a preservation format for digital images, with JPEG 2000, PNG, and other formats used for access copies. Portable Document Format (PDF) is also used as an access format for text documents.

For audio recordings, Waveform Audio File Format (WAV) and FLAC may be used as preservation formats. MP3 is far and away the most well-known file format used for access, although there are other formats such as Advanced Audio Coding (AAC), OGG, and Windows Media Audio (WMA). Audacity is popular open-source audio editing software. There are many proprietary software programs such as Sound Forge, Pro Tools, and Apple's Logic Pro X.

The CARLI Digital Collections Users' Group recommends Material eXchange Format (MXF) as the best preservation file type for video, but Audio Video Interleave (AVI) or QuickTime (MOV) are acceptable substitutes.[1] Other file types may be used for access files as appropriate to the platform including MP4, Matroska (MKV), and Windows Media Video (WMV), among others. Apple's Final Cut Pro X and Adobe's Premiere Pro are software programs that are used to process the digital recordings, and HandBrake is a popular open-source program for ripping DVDs.

Table 11.1. Digital File Formats

Object Type	Preservation Format	Access Format
Text document	TIFF	PDF
Still image	TIFF	JPEG 2000, PNG
Audio recording	WAV, FLAC	MP3, AAC, OGG, WMA
Video recording	MXF, AVI, MOV	MP4, MKV, WMV

Digital Library Management Systems

The digital library management system (DLMS) houses and provides access to the digital objects. These software solutions usually have a web interface for discovery and a database backend. As such, there is a front-end for library users to search and browse content and a way to present the digital objects to them. Library employees use a back-end interface to upload digital objects and assign metadata. Many DLMSs also expose metadata for harvesting by aggregators using Open Archives Initiative Protocol for Metadata Harvesting (OAI-PMH). In this way, items in the digital library may be discovered through unified or federated discovery interfaces that provide access to multiple sources of information.

DSpace and CONTENTdm were among the first widely used DLMSs and are still used by many institutions. Islandora and Samvera are solutions that are built on the Fedora Commons digital asset management system. Eprints and Digital Commons specialize as digital repositories and publishing platforms, whereas Omeka specializes as a lightweight platform for online exhibits.

COLLECTION AND SPACE MANAGEMENT

Another realm of library technology concerns the management of physical collections and of the myriad spaces in the library building. Room reservation software has been developed for study rooms, conference rooms, media viewing, and other specialty rooms. Many public libraries use specialized software for reserving computer workstations and displaying their availability on a website or kiosk. Buildings often have cameras featuring closed-circuit TV and DVR recording for security purposes.

Circulation Technologies

Aside from the inventory management features of the LMS, a number of other technologies aid in the management of physical collections.

Security Gates

A common feature found in libraries are the security gates that are meant to prevent theft. They are usually positioned at exits that library visitors pass through, and for a long time they have used magnetic *tattle-tape* security strips that are hidden inside book spines, DVD cases, and other items from the library collection. The gates are often electromagnetic, and when an item that has not been desensitized passes through, it triggers an alarm to alert nearby staff. A case can also be made that the presence of the gates and sound of the alarm is a deterrent to would-be thieves. RFID is used in some security gate systems as a newer alternative to the electromagnetic system and affords the possibility for additional functionality.

There is a recent trend away from the use of security gates as they reach their end-of-life and libraries must consider whether to replace them at a significant cost. Questions about their effectiveness are being raised,[2] and particularly about the return on investment when the cost is compared with the cost to replace lost items.

Electromagnetic security gates require the use of magnetic sensitizing and desensitizing stations as part of the circulation workflow of the item checkout and return process. The gates themselves require electricity to function and may also need an Ethernet connection, if they input information to a database.

Self-checkout

Much like self-check machines in grocery stores, self-checkout stations in libraries allow patrons to borrow library materials without interacting with library staff. The machines might use a barcode scanner to read a barcode that is affixed to each item or they might use RFID to determine what items are being borrowed. If the items have tattle-tape, the station desensitizes the tape so that the item can pass through the security gates without triggering the alarm. The station often features a touch-screen interface and a computer with proprietary software. In addition to power, it requires a network connection so that the software can update item and patron records in the LMS.

Book Lockers

Lockers that feature electronic locking and access are a newer trend for lending library items. These book lockers are useful for accommodating touchless delivery as well as the ability for patrons to pick up requested items twenty-four hours per day. A possible scenario involves a patron requesting an item through the library's discovery platform. An employee then retrieves the item, checks it out to the patron, and places it into a locker. The patron can then pick up the item at his or her convenience. If the lockers are placed outside of the building, or in a 24/7 accessible space, items can be picked up any time of the day or night without direct employee interaction.

Different models have different mechanisms for unlocking the appropriate locker for the patron: some scan a library card, some require a code to be entered into a touchscreen interface, and others can be used with a mobile phone app. Similar technology is used in shopping centers and even for Amazon Lockers.[3]

Some products integrate with LMSs and may include additional features such as a built-in security camera. They require power and network connectivity, with a wired Ethernet connection often preferred to wireless, depending on signal strength.

RFID in Libraries

RFID systems in libraries use tags that are placed on items and readers that are used at a short distance to activate and retrieve information from the tag. Libraries typically use passive tags that are composed of a microchip containing stored information about the item and an antenna that must be activated by a compatible reader to retrieve the information. Passive tags do not actively send out a signal, unlike active tags that have a power source incorporated and may be read at a much longer distance. Active tags are more commonly used in warehouses or toll collection systems.

RFID readers are used at self-checkout machines, staff workstations, and security gates. Handheld readers can also be used when processing items or conducting shelf audits. RFID can greatly speed up shelf inventory audits, which are normally done by manually looking at each individual item and checking against an inventory list. With a handheld RFID scanner, an entire shelf can quickly be checked to determine what is missing and what doesn't belong.

Because the tags are activated by an electromagnetic signal from the reader, it is not necessary for the tag to be visible to the reader—unlike a barcode. Consequently, tags can be placed within items and multiple items can be scanned simultaneously, for example, when placing a pile of books on a self-checkout machine.

There are some privacy concerns connected to the use of RFID, as there is the possibility for an unauthorized person to use an RFID reader of their own to scan items carried by a patron, and to associate the items with that patron, thus violating their privacy. A simple solution to this concern is to store minimal information on the tag, and to use a unique ID that is useful only when linked to the LMS in a way that only employees would have access.

Automated Storage and Retrieval Systems

An ASRS is a computerized system using robotic machines that move around in a high-density storage facility to perform the storage and retrieval of items. ASRSs are more commonly used in warehouses that handle manufacturing, retail, and distribution—but they have also found a home in some libraries.

Moving collections into an ASRS can create additional space in the library while keeping collections nearby and readily accessible. Although they are not browsable, requested items can be retrieved in short order—sometimes just a matter of minutes from when the request is placed to when the item is presented to the patron. General practice is to move collections that are less frequently used into the ASRS so that the more popular items remain available for browsing.

The system maintains an inventory of all items, which in part tracks the location of each item in the storage facility. Items are stored in steel bins, which may vary in height. Because the facility is not browsable by people, items do not have to be kept in call number order. Rather, the system tries to fill bins that have space in them according to the size of the item. The result is that an item probably won't go back into the same space—or even the same bin—from which it was retrieved, as the bin may have been filled by another item in the meanwhile. Best practice is to conduct ongoing audits to confirm the accuracy of the inventory.

In a common model used by libraries the storage and retrieval machine (SRM) moves down the aisle on tracks to the proper location, then raises to the correct height of the bin, whereupon the bin is withdrawn from the aisle, and finally returns to the end of the aisle where an operator can access the bin and pull out the appropriate item. The process of retrieving a requested item is known as a *pick* and the process for replacing an item is known as a *deposit*.

A complex system like an ASRS involves automated cranes, computer workstations, and specialized software to operate. Some basic troubleshooting such as bin misalignments can be handled by trained library staff; however, ASRS support can be dangerous if not conducted correctly. A vendor should be contracted to provide support as well as preventative maintenance. The system software includes an inventory database and requires a connection to the library management system to facilitate picks and update availability. Additionally, there is a computer workstation at the end of each aisle associated with the SRM located there.

Digital Signage

Digital signage may refer to wayfinding or other information displayed on a video monitor, digital kiosk, or other similar device, for library visitors. The most basic example is a monitor displaying a looping slideshow with pertinent information about available services or the space in which it is located. More advanced systems are connected to a networked server that distributes images, animation, and video to multiple digital signs. An administrator is able to designate information prepared for display to individual signs using a commercial software package. The library's parent organization might use a commercial solution to manage digital signage throughout the organization, with permissions granted to individuals to manage the signage within their department.

Another form of digital signage is the kiosk, which may feature a touchscreen interface so that the user can query directions, interact with a map, or learn more about featured collections and events. Placement of a kiosk makes a difference not just in encouraging use, but also when taking into consideration access to power and networking for the station.

People Counters

People counters are frequently found in libraries as they provide useful information such as the number of library visits, which can inform staffing levels and hours of operation. The most basic people counters may feature an infrared signal that increments a counter every time someone passes through. Slightly more advanced people counters are bi-directional, meaning that they can differentiate between traffic entering and exiting an area. Integrated people counters have become a standard feature of security gates. Some people counters require a network connection to continually update server software that may be accessible through a desktop client or web interface. People counters that are not networked will need an employee to retrieve the count from the device.

Other products use a camera with thermal imaging or a video feed to track the movement of people through a space. In addition to obtaining simple counts of people crossing a threshold, some are able to identify traffic patterns or create heat maps that can help analyze space use. Real-time statistics can provide current data about space occupancy as well as granular time-based traffic patterns. SenSource, D-Tech, and Bibliotecha are some vendors that provide such products, although some libraries have experimented with do-it-yourself solutions involving single-board computing platforms such as Arduino and Raspberry Pi and passive infrared sensors or ultrasonic distance sensors.

SUMMARY

Library technology has evolved along with libraries, and specialized systems have been created to solve the particular issues of libraries. Library employees in different functional roles have deep expertise with some of these systems, but the library technologist needs a general understanding of all of them to provide support.

The LMS is the primary enterprise software solution for all libraries. It facilitates the inventory management and discovery of library resources and is used throughout the library in activities such as acquisitions, cataloging, circulation, and discovery. Recent trends have libraries moving from locally hosted LMSs to vendor cloud-hosted library services platforms.

ERM is becoming ever more important as libraries increasingly adopt online resources such as e-books, digital articles, and streaming media. Authentication and access are two major technology concerns associated with electronic resources that are tightly controlled by DRM and license restrictions.

Digital libraries and institutional repositories are important services that libraries provide to make collections accessible to a greater number of people by digitizing them. Another concern of digitizing collections is digital preservation. There are many methods for digitizing physical resources as there is a huge variety of physical formats. Some even involve the use of legacy technology for converting them into modern digital formats.

A number of technologies have been adapted to suit libraries to manage their physical collections and building spaces. Circulation technologies include electromagnetic security gates, self-checkout machines, and book lockers. More recently, RFID has been adapted for use in collection management. Although not widely used, ASRS comes with many advantages for storage and space use but requires complex support.

KEY TERMS

Automated storage and retrieval system (ASRS)
Book lockers
Digital library management system (DLMS)
Digital preservation
Digital rights management (DRM)
Digitization
Discovery interface
Electronic resource management (ERM)
Institutional repository
Integrated library system (ILS)

Library management system (LMS)
Library services platform
Lossless compression
Lossy compression
Optical character recognition (OCR)
People counter
Radio frequency identification (RFID)
Security gates
Self-checkout

QUESTIONS

1. What functional roles does an LMS support?
2. Describe ERM.
3. What is DRM?
4. What is the difference between a preservation file and a derivative file?
5. Compare the differences between using lossy compression, using lossless compression, and not using compression at all to create a digital file? In what circumstances would you use each?
6. List specific examples of collection and space management technologies.

ACTIVITIES

1. Select an analog item that represents an imaginary (or real) collection and digitize it. Write a workflow procedure for imaginary colleagues to follow while digitizing the collection.
2. Investigate a library. List the collection and space management technologies that are being used. Is there a technology the library is not currently using that you believe it would benefit from? Why?

FURTHER READING

Ayre, Lori Bowen. "RFID in Libraries: A Step toward Interoperability." *Library Technology Reports* 48, no. 5. Chicago: ALA TechSource, 2012.

Breeding, Marshall. "2020 Library Systems Report: Fresh Opportunities amid Consolidation." *American Libraries*, May 1, 2020. https://americanlibrariesmagazine.org/2020/05/01/2020-library-sys tems-report/.

CARLI Digital Collections Users' Group and CARLI Created Content Committee. *Guidelines for the Creation of Digital Collections: Digitization Best Practices for Moving Images.* Consortium of Academic and Research Libraries in Illinois. Accessed on July 21, 2020. https://www.carli.illinois.edu/sites/ files/digital_collections/documentation/guidelines_for_video.pdf.

Engard, Nicole C. *The Accidental Systems Librarian*, 2nd ed. Medford, NJ: Oldsmar, FL: Information Today, 2012.

Kovalcik, Justin, and Mike Villalobos. "Automated Storage and Retrieval System: From Storage to Service." *Information Technology and Libraries* 38, no. 4 (2019). https://doi.org/10.6017/ital.v38i4.11273.

Pandian, M. Paul. *RFID for Libraries: A Practical Guide.* Chandos Information Professional Series. Oxford, UK: Chandos, 2010.

RFID in Libraries: Privacy and Confidentiality Guidelines. American Library Association, May 29, 2007. Accessed on July 25, 2020. http://www.ala.org/advocacy/intfreedom/statementspols/otherpol icies/rfidguidelines.

Sander, Janelle, Lori Mestre, and Eric Kurt. *Going Beyond Loaning Books to Loaning Technologies: A Practical Guide for Librarians.* Practical Guides for Librarians; No. 13. Lanham, MD: Rowman & Littlefield, 2015.

Xie, Iris, and Krystyna K. Matusiak. *Discover Digital Libraries Theory and Practice.* Cambridge, MA: Elsevier, 2016.

RESOURCES

Library Management Systems

Library Technology Guides: https://librarytechnology.org/

Digitization

Adobe Premier Pro: https://www.adobe.com/products/premiere.html
Apple Final Cut Pro X: https://www.apple.com/final-cut-pro/
Apple Logic Pro X: https://www.apple.com/logic-pro/
Audacity: https://www.audacityteam.org/
Avid Pro Tools: https://www.avid.com/pro-tools
Digital Library Federation: https://www.diglib.org/
HandBrake: https://handbrake.fr/
Sound Forge: https://www.magix.com/us/music/sound-forge/

Digital Library Management Systems

CONTENTdm: https://www.oclc.org/en/contentdm.html
Digital Commons: https://www.bepress.com/products/digital-commons/
DSpace: https://duraspace.org/dspace/
Eprints: https://www.eprints.org/
Fedora Commons: https://duraspace.org/fedora/
Islandora: https://www.islandora.ca/
Omeka: https://omeka.org/
Samvera: https://samvera.org/

Space Management

Bibliotecha: https://www.bibliotheca.com/
D-Tech: https://d-techinternational.com/us/
Google Kiosk apps, managed guest sessions, and smart cards: https://support.google.com/chrome/a/topic/6128720
Open Kiosk: https://openkiosk.mozdevgroup.com/
SenSource: https://www.sensourceinc.com/

NOTES

1. CARLI Digital Collections Users' Group and CARLI Created Content Committee, *Guidelines for the Creation of Digital Collections: Digitization Best Practices for Moving Images*, Consortium of Academic and Research Libraries in Illinois, accessed on July 21, 2020, https://www.carli.illinois.edu/sites/files/digital_col lections/documentation/guidelines_for_video.pdf.

2. Jonathan H. Harwell, "Library Security Gates: Effectiveness and Current Practice," *Journal of Access Services* 11, no. 2, (2014): 53–65, https://doi.org/10.1080/15367967.2014.884876.

3. "Amazon Locker Delivery," Amazon.com, accessed on July 22, 2020, https://www.amazon.com/b?node=6442600011.

12

Technology Planning

Plans help us to make informed decisions and the best use of limited resources. This is particularly important when it comes to IT—a complex topic at the best of times. New developments are taking place all the time, with exciting new technologies that promise greater efficiency and more productivity being released frequently. But not every new development is right for every library and we all have constraints such as policies, funding, time, and staffing that affect what we can and should attempt to accomplish.

Technology planning is an opportunity to assess and evaluate current technologies and services in the library as well as to investigate new solutions. It establishes a framework by which to prioritize initiatives and allocate time, money, and effort appropriately. Plans are used to provide justification for projects, to communicate and build support with administrators, and to request funding. A technology plan is the launching point for writing grant proposals, implementing projects, and addressing the needs of stakeholders.

This chapter addresses several broad areas that involve technology planning. Acquiring technology should be a deliberate process and take into account the actual need at hand and the constraints that must be worked within. This chapter discusses library budget structures and budget planning with technology in mind. It also discusses a technology selection process that can be used for small and large projects. Strategic technology planning is a major and sometimes neglected component of IT management. The chapter discusses the planning process and reviews the elements of the final planning document. The technology perspective of continuity planning and disaster recovery are also often neglected by libraries. This chapter reviews what goes into a continuity plan, discusses disaster response, and lists some risk-management strategies. The chapter ends with a brief discussion about managing change.

ACQUIRING TECHNOLOGY

Acquiring technology should be a deliberate decision-making process—no matter the scale—that involves an investigation of the need, a consideration of the total cost, and an evaluation of the potential solution. This should be true whether the project is a one-time software purchase for an individual employee or an enterprise-level solution such as a library management system. It is only the amount of resources brought to bear that changes depending on the scale of the technology needed.

Organizations likely have required processes to go through and approvals to obtain, and those may vary depending on the scope of the technology and the level of autonomy that the library has in making purchasing decisions. The IT department of the parent organization may have a say in certain (or all) technology-related purchases, while the finance department may have their own set of requirements, and the organization may require a review before entering into any contracts.

Likewise, library employees should not be allowed to make technology purchases at their whim. It would be terribly inefficient if you needed to regularly purchase twenty different types of toner to accommodate everyone's individual desktop printers. Some internal controls should be in place in which a technology support person in the library at least reviews purchase requests to ensure their compatibility with the current technology environment. If the library technology unit is expected to support the technology, they need to assess their own capacity and the most efficient way to support the need.

Technology Adoption

Establishing the need—whether to solve a problem, fulfill a request, or test a potential new service—is the first step in adopting technology. All technology needs do not have to begin with a problem, like a broken-down microfilm reader or out-of-date website. However, you should always consider the effect on resources and services adopting a certain technology will have. It is good to experiment and be creative with new technology, but don't adopt something bleeding edge as an essential service just because it is new and shiny.

Give library workers some freedom to try out new things with the understanding that it is a pilot or a trial before attempting a widespread implementation with something unproven or, worse, that doesn't actually serve a purpose for your library. On the other hand, you don't want to be so far behind as to be doing your employees and patrons a disservice. If technology staff are spending all their time patching up old technology, they could be wasting time that might be better used providing other services for library workers and patrons.

Budget Planning

Library budgets are complex, with multiple funding sources; stable or reducing income; and increasing costs for collections, salaries, and technology. It is often the case that technology budgets in libraries are not well established or else do not reflect the actual and whole of the technology expenses. Technology budgeting is further complicated by the fact that many technology projects can be expensive in the initial year, with ongoing maintenance that costs little in comparison, with an expensive refresh or upgrade that will have to take place a number of years down the road. It would be difficult for an organization to plan for a technology budget that fluctuates wildly from year to year, so we must do our best to carefully plan our spending out over multiple years in an attempt to have somewhat stable expenses.

A real example of spreading out expenses over multiple years is the technology refresh cycle for employee and patron computers. Because of bulk-purchase discounts, it is most cost effective to purchase all computers at one time, and to repeat this every three to four years. This results in a spike in expenses during every refresh with a lull in the intervening years. This is a difficult way for organizations to budget that may actually hurt the technology budget; it may appear to the organization as if the need does not exist in between refreshes, and so the technology budget could end up radically reduced. There is also the question of staff resources and whether the library can afford to have them entirely diverted to supporting a refresh of that scale once every few years. Instead, the best practice is to refresh a chunk of the computer inventory every year, resulting in a more stable budget and spreading out the labor involved.

Aside from regular expenses like technology refreshes and software licenses, projects with large one-time expenses are unavoidable. For these it is important to prioritize according to urgency and need, as well as how they fit into the library's mission. If there is room in the budget or funds (and other resources) become available, these projects can be tackled in order of priority. Doing the work to prioritize technology needs help to ensure that resources are being managed efficiently and with greatest effect for library services and employees.

Budget Structure

Pay attention to the fiscal year calendar for your institution. Although it usually does not line up with the calendar year (January 1–December 31), there is not a universal fiscal year, and it can actually differ quite a bit from one industry to the next. Educational institutions frequently employ a July 1–June 30 fiscal year so that the year-end falls during the summer months. The US federal government fiscal year runs from October 1 through September 30. Fiscal years are named for the year in which they end—therefore, fiscal year 2021 (FY2021) might be July 1, 2020, through June 30, 2021. This all matters to the technology budget because funds are usually made available according to the annual budget, with the deadline for spending the current-year budget falling sometime before the end of the fiscal year. Ending the spending prior to the end of the fiscal year gives the financial specialists of the institution time to process payments and make final budgetary adjustments. Sometimes spending is also paused at the beginning of a fiscal year while budgets for the new year are finalized and funds dispersed. Careful planning is needed not only to avoid going over budget but also to not come in too short. Failing to spend down a budget can make it appear as though the amount budgeted is not needed, and the budget may end up being reduced in the following fiscal year's budget.

Sometimes, unspent money that had been budgeted is allowed to "roll over" the end of the fiscal year into the next. More often, however, any unspent money is swept by the parent organization to help balance the budget. Because of the nature of spending on technology, careful planning is needed to make sure that funds are available when they are needed. Although it is more cost-effective to bulk purchase all of the computers needed for a refresh in one go, a steady annual budget cannot be maintained by making a large expenditure once every three or four years (depending on your refresh cycle). Instead, a refresh plan spreads those purchases out, with maybe a quarter of the computers being replaced every year. Major projects are often undertaken during the summer months at academic libraries when the effect on students and faculty is the lowest. Careful planning is needed to make sure that the spending falls in the correct fiscal year, or else permission is given to rollover some money—but be prepared to justify the rollover to the institution's finance department!

Do a survey of technology expenses made by the library. Even with significant control over a technology budget, many libraries will likely discover technology-related expenses paid from budgets or buckets of money that were not assigned for the purpose of buying or licensing technology. The most difficult situation is for technology expenditures to be spread out all over the library's budget. It is very difficult to plan for future projects and expenditures if you do not have a clear idea of how much you are already spending, and how much is available.

One-time monies are funds that are not a part of the regular budget but are outside of the regular budget as a one-time "bonus" that can help fund large or unexpected expenses. They may come in the form of a grant or money shifted from another part of the organization's budget. The nature of one-time money is that it is not ongoing, so it should not be used for anything that incurs ongoing expenses unless a consistent, ongoing funding source has been identified. It might be okay to spend one-time monies on a major infrastructure upgrade or a pilot project that has a predetermined end date. It would not be a good idea to purchase the first year of a software license unless there is a plan to pick up the tab in future years.

Be sure to budget for service and maintenance contracts. These are an ongoing obligation and should be part of the consideration before acquiring any new technology. Also reserve some money for unexpected expenses, such as for repairs or replacements or an opportunity to try a new technology product or service. Then if you find yourself near the end of the fiscal year with some funding left, you can turn to the prioritized list of projects to see what is needed, or perhaps keep a wish list of lower priority items that you can really only afford when there is a little extra money.

Evaluation and Selection

The process of ultimately selecting a technology product is described in figure 12.1. First you must have a thorough understanding of the need; next you can investigate for potential solutions. Having identified some potential solutions, they should be evaluated, and finally a decision can be made.

Figure 12.1 Technology selection process

Understanding the Need

The first step in acquiring any new technology is to come to a full understanding of the need. What is the goal? Is there a problem to be solved or a new service to launch? Who will use the technology and how will they interact with it? Clearly define the problem to be solved and the requirements for the solution.

An essential source for understanding the need are the stakeholders. Interviews, observations, surveys, and focus groups are all tools for gathering information. Pay close attention to the objective as well as the current practices and workflows used. Might the library already have an available solution (e.g., software) that meets the needs? Might additional training or adjustments to workflow solve the problem?

Be sure to also consider the constraints. Do you have the resources and infrastructure to implement and support a potential solution? At this point, you may not have a clear picture of the total cost of ownership (TCO), but with experience you can make an educated guess and begin to think about what it will take to solve the need as well as what solutions might be realistic.

Investigation

With a clear understanding of the need, you can now investigate potential solutions. This is where research skills come into play as you investigate many different resources such as white papers, product reviews, industry journals, and magazines. Keep an eye on industry trends. Vendor websites will go into some detail about the specifications and implementation requirements. Be sure to also reach out to colleagues at other institutions who may have solved similar problems. Listservs, association newsletters, library journals, and other library communities are also useful sources of information. Peer institutions can be a wonderful source of information. How have they solved a similar problem? Are they satisfied with the solution?

Focus on products that accomplish the objectives set out in the previous step. Try not to be swayed greatly by extra features that do not meet the established need. Is the technology well supported and widely adopted? Is the vendor preparing to replace it with the "next generation?" If so, are you prepared to support an obsolete technology or else make another migration to the next version soon?

Major technology acquisitions may have to go through a request for proposal (RFP) process wherein a call is put out detailing the technology environment and requirements for a solution, and vendors have the chance to respond in detail about how their solution will meet the needs described. As there may be multiple responses, the pricing can become a competitive process. The RFP response initiates the process by which the library may be able to negotiate some customizations of the product and the evaluation phase.

Evaluation

After you have identified some potential solutions, it is time to evaluate them. See if you can get a trial or demo version to test out. If the software or equipment is for library employees, have the actual employees who would use it as part of their work try it out with their real workflows, and get their opinion. Talk to colleagues at other institutions who may have the same product about how well it has met their need, how well it integrated into their technology environment, whether workflows had to be adjusted, and whether it introduced any inefficiencies.

For patron-facing technology, consider a pilot to test it out in a live environment with real patrons. Depending on the technology, consider some usability studies to determine if the user interface is satisfactory. Also consider accessibility for anything that has an interface, be it a digital or physical interface. Some organizations may require an accessibility review of any technology product before it is purchased.

If customizability is desired in the product, how customizable is it? Is there an additional cost for the vendor to produce a custom solution or can it be done in-house by library employees? Is there an additional cost for updates and upgrades? Make sure that it will work in your technology environment (i.e., with your infrastructure). Will your network accommodate the new system's requirements? How will it interface with other systems? What is the security of the system? If personally identifiable information will be stored or transmitted, is it secure? Does it use encryption and secure connections?

Compare alternative solutions and do not go with the first solution that presents itself. A common tool for evaluating products is the weighted-point evaluation. In this method you identify a list of factors that you wish to evaluate each product on. Then you apply a weight, or multiple, to each factor, with the most important factor receiving the greatest weight. This way, each factor can be rated using the same scale (e.g., one to five with one being worst and five being best) and the weight ensures the most important factors apply the greatest influence on the overall score.

Table 12.1. Sample Weighted-point Evaluation of Two Products

Criteria	Weight (multiple)	Product 1		Product 2	
		Score	Points	Score	Points
Criterion 1	50	7/10	35	5/10	25
Criterion 2	20	7/10	14	8/10	16
Criterion 3	30	9/10	27	6/10	18
Total Possible	100	Total	76	Total	59

Selection

Following the evaluation phase, a report can be drawn up that includes the pros and cons of each product, the weighted-point evaluation, and a comparison of specifications. From this, it should be fairly straightforward to make a recommendation for purchase. It may be that multiple solutions are satisfactory; in that case it is often decided by the cost of the solutions. If price quotes were not obtained from the vendors during the evaluation, they will need to be requested now, before the final decision is made.

Given what you have learned from the investigations and the quotes that have been obtained, be sure to revisit the TCO, including employee time to implement and support the technology, potential services and maintenance fees, extended warranty costs, and future updates or upgrades.

Purchasing Process

Depending on the type and scope of the technology, there may be multiple review steps involved before the product can be purchased or licensed. The process may also change depending on the dollar amount, with, for example, credit card purchases okay up to a certain threshold but those beyond requiring a different process. However, be wary of using a credit card—just because you can doesn't necessarily mean that you should. Organizations tend to have strict guidelines for what and when a company credit card can be used for purchases.

In general, you will submit the recommendations and quotes to the appropriate units or persons for review and approval. Again, depending on the technology and scope, it may have to go to various parties to review accessibility, security, infrastructure compatibility, and budgeting, as well as someone to review contract or licensing agreements.

Make sure that you are familiar with the terms and conditions of any warranties. Consider extended warranties for hardware and find out the cost of any service or support calls that are not covered by the warranty. Also be familiar with what may void the warranty, such as purchasing parts from a third party to conduct your own repairs.

STRATEGIC PLANNING

Technology develops rapidly, making it difficult to plan very far into the future. Nonetheless, a strategic plan is necessary to guide resource allocation and to ensure that the organization's goals are being supported. Strategic planning results in a multiyear plan that evaluates the current technology environment, prioritizes the projects and tasks that should be accomplished, and establishes a timeline for their implementation. It features detailed plans for the near future that can be acted on immediately, with less detail further out in acknowledgement that circumstances and technologies can and do change. The plan should be reviewed and revised regularly, perhaps on an annual basis. Do not expect that all of the projects will be implemented as planned. The annual revision presents an opportunity to make adjustments based on changes during the year and your success in following the timeline.

Nicole Engard reminds us, "Realize that your plan is not a 'wish list' describing the technology you would ideally like to have but a statement of what your library truly intends to do with technology in the foreseeable future."[1] This is an important point to keep in mind throughout the planning process. For the plan to be effective, it should address the actual needs of the library and do so in a sustainable way. The plan will be used to justify investing in new technology, so it is important to be thorough in determining priorities and realistic about what can be accomplished.

Sometimes the impetus for strategic planning comes from the parent organization or another group outside of the library. If this is the case, be clear about the objectives and keep your audience in mind. A plan written for a group external to the library is different from one meant only to be used internally. But the ultimate goal in any case is to provide a framework within which informed decisions can be made about technology-related projects and initiatives.

Planning Process

Although there isn't a prescribed way to create a strategic technology plan, most methods involve the steps described in this section. Many books outline different processes and documents, and much of it depends on the scope, circumstances, and available resources. With experience, you will be able to tailor the strategic planning process and document to your particular institution.

It is typical for the strategic planning process to take six months to a year from initiation to finalizing the document. Building off an existing strategic plan may make the process somewhat simpler, but it is important to be careful about making any assumptions based on the previous plan.

The first step in the planning process is to form a planning team or task force to do the work of conducting the research, making decisions about priorities, and writing the strategic plan. The team gathers relevant documentation, reviews the history of technology in the library, and gathers input from stakeholders. It is their job to evaluate the current technology environment and to make informed decisions about priorities of the library. Based on the priorities and a realistic assessment of resources, an implementation plan can be created. All of this information will go into the final document that is to be the written strategic technology plan.

Form a Planning Team

The planning process is initiated by the formation of a planning team. Because creating a strategic technology plan is a project unto itself, it is useful to employ project management tools. Establish a communication plan, create a timeline, and assign responsibilities. The team should be made up of members who represent a range of technology expertise levels as well as a range of library functions. Because technology is engrained in nearly every library function, it is important to have those stakeholders represented on the team.

Begin by reviewing the previous technology plan (if one exists), as well as the library's and parent organization's strategic plans. The team should refer to the vision and mission statements when determining future technology initiatives and priorities to ensure that they align with the library and parent organization's priorities. Review examples of strategic plans from similar institutions if possible, and review library and technology literature with particular focus on trend reports.

Gather Documentation and Inventories

Gather any relevant information and documentation to the technology plan. This includes technical documentation such as network maps, wireless heatmaps, infrastructure plans and details, and equipment maintenance logs. Complete a full inventory of library technology, including all hardware, and a separate inventory of websites and web services—whether they are hosted locally or by a vendor. All of this information is needed to describe the current technology environment of the library.

Other useful information might include relevant plans by external groups and vendors that provide services or otherwise affect library technology. Budget forecasts, timelines for planned technology, infrastructure and facilities projects, and technology refresh cycles all play a role. Review other institutional plans that may have expectations for technology support that the library will be required to fulfill. In particular, a library's strategic plan or departmental plans will likely have a technology component. Hopefully they will have consulted with the library's technology staff during their planning process, but in any case, the strategic technology plan may need to align with their scope and goals.

Gather Input from Stakeholders

Early in the planning process, the planning team should identify the primary stakeholders. This will likely include library employees and library patrons, but there may be additional stakeholders, or the team may desire to identify subgroups of stakeholders who have particular needs.

Stakeholder input plays an important role in determining priorities, so it is important to involve stakeholders from the beginning and to listen carefully. Input can be solicited through surveys, focus groups, observations, and interviews. Library employees are a good source of anecdotal evidence, such as general observations of patron behavior. Patron input can also be solicited by using suggestion boxes or web-based suggestion forms. However, be cautious with input that may come from a self-selected or biased source.

Evaluate the Current Environment and Establish Priorities

After the planning team has gathered all of the documentation and stakeholder input, it is time to come together and evaluate the current technology environment. Conduct an assessment of technology and technology-related services, using quantitative data when possible but also relying on information from stakeholders. Identify critical library activities and services, and assess the technology that supports them. The library management system is likely critical to the functioning of the library. The local network infrastructure is also very important. Are those systems performing up to expectations? Is an upgrade or expansion warranted?

Identify what library technology and technology services need to be improved or enhanced. Review the library and department plans for relevant goals and projects to make sure that they are reflected in the plan. Aside from evaluating individual services and technologies, holistic environmental assessment, such as an analysis of the strengths, weaknesses, opportunities, and threats (SWOT) can help to bring it all together.

Take all of the information that has been gathered—historical context, stakeholder input, the evaluation of current technology—and use it to establish future priorities. Be realistic about what can be accomplished. Find ways to always drive progress forward but consider constraints such as policies or funding when establishing priorities. It is common to have to identify external funding or one-time money to implement expensive projects, so make note of that need if it applies. Take other resources such as staffing and infrastructure into consideration. Will the current infrastructure support the desired technology? What will the effect of the project be on staff resources?

The priorities that are established should align with the library's mission and goals. If you discover projects that do not support the library's plan, then consider whether it actually is a priority or if in fact it would be detrimental to pursue at this time and should be dropped from the plan.

Create an Implementation Plan

Starting with the priorities established in the previous step, and taking into account budgetary and other resource constraints, create an implementation plan. This is the document that will guide the work to be done during the lifetime of the strategic plan. Realize that it will also be the most heavily modified part of the plan in coming years as the plan is revisited and revised according to actual circumstances.

The implementation plan should describe in general terms the projects, initiatives, and tasks that will be undertaken. List the necessary resources (including funding), the project owners and stakeholders, general implementation steps, and approximate time frame. Don't forget to account for resources that are needed to maintain the technology following implementation, or any training that will be required for technology staff or the users.

Develop a realistic timeline built on the established priorities and taking into account resource constraints and other things that may affect the calendar. This does not need to go into a great level of detail, but it should include all of the projects that are on the implementation plan. More immediate projects will probably have fairly accurate start and end dates whereas those further down the timeline will need to be estimated. They can always be adjusted when the plan is revised.

Based on the estimated necessary funding for each of the initiatives, and given the budget cycle of the organization, it should be possible to create a strategic technology budget. Start with ongoing technology expenses such as annual license fees and maintenance contracts. Then move on to the priorities that were identified. If the funding source is already known, be sure to note that. If external funding will be needed, such as grants or donations, this should be noted as well.

Take a step back and look at the implementation plan as a whole. Is it realistic? Does it take into account resource constraints? Will it make an impact? Be ambitious about forward motion but don't set yourself up for failure. Part of the implementation plan should also be to conduct a regular review to assess progress, consider unanticipated issues, and make revisions to the plan.

Plan Reviews, Approvals, and Implementation

Give stakeholders an opportunity to provide feedback on the plan, particularly library employees who will implement or be greatly affected by the initiatives in the plan. Depending on organizational structure and practice, it may be necessary to provide library administration and other organizational leadership the opportunity to review and comment on the plan. It may also be necessary to obtain approvals before the plan can be considered finished. Once the plan is complete and approved, it is time to implement it.

Document

The strategic technology planning document is the final product of the planning process. It includes a description of the current technology environment, an assessment of the technology, and the implementation plan. Additional documentation can be included in an appendix. The length of the plan itself varies depending on the scope of the plan. At its most basic, a library's strategic technology plan includes short-term goals and objectives as well as plans to accomplish those goals. It should be referenced frequently and serve as a guide for all technology efforts. It also serves as the foundation for the next strategic plan several years down the road.

Executive Summary

The first part of the document is often the last to be written. Reference the library's plan, mission, and vision statements. Include a vision statement for the technology plan, which briefly shows how technology will support the library's mission. Give an overview of the major goals and objectives of the technology plan and the resources that will be necessary. Make a high-level reference to funding that includes a breakdown of major funding sources, such as the operating budget and any external sources. Finally, describe how success will be evaluated and note the document revision schedule.

History

Historical context is important yet often overlooked. Having an understanding of how you got to where you are currently can greatly inform decision making about the future. Describe how technology adoption and use has developed in the library and major initiatives that have been undertaken in the past. Were those initiatives successful? Why? Which ones failed? Note major shifts in the way that library services are provided because of technological changes. Also note external influences that have had a major influence on technology such as a significant reduction in the budget, or the centralization of technology support staff. This section might conclude with a brief overview of the major initiatives currently underway—work doesn't pause during the planning process.

Current Technology Environment

A description of the current technology environment is formed from all of the inventories and documentation that was gathered. Depending on the amount of technology covered, this section can get quite lengthy. Detailed inventories can be included in the appendix, but this section should summarize all of the technology used by the library. Some of the information that should be covered here includes web services, infrastructure (such as networking and power), public and employee computing (hardware and software), servers, technology support staffing, specialized technology services (such as a makerspace or media lab), and other technology initiatives such as digitization efforts. The library management system should be highlighted, as a mission-critical piece of technology. If technology or support is provided by external units it should be noted here, and any memoranda of understanding (MOUs) or service-level agreements (SLAs) should be included in the appendix.

Technology Assessment

In the technology assessment the conclusions reached while evaluating the current technology environment are summarized. Cover all areas of technology in the library and provide a brief assessment of each one. Include evidence that supports the assessment, as this is used as justification for prioritization and budgeting. Also be sure to assess areas such as technology support services and library employee technology skills and expertise, and identify where additional resources or additional training would be beneficial.

Make a list of initiatives organized by priority, as established during the evaluation phase. It should be clear that these follow naturally from the assessment and support the mission and goals of the organization.

Implementation Plan

The implementation plan is described in detail earlier in this chapter. This part of the document summarizes the projects, initiatives, tasks, and other technology-related priorities that will be undertaken. Include a multiyear technology budget and identify funding sources where possible. A timeline of projects and milestones that spans the life of the plan includes more detailed information in the initial couple of years with more approximate dates and general information as the calendar progresses.

Whereas the executive summary is the section of the plan that will be of the most interest to administrators and external stakeholders, the implementation plan is the part that technology support staff and library employees who actually bring the plan to life will focus on.

Appendices

Supporting technical documentation such as inventories, network maps, infrastructure plans, MOUs, and SLAs should be included as appendices. Also include documentation that was generated while gathering stakeholder input such as focus group notes, survey questions and results, and workflow observations.

CONTINUITY PLANNING AND DISASTER RECOVERY

A continuity plan is a document that describes how an organization will continue operations in the event of a disaster that interrupts the normal course of activities. Interruptions and disasters include natural events such as earthquakes, floods, hurricanes, and wildfires, and artificial events like utility outages, arson, and sabotage. A library disaster plan will more than likely focus on collections, but may not address technology or services, which are more concerned with operational continuity. Nonetheless, the beginning point for a technology continuity plan is the library and parent organization's disaster plans. When formulating a plan, be sure to get advice from the institution's emergency management or public safety office. They can be very helpful and will probably be happy to serve as a resource while creating a plan.

Continuity Plan

Technology plays a critical role in a library's continuity of operations. Some interruptions or disasters may affect the library's technology directly—such as a power outage, a loss of internet service, or a flood in the server room, whereas in others the technology infrastructure may be unaffected but essential to maintain or even extend library services. Earthquakes, snowstorms, and nearby wildfires can all force the closure of library buildings while the expectation is that the library organization will continue to function and provide library services to their community. The COVID-19 pandemic saw widespread, extended building closures during which technology was needed to support large-scale telecommuting by employees and new services deployed such as rapidly scaled-up equipment lending and digitization of collections.

A continuity plan describes the types of interruptions that may occur and details the specific steps to mitigating the interruption and supporting continued operations. Creation of the continuity plan should take place in the same manner that other plans are often developed, with the formation of a committee to create the document, gathering information from stakeholders and experts, and producing a document that can be easily accessed if the need arises.

List the threats to library operations and group them according to which are more likely to occur. Is there a high risk or a low risk for any given threat? Consider local natural hazards that have a high probability, such as a tornado or a hurricane. Regional flood zone and earthquake hazard maps are useful sources of information. Develop scenarios that address the interruptions that operations will face during each threat and the general responses and mitigation that will enable operations to continue. Don't leave out relatively minor disasters, such as a failure of a mission-critical system like the library management system, or a burst pipe in the digitization lab. Be aware that it is possible for multiple types of interruptions to occur simultaneously or for problems to cascade.

In general, a continuity planning document might include the following sections:

- Emergency contact information and communication plan
- Risk assessment
- Disaster scenario response plans
- Data backup policies and procedures
- Data recovery procedures
- Emergency supplies list and storage locations

The disaster scenario response plans describe the details of how operations will continue in response to specific interruptions. Is it necessary to relocate operations? If employees are to telecommute, how will equipment be distributed and support provided remotely? Are there alternate means for accessing online resources? How will services continue if the library management system is unavailable? What are the steps for switching to backup generators in the event of a power outage?

Copies of the plan should be located in multiple locations, should one location be compromised. Additionally, the plan should be reviewed at regular intervals to reflect changes in threats, the technology environment, and organizational structure.

Disaster Response and Recovery

When an interruption or disaster occurs, the immediate priority is to ensure the safety of the employees and patrons. Next assess the damage that has occurred, and then enact mitigation efforts. With a disaster plan or continuity plan as a guide, employees can respond swiftly to address the most urgent issues.

Part of the disaster response is to make sure that any automatic measures took place as expected. If there was a power loss, did the emergency generator activate? Did stand-by systems come online? It is also desirable to keep operational downtime to a minimum, so as to minimize an interruption to services. Is it necessary to switch to alternative methods of accessing resources? Do backups need to be used to rebuild lost data? If the groundwork has been laid, recovery may be kept within an acceptable period of time. Of course, flexibility is also a key part of the disaster response. No matter how detailed the plan, things will not go entirely as expected. Backup systems may not operate correctly. Unanticipated issues may occur. Disasters can be compounded by multiple problems. But having a plan in hand will relieve enormous pressure and allow you to focus on the unexpected.

Mitigation involves reducing the effect of the disaster and moving into a phase that supports the continuity of operations. Enact backup plans to provide services during an extended disaster or salvage operations. Depending on the type of disaster, it may be necessary to relocate to a nearby backup site or to transition to remote operations entirely while salvage activities take place.

Recovery is the process of returning to normal operations and the restoration of full functionality. The recovery time is something that should be planned for and an acceptable period during which services are unavailable should be predetermined. Some data loss should be expected, depending on the service. How much data loss is acceptable should also be known ahead of time with mitigation procedures in place to meet those goals. Depending on the disaster, recovery may involve restoring data from backups, setting up replacement hardware and software, and the reconfiguration of systems.

Risk Management

In *A Guide to Computer User Support for Help Desk and Support Specialists*, Fred Beisse defines *risk management* as "the use of strategies and tools to reduce the threat to an organization from uncontrollable disasters or accidents and to help an organization recover from a disaster with reduced financial impact or customer service loss."[2] Risk management starts with a threat assessment followed by the implementation of measures that will help prevent, mitigate, and recover from disasters.

With the movement of many services to the cloud, including library management systems, much of the pressure on libraries to protect local systems has been alleviated. Instead, risk management involves becoming familiar with the data protection, security, and disaster recovery plans of the vendor. In this case, it is incumbent on the vendor to provide complete and accurate data recovery within an acceptable time frame. There may be an opportunity for negotiation when acquiring a cloud service.

Risk Management Strategies

Risk management strategies include the following:

- Virtualized server solutions with backups that can be quickly deployed
- Moving local servers to the cloud to remove them from local threats

- Virtual private network access for telecommuting work
- Electrical power backup generators
- Uninterruptible power supplies for servers and important workstations
- Local data backups that allow for frequent backups and the rapid recovery of lost data
- Off-site data backups stored at a separate location in the case the local backup is also corrupted or destroyed
- Mirrors of web servers to which traffic can be redirected
- Fire suppression systems
- Antivirus software
- Security measures
- Continual monitoring of the network, servers, systems, power, etc.

Be sure to test mitigation measures and procedures regularly, including a full test of backup generators that replicates a realistic loss of power. Run data recovery tests to make sure that backups are running properly and making complete and accurate backup copies. Keep all software-based measures up to date.

MANAGING CHANGE

A responsibility of technologists at all levels is to assist library employees and patrons with adjusting to change brought by new technologies. Change can be hard. Not everyone will be excited about the potential benefits of a new system and some will be reluctant to lose the expertise that they have developed with the old system. With experience, people develop mastery of systems, including complex workarounds that enable them to accomplish tasks in spite of the limitations of the system. There may be resistance to change even if the new system will allow them to be more efficient and productive because people are generally comfortable with what they know. There may also be fear associated with change and a feeling of uncertainty about their role or status.

Part of our job is to help people minimize the uncertainty to a manageable level. Communication is a key tactic for enabling change. Communicate early and often about expected changes. Large projects will benefit from a clear plan or roadmap that conveys the process to stakeholders. Involve stakeholders during the research and planning stages and encourage input and feedback. This helps establish some ownership of the process and develop buy-in if they feel that they have a role in the project and the ability to influence the selection and implementation of the new technology.

It can be difficult to please everyone, and unanimous agreement shouldn't necessarily be the goal. It is still the role of the technologist to leverage his or her knowledge and expertise when guiding a project within the technologist's wheelhouse. However, it is important to show stakeholders that their input is valued, and that plans will be informed by the opinions and experiences of the stakeholders. Suzanna Conrad discusses making the "complex sale," which involves "multiple decision-makers, often at various tiers of an organization." She goes on to describe the difference between compromise and collaboration, with compromise being an acceptable solution whereby each party finds wins, but collaboration is the best approach because all parties are involved and "the solution should theoretically fulfill the needs of everyone."[3]

Understanding the effect that a change will have on stakeholders is important. The planning and implementation team should be aware of the changes in workflow and practices that a new technology will bring. It is helpful to make sure that the stakeholders are aware of the benefits that a new technology will bring—don't exaggerate, but don't sell the technology short, either. Be realistic about both the challenges of the old technology and the benefits of the new technology. The point here is to be realistic. If you're not seen to be honest about the old system, then staff may not trust your decisions or the reasoning behind the change. Similarly, if you're not realistic about the new system then they may have inflated expectations that will inevitably lead to disappointment.

Training can help develop a basic comfort level with the new technology, but only experience will result in mastery. Provide ample training opportunities both before and after the implementation, and ample documentation that users can rely on while building their mastery of the new technology.

Change isn't always difficult, for example, when stakeholders feel that the old technology doesn't support their needs and doesn't accomplish what they want. This is particularly the case if they believe that it makes their work more difficult than it has to be. In this situation they may anticipate change as they believe that it will make their lives better. An organizational climate that encourages learning is helpful, as is a culture that encourages experimentation and rewards failure. This type of culture is one that leads to innovation across the organization.

SUMMARY

Technology adoption should reflect real needs and constraints and be determined through an intentional process—no matter the scope or scale. Library budgets are complex and represent a real constraint for technology adoption. It is key to be familiar with budgeting and the real technology expenses of the library to make the best use of organizational resources. With that foundation, it is possible to move through the technology selection process in response to a need. First you must have a thorough understanding of the need, and next you can investigate for potential solutions. Then, having identified some potential solutions, those solutions should be evaluated, and finally a decision can be made to select one.

Strategic technology planning is an important factor in making sure that resources are used efficiently, and the library's vision and goals are supported. The process of creating a strategic technology plan is a project unto itself. The process begins with the formation of a planning team, which gathers relevant inventories and documentation, gathers input from stakeholders, conducts an evaluation of the current technology environment, and finally creates the implementation plan. The document itself should be made up of an executive summary, a brief history of technology use in the library, a description of the current technology environment, an assessment of the current technology, and the implementation plan. The document can also include documentation and other information that was gathered in the appendix.

A continuity plan is a completely separate document from the technology plan that evaluates threats to the technology environment and describes how the library will continue operations in the event of a disaster. Disaster response is the immediate, and hopefully planned, actions that take place following a disaster. Mitigation involves reducing the effect of the disaster, and recovery is a return to normal operations. Risk management involves plans and actions put in place in advance of a disaster to reduce threats and mitigate a disaster when it does occur.

A responsibility of technologists at every level is to aid people in adapting to change. Communication, collaboration, and training are all tactics that can be used to manage change.

KEY TERMS

Budget planning

Risk management

Change management

Stakeholder

Continuity plan

Strategic planning

Disaster recovery

Technology assessment

Implementation plan

Technology planning

Mitigation

Technology selection process

Refresh cycle

Total cost of ownership (TCO)

Request for proposal (RFP)

Weighted point evaluation

QUESTIONS

1. What are some of the things to be taken into consideration when evaluating a technology acquisition?
2. Describe the technology selection process.
3. List some methods for gathering stakeholder input.
4. Describe the strategic planning process.
5. What are the sections of a strategic technology planning document?
6. What is a real threat (natural or artificial) to a library in your locality? What are some strategies for managing the risk?
7. List some risk management strategies.
8. Have you experienced a time when change was managed or received poorly? How would you approach a similar situation as someone in a role to help manage the change?

ACTIVITIES

1. Do a weighted-point evaluation of several products to solve a technology need.
2. Review a strategic technology plan, continuity of operations plan, or disaster recovery plan from a library. What information does it cover? How current is it? In your opinion, is it complete? What would you do differently?

FURTHER READING

Conrad, Suzanna. "Spinning Communication to Get People Excited about Technological Change." *Code4Lib Journal* 41 (2018). Accessed on August 12, 2020. https://journal.code4lib.org/articles/13641.

Jost, Richard, M. *Selecting and Implementing an Integrated Library System: The Most Important Decision You Will Ever Make.* Oxford: Elsevier Science and Technology, 2015.

Mallery, Mary, ed. *Technology Disaster Response and Recovery Planning: A LITA Guide.* Chicago: ALA TechSource, 2015.

Matthews, Joseph R. *Technology Planning: Preparing and Updating a Library Technology Plan.* Westport, CT: Libraries Unlimited, 2004.

NOTES

1. Nicole C. Engard, *The Accidental Systems Librarian*, 2nd ed. (Medford, NJ: Information Today, 2012), 167.
2. Fred Beisse, *A Guide to Computer User Support for Help Desk and Support Specialists*, 6th ed. (Boston: Cengage Learning, 2015), 262.
3. Suzanna Conrad, "Spinning Communication to Get People Excited about Technological Change," *Code4Lib Journal* 41 (2018).

Index

integrated library system (ILS), xiii, 9, 24, 163–65; history of, 3–4, 13; open source examples of, 140; security of, 92; who is responsible for, 6, 10. *See also* library management system

Intel, 34, 41

internet of things (IoT), 71–72, 74, 96–97, 157–58

Internet2, 70–71

iOS, 55–56, 65

IoT. *See* internet of things

issue tracking system, 19–22, 29

Java, 113, 130, 136

JavaScript, 113, 122, 132, 136; position uses, 115; web design use of, 119, 134; web server use of, 85

Jobs, Steve, 2

joint application development, 132

JSON, 113, 121

Jurkowski, Odin L., 117

Kerberos, 102–3

LAMP (Linux, Apache, MySQL, PHP), 81, 85, 111

LAN. *See* local area network

laser cutter, 150–51, 154, 158

LastPass, 98, 103

LDAP (lightweight directory access protocol), 50, 65, 68, 102–3

Lego, 132, 154

library automation, 2, 9–10, 164

Library of Congress, 2, 113, 121, 139, 164

library management system (LMS), 163–65, 170, 172, 173; application programming interface for, 139; automated storage and retrieval system use with, 171; cloud hosted, 82, 85; history of, 2; technology planning and role of, 184–86; user information collected by, 13; who is responsible for, 82. *See also* integrated library system

library services platform, 164, 172

linear network topology, 62; Linux, 43, 49, 70, 99, 135; Android version of, 55; Chromebook version of, 55; history of, 3; server use of, 80–87, 111; single-board computer use of, 153; user authentication for, 68

LITA (Library Information Technology Association), 157–58

LMS. *See* library management system

local area network (LAN), 3, 50, 65, 101, 129

log, 83, 87, 92, 116

lossless compression, 168

lossy compression, 168

MAC address, 66

machine-readable cataloging. *See* MARC

macOS, 42–43, 48–52, 135; history of, 3, 41; networking for, 65, 68, 70; print server for, 84; security for, 98–99, 101

mail server, 65, 77, 86–87

Make:, 148, 153

Makeblock, 133, 154

makerspace, 145–47, 150–55

malware, 42, 50–52, 56, 94–96, 104. *See also* antivirus software

Malwarebytes, 95, 98

MARC (machine-readable cataloging), 2, 13, 113, 121, 142

markup language, 102, 112–13

mass storage, 36–37, 43–44, 48, 65

McAfee, 52, 98

memorandum of understanding (MOU), 6–7

mesh network topology, 63; MFA. *See* multifactor authentication

microcontroller, 151–53, 155

Microsoft: HoloLens, 155–56; Office 365, 44, 82

Microsoft Windows, 42, 47–49, 51–53, 135; authentication for, 102; history of, 3–4; mobile device management for, 56; networking for, 65, 70; security for, 99–100. *See also* Windows Server

mitigation, 185–88

mobile application, 120

mobile device management (MDM), 25, 55–56, 58

mobile web design, 118–19. *See also* responsive web design

motherboard, 33–35, 39–40, 44

MOU. *See* memorandum of understanding

MS-DOS, 3, 135

multifactor authentication (MFA), 98, 103

MySQL, 85; *See also* LAMP

near-field communication (NFC), 71, 157

net neutrality, 71–72

network administration, 11, 67–70

network administrator, 11, 68, 72

network architecture, 59–65, 72

network interface controller (NIC), 39, 60, 66, 72

network security, 65, 67, 69, 101–4

network topology, 61–64

NIC. *See* network interface controller

normal forms, 137–38

object-oriented programming, 130, 134–36

OCLC, 2, 4, 82, 164

OCR. *See* optical character recognition

Oculus Rift, 155–56

Omeka, 140, 169

online public access catalog (OPAC),

OPAC. *See* online public access catalog, 2–3, 11, 13, 165

SQL (structured query language), 85, 97, 132, 134, 136–38, 140; programming in, 138–39
SSD. *See* solid-state drive
SSH. *See* secure shell
SSO. *See* single sign-on
stakeholders, 187–88; IT governance and, 5–6, 13; project management and, 27–28; technology planning and, 178, 181–85; web design and, 116–17
Stallman, Richard, 25
star network topology, 63
storage. *See* mass storage
strategic planning, 23, 128, 180–84
switch, 20, 62, 65–66, 72
syntax, 112, 114, 133–34
system administrator, 10–11, 77, 82, 105, 131
system changeover, 131
System Preferences, 48–49, 52, 101
system requirements, 48
System Restore, 51
systems development life cycle (SDLC), 129–32, 140

tablet computer, 25, 29, 55–56; history of, 4; networking of, 60, 65; web design for, 119; who is responsible for, 20
technology assessment, 182–84, 188
technology planning, 53, 175, 181, 183, 188
technology selection process, 178–80, 188
technology use policy, 53–54
Texas Instruments, 3
text editor, 112, 114, 122–23
textiles, 153, 155
TLS. *See* transport layer security
TOR, 100
total cost of ownership, 140, 175, 178
transport layer security (TLS), 100, 104
trojan, 95

Ubuntu, 43, 80, 83
uninterruptible power supply (UPS), 78–79, 187
universal design, 26
Unix, 2, 43, 48, 70, 82–84, 99
UPS. *See* uninterruptible power supply
usability testing, 115–16, 118, 120–21, 123, 131
USB (universal serial bus), 36–38, 60, 65, 94
user authentication, 50, 68, 72, 102–105, 165–66; security threats to, 93, 95–96; who is responsible for, 8, 11, 20
user-centered design, 120
user experience (UX) design, 8, 10–11, 114, 120, 123
user privacy, 12–14, 69, 92, 100, 104, 157
user support, 6, 8–9, 11, 17–21, 23, 29
user support tiers, 19, 29
UX design. *See* user experience design

video ports, 38–39
virus, 94
virtual desktop, 54–56
virtual network, 60–61
virtual private network (VPN), 61, 100
virtual reality (VR), 34, 145–46, 155–56
virtual server, 7–8, 11, 80–81
voluntary product accessibility template (VPAT), 26
VMware, 55, 80
VPAT. *See* voluntary product accessibility template
VPN. *See* virtual private network

W3C (World Wide Web Consortium), 27, 112, 122–23
WAP. *See* wireless access point
waterfall method, 27–28
WCAG. *See* web content accessibility guidelines
wearable technology, 153, 155, 157
web accessibility, 27, 29, 115, 118, 122, 125. *See also* accessibility
web analytics, 116, 121–22
web API. *See* web application programming interface
web application programming interface (API), 121, 123. *See also* application programming interface
web content accessibility guidelines (WCAG), 122–23
web design process, 116–18
web development, 6, 8–9, 11, 114–23, 125
web server, 77, 81, 85–86, 109, 111–12, 122; risk management for, 187; security of, 70, 96–97, 100, 102, 104
webpage layout, 110
weighted point evaluation, 179,
wide area network, 11, 65
Windows. *See* Microsoft Windows
Windows Server, 68, 83–84, 87. *See also* Microsoft Windows
wireframe, 118
wireless access point (WAP), 60, 67
wireless networking, 20, 25, 39, 60, 69, 104
Wordpress, 81, 112
work breakdown structure, 28
world wide web (WWW), 3, 59, 96, 109–10
WPA2, 69, 104
WYSIWYG (what you see is what you get), 114–15

XML (extensible markup language), 112–13, 121
XR. *See* extended reality

Yelton, Andromeda, 134

Z39.50, 3

About the Author

Jonathan M. Smith is interim assistant dean for technology and access services at Sonoma State University. He is the lead technologist for the library, where he drives technology development with a focus on collaboration and an eye towards student success. Throughout his career, he has led major projects in strategic technology planning, web development, and server migrations; launched two academic makerspaces and an institutional repository; and has taught graduate-level courses in systems analysis and database development. Jonathan is a 2018 Library Senior Fellow at UCLA, and has held faculty positions at California State University, San Bernardino and The Catholic University of America.

Jonathan regularly presents on technology topics at conferences, often focusing on emerging technologies. His published work includes a chapter on makerspace tools and technologies in the recent publication *Makerspaces in Practice* and a chapter on Arduino programming in *The Makerspace Librarian's Sourcebook*. Visit www.jonathanmsmith.net for more information about him. Jonathan holds an MSLS from The Catholic University of America and a BA from California State University, Fresno.

CPSIA information can be obtained
at www.ICGtesting.com
Printed in the USA
BVHW082149150321
602361BV00003B/6